Peacebuilding

This book aims to clarify some key ideas and practices underlying peacebuilding; understood broadly as formal and informal peace processes that occur during pre-conflict, conflict and post-conflict transformation.

Applicable to all peacebuilders, Elisabeth Porter highlights positive examples of women's peacebuilding in comparative international contexts. The book critically interrogates accepted and entrenched dualisms that prevent meaningful reconciliation, while also examining the harm of 'othering' and the importance of recognition, inclusion and tolerance. Drawing on feminist ethics, the book develops a politics of compassion that defends justice, equality and rights and the need to restore victims' dignity. Complex issues of memory, truth, silence and redress are explored while new ideas on reconciliation and embracing difference emerge.

Many ideas challenge orthodox understandings of peace. The arguments developed here demonstrate how peacebuilding can be understood more broadly than current United Nations and orthodox usages, so that women's activities in conflict and transitional societies can be valued as participating in building sustainable peace with justice. Theoretically integrating peace and conflict studies, international relations, political theory and feminist ethics, this book focuses on the lessons to be learned from best practices of peacebuilding situated around UN Security Council Resolution 1325 on Women, Peace and Security.

Peacebuilding will be of particular interest to peace practitioners and to students and researchers of peace and conflict studies, international relations and gender politics.

Elisabeth Porter is Head of School of the International Studies at the University of South Australia.

Routledge advances in international relations and global politics

Peacebuilding

Women in international perspective

Elisabeth Porter

Routledge
Taylor & Francis Group

LONDON AND NEW YORK

First published 2007
by Routledge
2 Park Square, Milton Park, Abingdon, Oxon, OX14 4RN

Simultaneously published in the USA and Canada
by Routledge
270 Madison Ave, New York NY 10016

Routledge is an imprint of the Taylor & Francis Group, an informa business

Transferred to Digital Printing 2008

© 2007 Elisabeth Porter

Typeset in Times by Wearset Ltd, Boldon, Tyne and Wear

British Library Cataloguing in Publication Data
A catalogue record for this book is available from the British Library

Library of Congress Cataloging in Publication Data
A catalog record for this book has been requested

ISBN10: 0-415-39791-X (hbk)
ISBN10: 0-415-47973-8 (pbk)
ISBN10: 0-203-93999-9 (ebk)

ISBN13: 978-0-415-39791-9 (hbk)
ISBN13: 978-0-415-47973-8 (hbk)
ISBN13: 978-0-203-93999-4 (ebk)

Contents

Acknowledgements

A book like this starts as a seed, with a kernel of an idea, and spurts a life of its own. This book has travelled a long way, in my head, in location and in realization. I doubt if I would have begun thinking seriously about peacebuilding had I not worked in Northern Ireland in 1990, 1994–1999 and 2004–2006, experiencing first-hand the incredible frustrations of political stalemates, the anticipation of tentative possibilities of new hopes for living with peace, security and justice and experiencing the effects that practical peacebuilding has on family life, for good and also in danger. Ideas on the book began to swirl around in the late days in idyllic Byron Bay, in northern New South Wales, while I was teaching on peace, war and international politics at Southern Cross University. Clarity for the content came about at the Leopoldskron Palace, Salzburg at a reconciliation seminar. Consolidation occurred while I was working at the University of Ulster at a time when, despite supposed ceasefires and a peace agreement, street violence and sectarianism continued. The book was completed while I am Head of the School of International Studies at the University of South Australia.

During my time as Research Director at INCORE (International Conflict Research), University of Ulster/United Nations University, I was privileged to meet a wide variety of international scholars and practitioners working to further peace and security. While at INCORE, I was grateful for highly competent research assistance from international interns including Jessica Blomqvist, Ekaterina Borissova, Jason Brookhyser, Lisa Brown, Johanna Karlsson, Shauna Meehan, Emma Plant, Asmara Gonzales Rojas and Hanna Nilsson-Sahlan. Living in Northern Ireland, I learned much through listening. In particular, I thank Monica McWilliams, leader of the former NIWC, for her friendship, humour and insight into the complexity of peace negotiations and her unfailing optimism in the possibility of peace. Gillian Robinson is an ever-considerate Director of INCORE who encouraged my work. I shared hours of serious, hilarious conversation with Cathy Gormley-Heenan, friend and colleague, as we drove up and down from Belfast to Derry. Thanks also to Phil Clark for the memorable hours of conversation spent over the dinner table in Belfast and for his incredible knowledge of African politics and reconciliation in Rwanda.

I have given many papers on feminist ethics and peacebuilding and learned much from shared conversations at conferences. I have been privileged to meet numerous peacebuilders from all over the globe whose personal narratives are inspirational, and their stories have influenced this book. I owe long-term intellectual debts to a wide range of theorists mentioned in this book, but particularly to Seyla Benhabib, Carol Gould, Martha Minow, Martha Nussbaum and the late Iris Marion Young.

Our children Shantala, Simon and Luke are always present in my mind as I write, and Sasha our granddaughter is a reminder of the joy of life. Without doubt, my greatest appreciation goes to my best friend, my amazing husband Norman Porter, whose deep insight into life's complexities and nuance never ceases to amaze me. His intellectual acumen is acute. He answers my questions with such wisdom. He cooks me wonderful meals. I owe him so much and love him dearly.

Abbreviations

CEDAW	Convention on the Elimination of All Forms of Discrimination Against Women 1979
CSW	Commission on the Status of Women
DAW	Division for the Advancement of Women
DDR	disarmament, demobilization and reintegration
DPA	United Nations Department of Political Affairs
DPKO	United Nations Department of Peacekeeping Operations
FARC	Revolutionary Armed Forces of Colombia
FAS	Femmes Africa Solidarité
FERFAP	Federation of African Women's Peace Networks
FGM	female genital mutilation
ICC	International Criminal Court
ICTJ	International Center for Transitional Justice
ICTR	International Criminal Tribunal of Rwanda
ICTY	International Criminal Tribunal of Yugoslavia
INSTRAW	United Nations International Research and Training Institute for the Advancement of Women
IR	International Relations
IRA	Irish Republican Army
LWI	Liberia Women's Initiative
MARWOPNET	Mano River Women's Peace Network
MIGEPROFE	Ministry for Gender and Women in Development
MONUC	United Nations Mission in the Democratic Republic of Congo
NGO	Non-Governmental Organizations
NGOWG	NGO Working Group on Women, Peace and Security
NIWC	Northern Ireland Women's Coalition
NURC	National Unity and Reconciliation Commission
PFA	Platform for Action
REDE	Feto Timor Loro Sae (East Timorese Women's Network)
RWI	Rwanda Women's Initiative
SCR 1325	Security Council Resolution 1325
SRSG	Special Representative of the Secretary-General

TRC	Truth and Reconciliation Commission
UNAMSIL	United Nations Mission in Sierra Leone
UNDP	United Nations Development Programme
UNHCR	United Nations High Commission for Refugees
UN OSAGI	United Nations Office of the Special Advisor on Gender Issues and the Advancement of Women
UN PBC	United Nations Peacebuilding Commission
UNIFEM	United Nations Development Fund for Women
UNMIK	United Nations Mission in Kosovo
UNRISD	United Nations Research Institute for Social Development
UNTAET	United Nations Transitional Administration in East Timor
WANEP	West Africa Network for Peacebuilding
WILPF	Women's International League for Peace and Freedom
WIPNET	Women in Peacebuilding Network
WIPSA	Women's Initiative for Peace in South Asia
WISCOMP	Women in Security, Conflict Management and Peace

Introduction

Questions of peace and security trouble the western world enormously, particularly in the post-9/11 era. For those living in conflict zones or divided societies, violence and insecurity are daily realities. In 2005, the Peace and Conflict Ledger (Marshall and Gurr 2005) rated 31 countries as being at great risk of conflict escalating to serious violence and government instability and another 51 countries as being very vulnerable to conflict. 'In short, half the world's countries have serious weaknesses that call for international scrutiny and engagement' (Marshall and Gurr 2005: 2).[1] Even when violent conflict fades, peace appears elusive and feeling safe and secure is something to dream about. While men, women and children are affected by the traumas of war, violent conflict and radical political insecurity, the specific experiences of conflict, loss and pain differ for women. The difference extends to the types of experiences, the depths of exclusion from political decision-making and participation in peace-negotiations and in many women's interpretations of what is necessary to build peace and practice reconciliation.

Hence, the main practical focus in this book is on women who live in areas prone to war or in transitional societies that are moving from a dominant state of violence to new democratic and peaceful structures. The theoretical analysis of central blockages to peace that are outlined in this book and the suggestions for ways to move towards progress in building peace are relevant to men and women. The book examines concepts that are crucial to all forms of peacebuilding regardless of gender, namely inclusion in peace processes, recognition of differences, coalitions, trust, justice, mercy, compassion, truth, memory, forgiveness, apology, healing and reconciliation. In developing these concepts, I draw liberally on examples of women's peacebuilding practices. It is not that men's contribution to peace is not significant, it is. Rather, it is that women's contributions to peacebuilding usually are informal, ad hoc and rarely part of formal peace processes, so their stories often drift, unacknowledged. This book gives women's contribution to peacebuilding due recognition. I am looking at peace-building in Track 2 diplomacy with unofficial actors working informally as 'citizen diplomacy' and in Track 3 diplomacy with unofficial interventions at the grass roots level, rather than Track 1 official peacemaking, negotiation and mediation toward a ceasefire agreement and settlement.

The book's discussion is situated specifically within an international context whereby the United Nations (UN) has sought to address the issues of women, peace and security. The Beijing Declaration and Platform for Action (PFA), which emerged after the Fourth Women's World Conference in Beijing (1995), identified 12 'critical areas of concern' which remain obstacles to women's advancement, including armed conflict and power and decision-making, two factors that influence women's contribution to peacebuilding.[2] The PFA identified strategic objectives to be taken by member states to remove the obstacles to women's advancement. Five years later, the UN Commission on the Status of Women (CSW) submitted an 'Outcomes Document' (2000a) reviewing the agreements and outlining further initiatives needed. This document recognizes the obstacles remaining given the relative absence of women from decision-making positions at all stages of peace processes. It also highlights the need for more specific attention given to gender equality and peace. In 2005, the Commission met to review this document and maintain the pressure for implementation.[3]

What is of major significance to furthering peacebuilding is the UN Security Council Resolution 1325 (SCR 1325) (2000a) on Women, Peace and Security. It is historical in being the first Security Council resolution to address the special needs of women in relation to peace and security. UN SCR 1325 expresses:

> Concern that civilians, particularly women and children, account for the vast majority of those adversely affected by armed conflict, including as refugees and internally displaced persons, and increasingly targeted by combatants and armed elements, and *recognizing* the consequent impact this has on durable peace and reconciliation.
>
> (S/RES/1325 2000:1; emphasis in original)

The Resolution calls for increased representation of women at all levels of decision-making to prevent, manage and resolve conflict. It calls for increased numbers of women to become Special Representatives of the Secretary-General (SRSG) and realizes the need to expand the contribution of women in UN field-based operations. A significant consequence of this resolution is a heightened understanding of the urgency to realize the goals in measurable ways. Not to do so means that the resolution stays at the level of fine rhetoric. Despite considerable effort by the UN, in particular, the UN Development Fund for Women (UNIFEM), feminist researchers, academics, non-governmental organizations (NGOs), grass roots level movements, peace activists and supportive church groups to encourage women's participation in conflict prevention, management and resolution, women remain seriously under-represented in the institutional, formal mechanisms of peace negotiations and security enhancement.

This under-representation exacerbates gendered inequality in peace processes and undervalues the unique contribution that women in conflict societies and transitional societies bring to peacebuilding. To address this concern, the international community of scholars, activists, NGOs and UN divisions seek out lessons that can be learned from actual experiences in peace processes (UNRISD 2005; Vlachová and Biason 2005; International Alert and Women Waging Peace 2004). The lessons include insight into the barriers still to be overcome in order to achieve women's equal participation in all strands of peace processes and positive examples of practices and experiences that have facilitated women's inclusion in peace negotiations. SCR 1325 has been criticized for its conceptual gaps, for the lack of guidelines in practical application and for the failure in implementation. However, its efficacy as a global advocacy tool is without doubt. Stories of women from Afghanistan, Kosovo and East Timor who testified to the Security Council in 2001, honouring the first year of the Resolution, provide some evidence of its significance. This book seeks to outline positive instances of the importance of SCR 1325 and to situate examples of women's actual experiences within gender-inclusive conceptual clarifications of the nature of peacebuilding.

Women, war and peace

There are important qualifiers I need to make. All women are not natural peace-makers; some women are aggressive combatants (Alison 2006), particularly in Algeria, Eritrea, Ethiopia, Liberia, Mozambique, Nicaragua, Namibia, Sierra Leone, Sri Lanka, South Africa and Zimbabwe.[4] 'Over the last decade, girls have been part of fighting forces in 55 countries and involved in armed conflict in 38 of these countries, all of them internal conflicts' (Bouta 2005: 5), particularly in Angola, Columbia, the Philippines, Sri Lanka and Uganda (Fox 2004). Women have fought as 'freedom fighters' in Nicaragua, Sri Lanka, South Africa, Sudan and Vietnam. Indeed, 'in Eritrea, Sri Lanka, South Africa and across Latin America, women make up a third of the forces in guerrilla armies' (International Alert and Women Waging Peace 1999: 11). In some conflicts, women are abducted to join irregular armies and young girls are forced into 'jungle marriages', 'bush marriages' or 'AK-47 marriages' (Rehn and Johnson-Sirleaf 2002: 116). Some women act as spies, couriers or providers of refuge for combatants in hiding. Many women in Northern Ireland were strong supporters of men in paramilitary organizations and foster sectarian attitudes and during the violent conflict, hid weapons or fugitives. Some Rwandese women incited violence and encouraged revenge for the dead. Wherever there are deep ethnic, religious or tribal divisions, many women, like many men, instil in the young notions of the enemy as hated 'other'. Women ex-combatants sometimes join peacetime armies or security personnel or become peacekeepers.

However, because women universally are the prime nurturers in relationships, families and communities, they play crucial roles in peacebuilding, often in very informal, unofficial ways. These roles often emerge out of the experience of oppression, knowing what it is like to be excluded and seeking a society that is truly inclusive. Some women become peace activists, advocating strongly for non-violent ways of relating. Other women are mediators, trauma healing counsellors and policymakers working to address the root causes of violence and ways to transform relationships. Many women are educators and group facilitators, contributing to building the capacity of individuals, communities and nations to resolve conflict and prevent further surges of violence. Some women are humanitarian aid workers or peacekeepers. Many women facilitate dialogue between warring factions, tribes, clans or ethnic groupings by convincing husbands, brothers, uncles and sons to lay their spears, machetes or guns aside. Women often are willing to bridge divides across traditional ethnic, religious and cultural divisions, coming together on matters of commonality that generally revolve around their familial responsibilities in order to take care of the practicalities of life, such as food, shelter, health care, education and safety for their children. As a worker for KwaZulu Community Services explains quite simply, 'after the war situations it's women who start to put the fabric of life together' (in Mindry 2001: 1197). There is little choice – they are left with children, the aged and ill, amid devastation and have to find ways to survive. During war, women often are victims of rape and the loss of loved ones and grief, poverty and intense trauma sets in. Yet, an overemphasis on victimhood obscures women's agency and power to overcome massive obstacles. Further, 'in the very breakdown of morals, traditions, customs, and community, war also opens up and creates new beginnings' (Turshen 1998: 20).[5] Throughout the book, I offer examples of women who grasp this window of opportunity that transitional democracies allow to further gender justice, equality and rights. The impact of women's contributions to peacebuilding is significant in global terms, as the examples will demonstrate.

Feminist ethics in international relations

I am concerned to represent women's voices by respecting the integrity of their intentions in context, but I have not conducted interviews with women or analysed questionnaires. To do this would end in a different book. Instead, I have relied predominantly on other women's research on women,[6] NGO reports, up-to-date information available on the internet, academic literature and my own experience of working in Northern Ireland. I realize that this opens up potential gaps in understanding the nuance in context in which the examples are used. However, the chief aim of this book is to articulate a range of conceptual stances on the diverse range of ideas surrounding peacebuilding, ideas that are applicable for men and women. The examples of women's activity highlight the practical expression of these ideas. There are sound methodological reasons for the use of seemingly disparate global examples given throughout the book. Each share a significant factor, namely the urgency for women to thrust aside those divisions that cause conflict in order to find those commonalities which allow coalitions to form. When this happens, antagonistic differences that cause or exacerbate conflict in places such as Northern Ireland, Rwanda, South Africa, Sudan and Uganda are set aside, allowing a measure of trust to be built; only then, when the 'other' is no longer perceived as an enemy, can differences be interrogated constructively in order to be understood or, minimally, respected.

The common ground that draws women together usually lies in women's commitment to family and community ties and the shared urgency to pool resources and meet everyday basic needs, despite being surrounded by chaos and destruction.

Accordingly, this book analyses the range of meanings underlying key ideas of peacebuilding and offers practical and encouraging examples. I have chosen to highlight, in the main, positive examples of women's peacebuilding. I am neither underestimating the seriousness of prevailing blockages to women's participation in peace processes, nor romanticizing their involvement. I aim to do two things: first, to allow women's voices to express the personal significance of their active participation; and second, to demonstrate the extent of women's agency as peacebuilders. My overall argument in this book is that while women are active peacebuilders, their contribution often is informal, behind-the-scenes, unpaid, collaborative and unrecognized as actual peacebuilding, and thus they consistently are excluded from formal peace negotiation processes and public, political decision-making. 'While women will often have been at the forefront of peace initiatives throughout the conflict, peace agreements are usually negotiated predominately, if not exclusively, by men' (Bell *et al.* 2004: 320). What I suggest is needed relates directly to the two aims of this book. First, there needs to be greater recognition of women's activity as peacebuilders which translates into the inclusion of women more fully in all stages of peacebuilding. Second, peacebuilding itself needs to be understood broadly as a process that encompasses pre-conflict, conflict and post-accord transformation in formal and informal settings.[7]

Before explaining the direction of my argument, I should explain that there are issues related to women, peace and security that this book does not cover in depth.[8] It does not examine in detail gender research in violently divided societies (Baines 2005); the effects of war on women (Gardner and El Bushra 2004; Lorentzen and Turpin 1998; Turshen and Twagiramariya 1998; Bennett *et al.* 1995); the impact of 'crimes of honour' against women (Welchman and Hossain 2005); women refugees and displaced persons (Baines 2004);[9] war rape (Ellsberg and Heise 2005; Nowrojee 2005; Vlachová and Biason 2005; Corrin 2004; Krog 2001; Enloe 1993); peacekeeping (Olsson and Tryggestad 2001);[10] trafficking and prostitution as the only way to provide for one's family (Corrin 2004); girl soldiers (Brett and Specht 2004); disarmament, demobilization and reintegration (DDR) of ex-combatants (Bouta 2005); issues of land ownership that are crucial in post-war settlements and the economic livelihood of the many women who are left as widows in war-torn societies (Date-Bah 2003); the role of formal peacemaking and constitution-writing (Coomeraswamy 2004); or the children left to head households or who fight in almost 75 per cent of today's armed conflicts where 'nearly a third of the militaries that use child soldiers include girls in their ranks' (Mack 2005: 35).[11]

The reasons for not dealing in detail with these important issues are twofold. First and quite simply, to do so would be to write a different book. I am developing an analytic approach to peacebuilding through exploring a range of ways to understand different aspects of building the peace as developed by peace studies theorists and practitioners and as practised by peacebuilders. I do so through concentrating on the practical aspects of women's peacebuilding to draw attention to their often-unacknowledged informal contributions, and because women often articulate conflict and peace in different ways to men. The many valuable reports, handbooks and toolkits that are emerging highlight beneficial practices, but provide scant scholarly explanations for the underlying concepts to peacebuilding.[12] Second and importantly, rather than concentrating on women as victims of war, I provide instances of women's agency, the strength of their contribution as peacebuilders that slowly is being recognized and valued. Although women have shared their difficulties, 'fewer women have come together on the issue of peacebuilding to compare notes about *what* has worked and why, *and how to document best practices*' (Karam 2001: 21). My response is to try to assess what difference SCR 1325 is making on women's lives since 2000.[13] In fulfilling these two goals, of developing a conceptual articulation of peacebuilding and highlighting women's agency as peacebuilders, particularly in terms of post-SCR 1325, I am addressing a vastly underresearched area.

The central arguments developed throughout the book draw predominantly on the ideas and practices within feminist ethics of justice and care, primarily to interrogate and disrupt harmful dualisms which imply that we can have justice but not care, or mercy without justice, and thus to give substance to clichés such as 'peace with justice'. This book is explicitly feminist in challenging restrictive, oppressive, unequal, unjust and exclusionary relationships between men and women and in looking at examples of peacebuilding drawn from women's lives. I am defending a feminist ethics of justice and care as a way to break down dualisms and as a novel approach to integrate political theory, ethics, international relations (IR), human rights discourse and peace studies. This position directly challenges gendered dualisms, such as the idea that men are suited to the public world of transitional justice and political negotiations and women are suited to the private world of personalized care and picking up the emotional pieces after war. I have argued elsewhere that feminist ethics is focused on women's experiences and is cross-disciplinary in seeking alternatives. 'These alternatives emphasize personal experience, context, nurture and relationships' (Porter 1999: xi). I am assuming, and will explain why in the following chapters, that political decisions about peace and security are ethical priorities, as much as they are concerned with foreign policy. Moral deliberation about peace and security is coupled with contextual adaptability; there is no scope in peace negotiations for inflexible intransigence. Such deliberations must take into account the multifaceted nature of political, moral dilemmas. Hence, I draw on a wide array of multidisciplinary literature, bringing in political theory, IR theory, peace studies, human rights discourse and feminist ethics. Admittedly, this contributes to 'a hybrid approach' that leads to accusations of 'disciplinary messiness' (Baines 2004: 16), but like Erin Baines, I am comfortable with this.

In this book, I focus on a broad range of normative theories,[14] those that offer suggestions on how to make the world a better, safer, more equal inclusive world, and while I do not situate my work exclusively within feminist IR theory, it is appropriate to explain the significant contribution that it makes.[15] As Gillian Youngs explains, central tasks for feminist IR have 'been both deconstructive and reconstructive' (2004: 76), offering a critique of 'the masculinist limitations of mainstream approaches' (2004: 77), but also developing substantive alternatives to compensate for the earlier absence of women's voices from the international stage. These tasks draw attention to women as subjects rather than as victims or objects. 'Contemporary feminist perspectives on international relations are based on ontologies and epistemologies that are quite different from those that inform the conventional discipline' of IR (Tickner 1997: 629). They grow out of ontologies based on gendered social relations, often of marginalization and powerlessness and develop alternative notions of 'self-in-relations' (Porter 1991). Feminist epistemologies are grounded in the everyday lives of knowing subjects. They do not assume the inevitability of global anarchy, power struggles or violent conflicts. In understanding the complexity of global politics, sometimes 'we must go outside of international relations to find what we are looking for' (Maiguashca 2000: 134), and I go particularly to political theory, peace studies and feminist ethics.

I stress again the importance in emphasizing positive examples of women's peacebuilding. This book is deliberately upbeat, while being grounded in realistic examples. Remember, the examples come from the horror of war. Let me explain my idealism. I adopt a similar approach to John Paul Lederach's view of the moral imagination.[16] Lederach defines the moral imagination 'as the *capacity to imagine something rooted in the challenges of the real world yet capable of giving birth to that which does not yet exist*' (2005: ix; emphasis in original). Lederach's approach resembles feminist ethics, whereby:

> The moral imagination requires the capacity to imagine ourselves in a web of relationships that includes our enemies; the ability to sustain a paradoxical curiosity that embraces complexity without reliance on dualistic polarity; the fundamental belief in and pursuit of the creative act; and the acceptance of the inherent risk of stepping into the mystery of the unknown.
>
> (Lederach 2005: 5)

I attempt to be idealistic and realistic. Peacebuilding invariably is grounded in the everyday real challenges of violent societies and destructive patterns of relationships, yet it must have the capacity to transcend the grind and believe that there are alternative ways of relating that create constructive initiatives to further peace and security.

Overview

Chapter 1 provides historical background to why SCR 1325 was necessary and analyses its achievements to date. In this chapter, I challenge typical UN and orthodox peace scholars' understandings of peacebuilding as being located solely in formal peace processes or primarily as part of post-conflict reconstruction. I argue instead that these views of peacebuilding miss the informal practices of mediation, advocacy, conflict management and reconciliation in which many women are involved informally. The changing nature of violent conflict means that most wars are civil wars fought internally, close to villages, markets and essential infrastructure and where women, children and the aged are vulnerable. In this first chapter, I maintain the importance of understanding peacebuilding as an ongoing process. I explain how and why I broaden the conceptual parameters of peacebuilding to include all the processes needed to gain equal, just, inclusive, peaceful security. Official UN peacebuilding missions deploy 'military and civilian personnel from several international agencies, with a mandate to conduct peacebuilding in a country that is just emerging from a civil war' (Paris 2004: 38) and operate at a formal level.[17] While I include some examples that emerge from these missions, this is not the main focus of this study. My focus is on informal peacebuilding as an ongoing process.[18]

Chapter 2 explains the harm of polarization, that particularly since 9/11 2001 when President George Bush uttered the infamous 'if you're not with us, you're against us' ultimatum, there has been an entrenchment of an either/or, them/us and included/excluded mentality with devastating ramifications on marginalized groups. These groups include refugees, displaced persons, Muslims and those who appear Middle Eastern. It also includes many groups of women. I argue that the harm of dualism is a moral harm in that its effect is to fail to respect the dignity of the 'other'. Consequently, building cooperative relationships with those who are different is unlikely. I argue further that the moral harm lies in the demeaning nature of destructive dualistic thinking and practices which cannot avoid undermining the integrity of those who are different. My defence of feminist ethics is to overcome this harm of dualism. Specifically, I seek to incorporate both a universalistic defence of justice, equality and rights as intrinsic to peace and a particularized practice of care that is directed toward meeting the specific needs and responsibilities of those seeking peace with justice. My intention is to move beyond seemingly irreconcilable, optional or contradictory dualisms that presuppose either/or decisions. My reason for doing so is that such decisions usually exclude marginalized groups and fail to take into account context, complexity and the need for compassion. My aim is to demonstrate the positive benefits of an inclusionary politics which incorporates principled justice and practices of care. Chapters 3 to 6 demonstrate the importance of defying dualism: that given the appropriate conditions, it is possible to recognize specific identities and include differences as integral to building peace; combine justice with compassion; respect memory truthfully; and apologize and forgive where appropriate in order to embrace difference in a spirit of reconciliation.

Chapter 3 examines the worth of recognizing individual self-identity and collective identities. For example, in societies divided by ethnic and religious conflict, there are intense feelings of antagonism, rivalries, bitterness and fear which have deep historical roots affecting people in personal ways. In such societies, certain individuals and groups feel unrecognized, unappreciated, discriminated against and marginalized. Legislators, policymakers and politicians in transitional societies often are reformed fighters or warlords who, when trying to overcome discrimination, are accused of bias, surrendering tradition to appease rival groups or granting undue favours to 'the other side'. I argue strongly for the importance of pluralism and multi-faith inclusivity in overcoming divisions and demonstrate why it is necessary to go beyond mere tolerance and coexistence to advocate for deeper notions of mutual understanding and respect. Accordingly, I provide practical instances where women have been fully recognized and included in processes that enhance peace and security, paying particular attention to women who have experienced the trauma of war. For many women, personal recognition comes through their coalition-building across ethnic or religious differences.

Justice and compassion seem to be contradictory, in that one prevents the working of the other. Particularly where there have been instances of significant injustice and deep personal and political loss, political negotiators sometimes are accused of being weak, giving blanket amnesty to perpetrators of violence or not understanding the need for retribution or compensation. Chapter 4 argues for the importance of integrating both universal justice and particular compassion into the conceptual and practical framework of peacebuilding. That is, the universality of principles of justice, rights and equality undergird my articulation of the particularity of women's injustice, inequality and denial of rights in conflict zones. It also provides normative guidelines of what peacebuilders should be aiming to achieve. I argue that attention to need, listening and responding wisely are part of a political compassion that responds meaningfully to peace with justice. I substantiate these arguments by providing examples of restorative justice: a justice that is relational and seeks to restore broken relationships between victims, perpetrators of violence and their respective communities. This chapter examines what it means to feel that one is a victim who knows war-related grief, trauma, suffering and loss. My argument extends moral obligations to all victims who suffer and need care.

In seeking peace and security, those who have suffered deeply struggle with the enormous pain of what has happened to them, their family, communities and nations. Chapter 5 looks at the difficulties of dealing with the past and facing up to memory and truth. I begin with an analysis of evil, showing how sometimes, it is important for people to remember what has happened to them; other times, people choose to forget the awfulness of evil: war rape, torture, 'ethnic cleansing', murder of loved ones, destruction of homes or group discrimination are too painful to bear. Where people have been subject to the trauma of violence, providing forums for truths and confessions are crucial, but women often are silenced in these events, fearing the shame of talking about their traumas, particularly of sexual assault. Each culture is dealing with the past in different ways. What is appropriate in South Africa may not be suitable in Northern Ireland, Serbia-Montenegro, Sierra Leone, Guatemala or Cambodia. This chapter gives instances of how people are choosing to deal with the memory of the past and the need for avenues of truth to enable healing to occur. I look in particular at the special women's hearings at the South African Truth and Reconciliation Commission (TRC). I examine how redress differs for different injustices. I argue that moral agency is central in dealing with the past, facing the truth, admitting wrongdoing and dealing with shocking memories.

Closely connected with truth and memory is a controversial topic of Chapter 6, namely that of apology and forgiveness. I offer an analysis of what constitutes reasonable apology and explain the boundaries of forgiveness. What should be forgiven and what cannot? The answers are personal, but there is increasing evidence that without some acceptance of the need for admittance of wrongdoing and forgiveness,[19] there can be little healing of relationships. I offer instances of apology and forgiveness, and argue that those who have been harmed determine the boundaries of forgiveness. Again, my stress is on moral agency whereby victims become survivors. Chapter 6 concentrates on the topical issue of reconciliation and difference. Reconciliation is a term that is used loosely, so I pay considerable attention to outlining multiple understandings of reconciliation. Reconciliation involves processes that address conflictual, fractured and antagonistic relationships in order to heal past wounds and foster cooperative relationships in a spirit of open, fair and tolerant engagement. In order for these processes to begin, there must be a willingness to change personal and cultural attitudes and practices of prejudice, fear, suspicion and mistrust toward the 'other'. Once there are workable relationships, there can be the development of a shared vision for an interdependent future that permits reconciled relationships to work cooperatively. Each reconciliation process is unique. Examples are given of ways in which women cultivate practices of reconciliation through embracing differences, with a focus on Rwanda. In Chapter 6, many of the interconnected themes discussed in earlier chapters come to the fore.

The book concludes with a brief overview of the need for peace with justice and security. My conclusion reiterates my central arguments that to include women in political decision-making in transitional societies is to take seriously gender justice, gender equality, women's human rights and the rebuilding of relationships in demilitarized societies. Peacebuilding is a process that is important in pre-conflict, conflict and post-accord stages in both formal and informal settings. For reconciliation to be more than a trendy catchphrase, practical peacebuilding must be truly inclusive of women and men from all branches of life.

1 Peacebuilding as process

United Nations Security Council Resolution 1325

Historical background to UN Security Council Resolution 1325 (2000)

UN Security Council Resolution (SCR) 1325 reaffirms:

> The important role of women in the prevention and resolution of conflicts and in peacebuilding, and *stressing* the importance of their equal participation and full involvement in all efforts for the maintenance and promotion of peace and security, and the need to increase their role in decision-making with regard to conflict prevention and resolution.
>
> (S/RES/1325 2000: 7; emphasis in original)

Women experiencing the direct effects of war and conflict from diverse parts of the globe may appear to have little in common, given the stark differences in their history, culture, tradition, systems of governance, causes of conflict and duration of conflict. Probe deeper, and similarities surface between local women peace activists, negotiators and community workers, particularly in relation to the nature of obstacles that they face in having limited access to political decision-making, strategizing for peace and building coalitions across antagonistic, destructive barriers. This book looks at both the differences between women peacebuilders and the commonalities.

For women and girls living amid violent conflict there are similar elements. In particular, wars and violent conflict generally are internal, intra-state conflicts often rooted in long historical bitterness which has deep ethnic, religious and cultural roots. Triggers are numerous and internally, include economic crises, fights over resources, revenge killings, rebel insurgencies and tribal rivalries. External triggers include invasions and terrorist attacks. The combatants are soldiers, militants, paramilitaries, guerrilla fighters, drug dealers, warlords, rebels, political ideologues, disenfranchised youth, child soldiers or mercenaries. Western capitalists, greedy for diamonds, minerals, oil or a market for weapons, provoke violent conflict. State actors are part of the landscape of conflict, even if admittance of culpability is rare. Some might say that even peace itself is becoming more militarized,[1] with soldiers as peacekeepers. Given the complexities of modern war, issues related specifically to women and gender justice include: rights, economic development, sexualized violence, children born as a result of war rape, child abductions, trafficking, HIV/AIDS, specific health needs, lack of land and property rights, women-headed households, girl-headed households, orphans, asylum status with gender-based persecution, psychological trauma, women and girls as refugees, returnees and internally displaced persons (UN Secretary-General 2002a, 2002b). In attending to these complexities, the interdependence between gender equality, social justice, sustainable development and peacebuilding cannot be overstated.

United Nations and the Beijing Platform for Action

It is important to understand the international context in which women's peacebuilding occurs. The Convention on the Status of Women (CSW) was set up in 1946 and monitors the situation of women and promotes their rights. It establishes universal standards regarding equality between women and men, including the Convention on the Elimination of All Forms of Discrimination Against Women (CEDAW) adopted in 1979, entered into force in 1981 and monitored by the Committee on the Elimination of Discrimination against Women. The Committee is serviced by the Division for the Advancement of Women (DAW), which is the focal point for coordination of activities for women in the UN system. DAW is, understandably, grounded in the vision of equality of the UN Charter. UNIFEM is an autonomous organization working in close collaboration with the UN Development Programme (UNDP) on gender mainstreaming, women's empowerment strategies, engendering governance to increase women's participation in decision-making, promoting women's human rights and making women's perspectives central to peace.[2] The Office of the Special Advisor on Gender Issues and the Advancement of Women (UN OSAGI) promotes the implementation of the Beijing Platform for Action (PFA) and acts as an advocate for gender mainstreaming.[3]

The UN Fourth World Conference on Women held in Beijing in September 1995 was the largest UN conference ever organized, with 189 governments participating. The war in Bosnia and the genocide in Rwanda were vivid in participants' minds and the experiences of some present. The forum of NGOs brought together 30,000 women around the world and was held in parallel with the intergovernmental conference. The Beijing Declaration and PFA that emerged from the World Conference was enormously significant in raising global awareness of gender inequalities. Twelve areas of 'critical concern' were identified as stumbling blocks to women's progress: poverty, education and training, health, violence, armed conflict, economic considerations, power and decision-making, institutional mechanisms for the advancement of women, human rights, the media, environment and the girl-child. Strategic objectives were outlined to address these concerns. Recommendations were made for each concern. The PFA set an agenda for women's empowerment. Its success requires a strong commitment by the international community, governments, institutions, NGOs and local groups. Questionnaires were sent by DAW to governments to ascertain how they would implement the Beijing PFA. Governments were to set national action plans to respond to these recommendations. CSW was given the mandate to monitor the implementation of the PFA.

The conference was a watershed in the global quest for advancing women's concerns and prompted a renewed international commitment to equality, development, human rights and peace. At the civil society level, 'the PFA re-energized the women's peace movement, spawning a multitude of new NGOs, grass roots groups and regional and international networks' (Anderlini 2000a: 12).[4] For example, the Northern Ireland Women's Coalition (NIWC) was formed in 1996 from women's grass roots groups and won two seats at the official peace negotiations table. The Liberia Women's Initiative (LWI) was formed in 1994, and after Beijing, informed the international community of the solutions provided by women. The Jerusalem Link is led by high-level Israeli and Palestinian women and engages grass roots and national level peace efforts, offering parallel solutions to the official peace process, and was spurred on by the international women's peace movement. However, while there seemed to be a global commitment to gender equality in the mid-1990s, formal government responses often had little basis in reality.

At the international level there have been positive achievements since the Beijing PFA was adopted. For example, the Optional Protocol to CEDAW was adopted in 1999 and came into force in December 2000, but not signed by all member states. States who ratify the Protocol recognize the competence of the Committee on the Elimination of Discrimination Against Women to consider complaints of violation of rights from individuals or groups in its jurisdiction. The Rome Statute of the International Criminal Court (ICC) came into force on 1 July 2002 and explicitly: recognizes that certain gender-related crimes such as rape and other forms of sexual violence of war crimes amount to crimes against humanity. There is increased awareness that violence against women and girls is a human rights violation requiring the prosecution of abusers. There is a wider recognition that armed conflict has a different impact on women and children than on men. However, there is very slow recognition of women's contribution to conflict resolution.

Concern about limited progress prompted a special Beijing +5 UN General Assembly Special Session 9 June 2000 entitled 'Women 2000: Gender Equality, Development and Peace for the Twenty-First Century'. Informal sessions previewed the relevant document. Negotiations occurred between three blocks: G77, including 134 developing nations plus China; Juscanz, including Australia, Canada, Iceland, Japan, Liechtenstein, New Zealand, Norway, Switzerland, USA, and the EU block and the Holy See. There were also regional preparatory meetings in five regions in Addis Ababa, Ethiopia; Bangkok, Thailand; Beirut, Lebanon; Geneva, Switzerland; and in Lima, Peru. Governments reaffirmed their responsibility to implement the PFA. International Alert and Women Waging Peace was the secretariat of a global 'Women Building Peace' campaign and an active member of the NGO Caucus on Women, Armed Conflict and Peace. Caucus members worked hard to ensure that critical issues were put firmly on the Beijing +5 agenda. These issues can be aptly summarized as the desire for equal participation in decision-making in conflict prevention, conflict resolution, peacemaking, peacebuilding, peacekeeping, post-conflict reconstruction and reconciliation. Over 100 alternative reports were produced by women's NGOs, reminding the world of strategies needed to further gender equality. Experiences and strategies were shared across cultural, racial and national boundaries. What occurred was disturbing. In the preparatory sessions, some governments challenged the basis of what was reaffirmed in Beijing, namely that women's rights are human rights, thereby weakening the explicit rights language. In particular, there was an alliance between the Holy See, Algeria, Iraq, Libya, Morocco, Nicaragua, Pakistan and Syria.

The CSW submitted an 'Outcomes Document' with 188 countries as signatories and reviewed the agreements made by governments in 1995, as well as outlining further actions needed for implementation (CSW 2000a). Within the Outcomes Document, women's groups deplored the watering down of a commitment to women's rights, the lack of concrete benchmarks, numerical goals, time-bound targets, equality indicators and material resources needed to implement the PFA. The aim was to review the implementation of the Platform, not to renegotiate or rewrite it. However, while the Outcomes Document is not binding, signatories do commit themselves to taking action and thus can be held accountable with regard to a host of agreements on women's role in conflict resolution and peacebuilding.[5] The implementations were reviewed by the UN Economic and Social Council[6] and reiterate the language of the Platform, that peace is inextricably linked to gender equality. It also notes that progress has been made in strengthening peace organizations. Further actions and initiatives needed to implement the PFA were presented as a resolution adopted by the General Assembly.[7] This resolution notes that 'the underrepresentation, at all levels, of women in decision-making positions' and the lack of gender awareness in these areas, present serious obstacles to gender equality (CSW 2000a: 8, para 16). It notes that 'notwithstanding substantial improvement of *de jure* equality between women and men, the actual participation of women at the highest levels of national and international decision-making has not significantly changed' since Beijing 1995 (CSW 2000a: 10, para 23). Many sensible suggestions were made for the actions needed to remedy these obstacles. As Lul Seyoum of Eritrea notes, 'The issue of equal participation by women in post-conflict societies is not simply an issue of gender equality and human rights but could represent the decisive factor in maintaining peaceful development in a troubled region' (in Anderlini 2000a: 29). This is not merely a bold feminist statement, but as we will see throughout the book, many women work hard at building and sustaining practical peace measures.

Despite UN conventions and international agreements on legal standards regarding human rights and the conduct of conflict, there are serious obstacles to women's empowerment and security. Violence against women continues to be a strategic weapon of war, where 'raping enemy women is one measure in a series of measures to achieve victory in war' (Philipose 1996: 54). Women bear a large brunt of the burden of conflict, yet have little say in issues relating both to war and peace. Women, like men, are victims of and actors in armed conflict. However, there are more women who are involved actively in building peace than in destroying lives. Given the immense resistance to women's involvement in decision-making on security and conflict resolution, a further mobilization of global efforts was needed beyond the recommendations of Beijing +5.

'Women, Peace and Security': Resolution 1325

The lead up to the Security Council open debate on 'Women, Peace and Security' was of immense significance to the eventual success of the resolution. In May 1999, International Alert and Women Waging Peace launched a global campaign called 'Women Building Peace: from the Village Council to the Negotiating Table'. This was an international campaign to promote the role of women in peacebuilding and to help build a new vision of development, security and peace based on inclusivity and equality. The Security Council circulated a background paper outlining the contributions that it 'could make to improve women's protection in armed conflict and to ensure their centrality to conflict prevention and peacemaking, peacekeeping and peacebuilding' (UN Security Council 2000b: 1). The paper proposed the idea that the Security Council might 'call for the inclusion of peacebuilding elements in the process of consolidating a peace agreement and in the mandates of peacekeeping operations' (2000b: 5), specifically calling for attention to children and women's specific needs during repatriation, resettlement, rehabilitation, reintegration and post-conflict reconstruction. The paper affirmed the importance of gender equality and inclusion as the fundamental values on which peacebuilding and democracy should be based.

An NGO Working Group[8] on Women and International Peace and Security (NGOWG), comprising International Alert and Women Waging Peace, the Women's International League for Peace and Freedom (WILPF), Amnesty International, International Women's Tribune Centre, the Women's Commission for Refugee Women and Children, Women's Caucus for Gender Justice and the Hague Appeal for Peace, in collaboration with UNIFEM, played a leading role in bringing significant issues to the attention of Security Council members and provided crucial background information, recommendations and advice in informal bilateral discussions. On 23 October 2000, the Security Council held an Arria Formula meeting[9] where representatives of women's groups met privately with NGOs and Council members and presented their views. The statement by NGOWG reiterated the absence of women's voices at peace deals and high-level negotiations, despite the fact that women typically head households after war and know much about the practical aspects of what is needed to rebuild peace. On 24 October, an open debate of the Council permitted non-Security Council members to offer their views. Noeleen Heyzer, Executive Director of UNIFEM, asked the pertinent question: 'How can we, in good conscience, bring warlords to the peace table and not women?' (2000: 2). The resolution was circulated among Council members and adopted on 31 October 2000.

In her statement to the Security Council discussion, Angela King, Assistant Secretary-General and Special Advisor on Gender Issues and Advancement of Women, drew attention to the importance of understanding the role of societal dynamics as a guide to finding entry points into resolving disputes. She contended that all potential 'groups must be part of all stages of the peace negotiations' in future planning, rebuilding and crafting preventive strategies (King 2000: 2). As evidence of the value of women's participation in peace operations, King cited the three-year study that led to the Windhoek Declaration: The Namibia Plan of Action on 'Mainstreaming a Gender Perspective in Multi-dimensional Peace Support Operations' (S/2000/693), which looked at Bosnia-Herzegovina, Cambodia, El Salvador, Namibia and South Africa. The Declaration was to ensure that principles of gender equality permeate peace-keeping missions in every aspect of the peace process, contributing to a situation of political stability. King highlighted the findings: a critical mass of at least 30 per cent of women in peacekeeping missions encourages local women to become mobilized to join various committees, as occurred in South Africa and Namibia; it fosters confidence and trust among locals, as occurred in El Salvador and South Africa; women's participation expands debates to encompass diverse subjects; women usually are non-hierarchical, listen more and have insights into the root causes of conflict; local women who have been raped or subject to sexual violence, as occurred in Bosnia-Herzegovina, are more likely to confide in women peacekeepers; women are active negotiators, able to see the issues that effect women differently to men; and women's participation in all aspects of the mission helps to break down stereotypical views of women, which encourages the participation of local women in post-conflict decision-making.

Yet there is a profound contradiction between these findings and general practice, a contradiction I will refer to repeatedly throughout this book.

> Women are active at both the formal and informal levels. With few exceptions, women are not present in formal peace negotiations ... women at the local level are a rich resource waiting to be systematically tapped by the international community.
>
> (King 2000: 3)

The importance of King's affirmation of civil society groups,[10] particularly women's groups, is to counter the Security Council's traditional emphasis on resolving conflicts by focusing on warring sides who are negotiating for peace.

> Allowing men who plan wars to plan peace is a bad habit....While most men come to the negotiating table directly from the war room and battle-field, women usually arrive straight out of civil activism and – take a deep breath – family care.
>
> (Hunt and Posa 2001: 1)

The former Secretary-General Kofi Annan's comments at this debate on 'Women, Peace and Security' affirmed women's role 'as peace educators, both in their families and in their societies' and he noted the undervalued 'potential contribution of women to peace and security' (2000: 1).

The adoption of SCR 1325 (2000a) by the Security Council, under the Namibian Presidency, on 31 October 2000 builds on earlier Resolutions and Conventions.[11] It is unprecedented in acknowledging the importance of involving women in all peacebuilding measures. Its final clause, '*decides* to remain actively seized of the matter' (UN Security Council 2000a: 4; emphasis in original). The 18-point resolution calls upon the Council, the UN Secretary-General, member states and all parties to take action in four interconnected areas:

1   increasing the participation of women in decision-making and peace processes;
2   including gender perspectives and training in peacekeeping;
3   encouraging the protection of women; and
4   integrating gender mainstreaming in UN reporting systems and programmatic implementation mechanisms.

Sanam Naraghi Anderlini (2000a) provides insight into the implications of each of these actions. First, with regard to the participation of women in decision-making and peace processes, the explicit endorsement of women's groups and civil society participation in peace processes is unprecedented. However, the absence of actual quotas for women in high-level positions, benchmarks and timelines is of concern. Second, with regard to gender perspectives and training in peacekeeping, there is a clear endorsement of the need 'for gender training for peacekeepers and civilian personnel in peace support operations. *But* without the core commitment of governments to provide additional funds – these measures can be ignored or not implemented adequately' (Anderlini 2000a: 36). Third, in terms of the protection of women, all state and non-state actors in conflict are accountable for violations against women, and all have a responsibility to protect all citizens. '*But* without an effective monitoring and evaluation mechanism and incentives for compliance … it is likely that the necessary changes are not made' (2000a: 36). Fourth, in terms of gender mainstreaming, 'more needs to be done for this rhetoric to translate into concrete action' (2000a: 37).[12] SCR 1325 undoubtedly is significant and its history is worth remembering.

Achievements of SCR 1325

At the anniversary of SCR 1325, the Security Council convened a second Arria Formula and heard from women affected by conflicts in Afghanistan, the Democratic Republic of Congo, East Timor and Kosovo. Women peace leaders talked about violations committed against women. Elisabeth Rehn, the

UNIFEM-supported Independent Expert on Women and Armed Conflict, addressed the Council on the need for gender units to be included within all peacekeeping missions; the need for UN peacekeepers to be trained on the gender implications of their work with regard to sexual violence, forced prostitution and trafficking; the horror of HIV/AIDS being used as a weapon of war; the difficulties of DDR of female ex-combatants; and the persistent cry of women from diverse countries who want to participate in deciding how to rebuild their countries. Achievements were noted, such as the new developments of gender-awareness guidelines and training manuals for peacekeepers developed by the UK Department for International Development and the Canadian Department of Foreign Affairs and Trade.[13] Also noted were the groundbreaking results of the Gender Affairs Unit in East Timor, which has resulted in unprecedented levels of women's participation in public life (and will be elaborated on in subsequent chapters). Visits by international organizations to the Democratic Republic of Congo, East Timor and Sierra Leone made a positive difference to regional women's organizations.

Part of the recommendations of SCR 1325 was for the Secretary-General to initiate a study on the impact of armed conflict on women and girls, the role of women in peacebuilding and the gender dimension of peace processes and conflict resolution. Kofi Annan's Special Advisor on Gender Issues and Advancement of Women supervised the preparation of this study in close cooperation with the Inter-Agency Task Force on Women, Peace and Security. Elisabeth Rehn and Ellen Johnson-Sirleaf[14] were appointed as Independent Experts and travelled to many of the world's conflicts during 2001 and 2002. They focused on understanding the impact of armed conflict on women and highlighting women's roles in peacebuilding. They visited Bosnia-Herzegovina, Cambodia, Colombia, the Democratic Republic of Congo, East Timor, the former Yugoslav Republic of Macedonia, the Federal Republic of Yugoslavia, including Kosovo, Guinea, Israel, Liberia, occupied Palestinian territories, Rwanda, Sierra Leone and Somalia. They write:

> We realize how little prepared we were for the enormity of it all: the staggering numbers of women in war who survived the brutality of rape, sexual exploitation, mutilation, torture and displacement. The unconscionable acts of depravity. And the wholesale exclusion of women from peace processes.
>
> (Rehn and Johnson-Sirleaf 2002: vii)

Their account of the horrors that they found is vivid, yet they also tell of women surviving trauma and finding courage to rebuild communities. They were reminded of the need to implement, monitor and evaluate policies. 'Time and again women described the wonderful documents that had been created and signed – and the failure to implement most of what have been promised' (Rehn and Johnson-Sirleaf 2002: 84). For example, Asha Hagi Elmi of Somalia calls the National Charter of Somalia 'one of the best in the Muslim world' in terms of women's rights, yet Somalia today is one of the most dangerous places on earth, ruled by warring factions that have no commitment to honouring the National Charter (in Rehn and Johnson-Sirleaf 2002: 84). The Independent Experts call for 22 substantial requirements needed to implement SCR 1325. They stress that:

> Resolution 1325 is a watershed political framework that makes women – and a gender perspective – relevant to negotiating peace agreements, planning refugee camps in peacekeeping operations and reconstructing war-torn societies. It makes the pursuit of gender equality relevant to every single Council action.
>
> (Rehn and Johnson-Sirleaf 2002: 3)

In assessing SCR 1325 after two years, there was a follow-up report to the Security Council by the Secretary-General (2004a) giving illustrative examples of progress and identifying gaps. NGOWG also released an alternative report which documents activities outside of the UN, looking at civil society and NGO initiatives in Africa, Central and South America, Europe, North America, South Asia, South-East Asia/Pacific and the Middle East and West Asia (NGOWG 2004). This group identifies the remaining challenges of the Resolution in the weakness of the language; the lack of political will among member states; and that most people do not know that it exists. Strengths lie in its global consistency, that it is used as an advocacy tool across a broad cross-sector. What was the state of global politics two years on from SCR 1325? In October 2002, there were 31 areas in conflict and post-conflict situations including: Afghanistan, Algeria, Angola, Bosnia-Herzegovina, Bougainville, Burundi, Central African Republic, Chechnya, Colombia, Cyprus, Democratic Republic of Congo, East Timor, Eritrea, Ethiopia, Georgia, Guatemala, Guinea Bissau, Haiti, India, Israel, Kosovo, Liberia, Pakistan, Palestine, Rwanda, Sierra Leone, Somalia, Sri Lanka, Sudan, Tajikistan and Western Sahara. In only three of the 15 UN peacekeeping operations were there gender advisors (Democratic Republic of Congo, East Timor and Sierra Leone); women serving in UN operations totalled only 4 per cent of the police and 3 per cent of the military and there were no women at all in military peacekeeping missions in Afghanistan, Burundi, Cambodia, Golan Heights, Liberia or Tajikistan (International Women's Tribune Centre 2002). Clearly, there is a need for specific targets and benchmarks to monitor and evaluate the implementation of SCR 1325. Rehn and Johnson-Sirleaf see the obstacle in improving the gender balance in the staffing of peace operations as 'a misperception about what is required to serve in a position of leadership in a peacekeeping force' (2002: 65). They argue that the ideal criteria for leading peace operations are not military or political, but 'skills that can lead a war-torn society through a process of nation-building, economic development and reconstruction' (2002: 65).[15] Recent reports note that the common challenges to the implementation of these recommendations include the lack of funding, political will, capacity, coordination, monitoring and evaluation (INSTRAW 2006).

Some research finds that despite SCR 1325 and UN initiatives such as the Department for Disarmament Affairs Gender Action Plan to commit member states to include gender considerations in post-conflict DDR, 'gender concerns have been blatantly ignored in the planning and execution of such processes' (Schroeder *et al.* 2005: 5), and this exacerbates inequality because 'women and men have different needs in DDR' (2005: 6). For example, once the Afghan DDR programme began in October 2003, there were no gendered initiatives implemented and despite a gender office, 'it employs only one young Afghan woman' (2005: 14). The Afghan Women's Network campaigned for disarmament but its recommendations were not incorporated into official processes. And then there are clearly controversial responses to SCR 1325. As its contribution to fulfilling the commitments of SCR 1325, the Dutch military is recruiting more women into the military, arguing that the effectiveness of military peacekeeping missions would increase as numbers of women peacekeepers increased. Certainly, in Somalia the presence of women soldiers helped to lessen extreme behaviour such as human rights abuses. Whether this militarizes peacekeeping needs to be questioned.

Beijing +10

The ten-year review and appraisal of the PFA and the Outcomes Document presents a further opportunity to ascertain the advancement of gender equality and sustainable peace. With regard to the Critical Area E of the Beijing PFA, 'Women and Armed Conflict', UN OSAGI offers a stark appraisal of how women continue to struggle with the horrors of war and violence:

> Women's voices are still insufficiently heard at the tables of peace negotiations, their needs and interests are not reflected in peace treaties and ceasefire agreements and they are rarely among those making the decision to go to war. The actions mandated by the Beijing PFA in order to address women and armed conflict remain all-too relevant ten years after they were first called for.
>
> (UN OSAGI 2004a: 2)

Yet despite longstanding conflicts and continuing violence in many parts of the world, there have been positive developments.[16] The July 2002 entry into force of the Rome Statute of the ICC criminalizes sexual and gender violence as war crimes and crimes against humanity. (In subsequent chapters, the full impact of these advancements will be explained.) There have been many significant NGO reports, the UN Secretary-General's study on 'Women, Peace and Security' (2002a) and as mentioned above, UNIFEM's study on 'Women, War, Peace' (Rehn and Johnson-Sirleaf 2002). There is a greater availability of up-to-date information, manuals and guidelines on gender equality and peace and security.[17] Yet, 'women's participation or the inclusion of gender issues in conflict-resolution processes is consistently considered less "urgent" and therefore less important than other priorities' (UN OSAGI 2004a: 5). Chief obstacles to equality include lack of political motivation to lobby for women's inclusion, scarcity of funds for women's organizations, institutionalized sexism and patriarchal cultural mores.

The document *Beijing Betrayed* (Zeitlin 2005) presents women's realities and concerns from 150 countries across Africa, Asia, the Caribbean, Europe, Latin America, North America and the Pacific. June Zeitlin suggests that there are global trends creating an environment that is hostile to women's advancement, including the predominance of the neo-liberal economic framework, a growing militarization post-9/11 framed by the US-led 'global war on terrorism' and the invasions of Afghanistan and Iraq, and rising fundamentalism, both secular and religious (2005: 7). The document suggests that the linkages between the PFA's 12 Critical Areas of Concern are intertwined and captured in seven themes:

1   human rights;
2   peace and security;
3   power and decision-making;
4   poverty eradication;
5   education;
6   natural resources; and
7   environmental security and health.

The subregional reports found that government inaction continues to stall progress on national implementation of global commitments to SCR 1325. 'The rhetoric has failed to play out in the reality of women's lives', with governments adopting a piecemeal approach that cannot fulfil the promises of Beijing (Zeitlin 2005: 11). There is a proliferation of important reports on women, peace and security which concentrate on positive lessons that can be gained by sharing global stories. This book attempts to combine a theoretical analysis of many key concepts of peacebuilding with practical examples.

Peacebuilding as process: pre-conflict, conflict and post-accord

I have outlined the historical background to the importance of the Beijing PFA and SCR 1325. Significant achievements have been noted and remaining challenges emphasized. I now explore some of the many different ways to understand peacebuilding. First, I examine UN understandings of peacebuilding and peace processes. Second, I explore broader understandings of peacebuilding and explain what I mean by peacebuilding as a process. This explanation establishes the foundation of my argument that peacebuilding is an ongoing process in pre-conflict, conflict and post-accord stages in formal and informal contexts.

UN understandings of peacebuilding

In 1992, former UN Secretary-General Boutros Boutros-Ghali wrote *An Agenda for Peace*, a document that differentiates the UN's understandings of peacekeeping, peacemaking and peacebuilding. In this document, he distinguishes between preventive diplomacy to avoid a crisis, peacemaking as a prelude to peacekeeping and adds 'post-conflict peacebuilding' with an emphasis on the prevention of the recurrence of conflict (1992: 5).[18] Peacebuilding for Boutros-Ghali refers specifically to structural peacebuilding in post-conflict societies, 'rebuilding the institutions and infrastructures of nations torn by civil war and strife; and building bonds of peaceful mutual benefit among nations formally at war' (1992: 8). In 1995, Boutros-Ghali presented the *Supplement to An Agenda to Peace*. While he located most peacebuilding activities within the UN offices, agencies and programmes with 'responsibilities in the economic, social, humanitarian and human rights fields' (Boutros-Ghali 1995: 9), he does consider two types of situations where the UN might perform post-conflict peacebuilding. First, as part of traditional peacekeeping, with the stress on creating structures for institutional peace. Second, his suggestions focus on early warning systems as preventative peacebuilding. A new dialogue about peace was beginning. Boutros-Ghali established a task force to report to the Security Council on the availability of tools for post-conflict peacebuilding. The report (UNDP 1996) kept Boutros-Ghali's 1993 definition of peacebuilding linked to peace settlements. Consequently, the peacebuilding tools that the report considers remain in the post-conflict reconstruction stage.[19]

In 1999, former Secretary-General Kofi Annan, in his *Prevention of War and Disaster* document, writes that 'post-conflict peacebuilding seeks to prevent the resurgence of conflict and to create the conditions necessary for a sustainable peace in war-torn societies' (UN Secretary-General 1999: 101) and designated the UN Department of Political Affairs (DPA) as the focal point for post-conflict peacebuilding.[20] In 2000, Lakhdar Brahimi's *Report on Peace Support Operations* acknowledged 'the need to build the United Nations capacity to contribute to peacebuilding, both preventive and post-conflict' (2000: 1). Peace operations entail three principal activities: conflict prevention and peacemaking; peacekeeping; and peacebuilding. Peacemaking tries to bring conflicts to a halt through diplomacy and mediation. The DPA covers peacemaking as the diplomatic means to persuade conflicting parties to cease hostilities and negotiate a settlement and encompasses peacebuilding before, during and after conflict. Yet sometimes, DPA discourse refers to peacebuilding in post-conflict situations only. Peacekeeping incorporates military and civilian elements working together to build peace in the dangerous aftermath of civil wars. The UN Department of Peacekeeping Operations (DPKO) covers peacekeeping as a way to help countries torn by conflict to create conditions for sustainable peace. Peacemaking, peacebuilding and peacekeeping sometimes slide together.

To return to Brahimi's understanding, he defines peacebuilding as 'activities undertaken on the far side of conflict to reassemble the foundations of peace and provide the tools for building on those foundations something that is more than just the absence of war' (2000: 2–3). Brahimi includes activities such as reintegrating former combatants, strengthening law to improve respect for human rights, providing technical assistance for democratic development and promoting conflict resolution and reconciliation techniques (2000: 3). Brahimi acknowledges complex interrelationships: 'while the peacebuilders may not be able to function without the peacekeepers' support, the peacekeepers have no exit without the peacebuilders' work (2000: 5). In Haiti and Tajikistan, peacebuilding support offices were established as follow-ons to other peace operations and established as independent initiatives in Guatemala and Guinea-Bissau. Brahimi acknowledges that peacebuilding is only effective when there is active engagement with the local parties 'and that engagement should be multidimensional in nature' (2000: 7), but he says nothing about women's active role in peacebuilding processes. The report admits to ambiguity in peacebuilding in embracing multiple sectors of activity including political, legal, military, diplomatic, developmental, human rights, child protection, gender issues and humanitarian concerns. To summarize, peacemaking resolves conflict, peacekeeping preserves peace and peacebuilding rebuilds institutions, infrastructures and personal bonds. While peacebuilding is defined as part of the peace process continuum, within most UN departments it is usually qualified as predominantly 'post-conflict'. The Brahimi Report notes that a clear division of labour had not yet emerged in the UN system, neither in 'the formulation of comprehensive peacebuilding strategies, nor in their implementation' (UN 2000: 5). This lack of clarity is not academic, but has practical relevance for who does what, who is recognized for doing what, and who is supported for doing what in transitional societies.

It is important to note that UN peacebuilding support offices have only existed for a short time and are 'somewhat experimental' (DPA 2002: 2), needing to be flexible, strategic and responsive to different political situations. They are small operations, only employ a few UN staff in addition to civilian staff and exist in countries which have undergone civil war and entered a post-conflict stage. The first office was in Liberia in 1997. Others have been set up in the Central African Republic, Guinea-Bissau and Tajikistan. Smaller political offices in places such as Bougainville undertake peacebuilding activities. A prime part of peacebuilding is to get countries to work together towards a common goal of DDR. The distinctions between peacebuilding and humanitarian activities are not always apparent given the goals of DDR, democratization and good governance and poverty alleviation. Also, the motivations for peacebuilding cannot be taken for granted, particularly when instigated by formal structures. Alejandro Bendaña explains how, in the post-Cold War period, the ideal of peacebuilding as set out in Boutros-Ghali's (1992, 1995) documents was optimistic, but in the light of events in the Balkans and elsewhere, the ideals of peacebuilding as being driven by civil society groups gave way to 'peace-enforcement from above and the outside' (2004: 1), with a conceptual and practical confusion between peacekeeping, 'humanitarian' intervention and peacebuilding. That is, 'legitimating political intervention laid the basis for legitimating military force, from peacebuilding to nation-building' (2004: 1). Bendaña's argument is strong, that in a post-9/11 context of the US-led 'war on terrorism', the way that nation-building is defined may have little to do with democracy, autonomy and sustainable peace.[21] In Bendaña's terms, peacebuilding often 'becomes the smokescreen behind which equally self-serving political and economic practices are enforced upon the State and the people' (2004: 7). His plea is for a normative restoration of peacebuilding, nation-building and state-building, divorced from a corporatist neo-liberal and militarist superpower agenda. My defence of peacebuilding supports his plea.

Take, for example, democratization and women's equality. Equality and civil rights are, as Mary Caprioli argues, implicit in democratic principles, 'therefore, women should enjoy higher levels of security in democratic states, based on higher levels of equality' (2004: 415–416). Yet, as she points out, despite claims of adhering to democratic principles, cultural norms in new democracies remain powerful. During a parliamentary debate in Papua New Guinea, a member of parliament states, 'wife beating is an accepted custom … we are wasting our time debating the issue' (in Caprioli 2004: 416). Claims to be practising democracy cannot ensure women's security, as Afghanistan and Iraq testify. Certainly, democracy is 'good for domestic peace' because democratic principles support representation, human rights, international law, diversity, pluralism and peaceful conflict resolution through negotiation and compromise, but as developing and post-communist countries testify, there are tensions between peacemaking, peacebuilding and 'processes of democracy-building' (Burnell 2004: 1–3). For example, in Afghanistan, cultural mores remain powerful, thereby restricting many changes. The Northern Alliance is as prohibitive toward women as the Taliban. The upshot of this analysis is not to discard the goal of 'democratic peace', but it highlights the tensions between the important ideals within democratic principles and the realities of cultural gendered inequality that suppress their realization. (I return to this tension in Chapter 4.)

In recognition of the need for greater coordination of UN departments in peacebuilding, in September 2003, Secretary-General Kofi Annan appointed a high-level panel to propose major UN reforms and the creation of a UN Peacebuilding Commission (PBC) was one recommendation. Annan acknowledges a mixed record with success in managing and resolving conflicts as well as peacebuilding in Eastern Slovenia, East Timor, El Salvador, Guatemala, Mozambique, Namibia and South Africa and failures in Angola, Bosnia, Rwanda and Somalia (UN Secretary-General 2004b: 2). In Annan's (UN Secretary-General 2004b) report on *A More Secure World: Our Shared Responsibility*, he recognized the gap in the UN's peacebuilding capacity. His response to this panel refers to peacebuilding as 'post-conflict'. In 2005, his report *In Larger Freedom: Towards Security, Development and Human Rights for All* (UN Secretary-General 2005) endorsed the proposed PBC that was agreed at the 2005 UN World Summit. The draft resolution for the PBC recognizes the contribution of civil society organizations in peacebuilding efforts, including women's organizations to prevent and resolve conflicts. However, UNIFEM and NGOWG (2005) raise concerns regarding the need for staff positions dedicated to liasing with civil society, particularly women's organizations. They stress the need for local people who are most affected by conflicts to be able to voice their perspectives and the need for the inclusion into the PBC of gender experts drawn from a range of UN offices. Despite frequent acknowledgement of women as 'untapped resources' (UNDP 2003) and the significance of SCR 1325, the creation of the PBC is no guarantee that women's voices will be heard, or their role enhanced. I aim to show that the conceptual ambiguity on peace-building outlined in this section unwittingly undervalues the actual, informal work done at all stages of peace processes, not merely in the post-conflict stage.

Broadening the idea of peacebuilding

I have noted above some of the haziness in orthodox UN usages of the term *peacebuilding* and shifting understandings in peacebuilding practices. Before explaining why I believe the idea of peacebuilding needs expanding, it is worth clarifying further the central concepts of peace, peace processes and post-conflict peacebuilding as used by a range of theorists. Kenneth Boulding was the first to present the idea of 'stable peace' as 'a situation in which the probability of war is so small that it does not really enter into the calculations of any of the people involved' (1978: 13).[22] Understandings of *peace* have expanded from negative peace as merely the absence of war, armed conflict or violence, to positive peace, which requires the resolution of root causes of conflicts and the maintenance of sustainable peace. Notions of positive peace drive toward ideals of how a society should be, with goals of equality and inclusive, participatory and democratic structures with open, accountable government. These ideals open the field of peacebuilding up 'to include the promotion and encouragement of new forms of citizenship and political structures which will develop active democracies' (Pankhurst, 1999a: 6). The influential peace theorist Johan Galtung writes, '"peace", in my view, is another word for equality, equity, equal rights/dignity, symmetry, reciprocity, diversity/symbiosis' (2004a: 1). There is a lot entailed in such an understanding of peace. In order to realize positive peace, the root causes of conflict need to be tackled. (Questions of guilt, innocence, a human rights culture, impunity and justice, forgiveness, amnesty and reconcili-ation are all implicated and developed in forthcoming chapters.) Hastily drawn peace settlements may lead to a temporary cessation of violence, but they may not provide the substantial grounding for a lasting peace, where Galtung's understanding of peace comes into fruition. For example, peace advocate Lul Seyoum of Eritrea says that despite the Eritrean Popular Liberation Front policy of total gender equality during the war, with the advent of independence and elections, the country 'has generally sought to return to the traditional ways which discriminates severely against women' (in Pankhurst, 1999a: 9). Positive peace is a rich and demanding concept.

Peace processes consist of a complex range of informal and formal activ-ities. Informal activities include peace marches and protests, inter-group dia-logue, the promotion of inter-cultural tolerance and understanding and the empowerment of ordinary citizens in economic, social, cultural and political spheres. A range of actors, such as UN entities, international, regional, national and local organizations, and grass roots organizations, including peace groups, NGOs, women's groups, religious organizations and individuals, conduct the activities. Formal peace processes (as previously outlined) include early warning strategies, preventive diplomacy, conflict prevention, peacemaking, peacebuilding and global disarmament. Activities include conflict resolution, peace negotiations, reconciliation, reconstruction of infrastructure and the provision of humanitarian aid. These activities are conducted by political leaders, the military, international organizations such as the UN, regional and subregional organizations such as the Africa Union, the Organization for Security and Cooperation in Europe, the Organization of American States or the Economic Community of West African States, as well as governmental, non-governmental and humanitarian organizations. A UN report by Annan acknowledges that 'the contributions women can and do make to peacebuilding through informal processes is increasing' (UN Secretary-General 2002a: 5), thereby acknowledging informal peacebuilding. This is significant. At a residential workshop with 16 South African women who define their work as encompassing peacebuilding, Cheryl de la Rey and Susan McKay say that the 'perception of peace as a process was pervasive' (2006: 142) and it is directed toward meeting 'basic needs such as the need for food, water, and shelter' (2006: 147). As I will demonstrate repeatedly, how many women understand peace processes differs from the norm – typically it includes attending to practical material needs that further a sense of security. It is hard to feel secure if you are starving, your shack has been destroyed or your water source polluted.

What, then, is meant by *post-conflict peacebuilding and reconstruction?* Much of the literature and strategies for peacebuilding concentrate on the post-conflict stage, and refer to the 'long-term process that occurs after violent conflict has slowed down or come to a halt' after peacemaking and peacekeeping (Maiese 2003: 1). Roland Paris is explicit: 'peacebuilding begins when the fighting has stopped. It is, by definition, a post-conflict enterprise' (2004: 39). Some scholars and practitioners understand peacebuilding as post-conflict, while others mean more. Eric Brahm, in describing stages of conflict as no conflict, latent conflict, emergence, escalation, stalemate, de-escalation, settlement/resolution, post-conflict peacebuilding and reconciliation, concludes that 'finally, if and when an agreement is reached, peacebuilding efforts work to repair damaged relationships with the long-term goal of reconciling former opponents' (2003: 2). Michelle Maiese defines peacebuilding as 'a long-term process that occurs after violent conflict has slowed down or come to a halt' (2003: 1). She states explicitly, 'it is the phase of the peace process that takes place after peacemaking and peacekeeping' (2003: 1). Maiese expands further that many NGOs use peacebuilding as 'an umbrella concept', which encompasses long-term transformative efforts including early warning and response efforts, violence prevention, advocacy, humanitarian assistance, ceasefires and the establishment of peace zones (2003: 1).[23] I am maintaining that informal, long-term peacebuilding that addresses the underlying substantive root causes of conflict fall under this umbrella.

As noted, in the UN, peacebuilding typically refers to formal approaches used in post-conflict reconstruction. However, I maintain that in order to appreciate fully the work of grass roots peacebuilders, it is important to expand the concept of peacebuilding to include all stages of peace processes. Cordula Reimann and Norbert Ropers suggest that those working in the peace practice field are responding to the post-9/11 remilitarization of foreign policy through 'a revitalization of the normative references to their noncoercive peacebuilding work as the only acceptable and successful alternative to long-lasting peace processes and structures' (2005: 32). Within the UN, the CSW talks of 'post-conflict peacebuilding'.[24] UNIFEM explicitly defines peacebuilding from women's perspectives at all stages of peace processes, which contrasts with orthodox UN emphases on structural reconstruction.

Others are broadening the idea of peacebuilding. Louise Diamond and John McDonald (1996), of the Institute for Multi-Track Diplomacy, use the term 'peacemaking' in a generic fashion to include peacekeeping, peacebuilding, peace research, peace studies, peace education and conflict resolution. James Notter and Louise Diamond provide a broader theoretical definition of peacebuilding activities as 'creating the tangible and intangible conditions to enable a conflict-habituated system to become a peace system. Peacebuilding can be done, therefore, before, during or after violence erupts' (1996: 5). They suggest that to achieve conflict transformation, political, structural and social peacebuilding are necessary. Political peacebuilding involves the efforts of governments to focus on agreements and deals that establish sound political arrangements and build legal infrastructure. Structural peacebuilding creates the structures that support the implementation of a more peaceful culture, such as funding, economic provision and community relations. Social peacebuilding is the grass roots work that is done around human relationships and includes the beliefs, attitudes, values, feelings, emotions and opinions of all citizens. Despite political and economic progress in a nation emerging from conflict, when people are unwilling to counter prejudices of sexism, sectarianism, racism, ethnic hatred or economic domination over others, it is possible to have political and structural peacebuilding that does not contribute to social peacebuilding or a culture of peace.[25] This book concentrates on this third form of social peacebuilding, but of necessity includes bridge-building, capacity-building and institution-building, part of political and structural peacebuilding, in order to highlight where women remain marginalized from full participation.

The Peace and Conflict Ledger rates countries according to their peacebuilding capacity. A country's peacebuilding capacity is rated high when it avoids outbreaks of armed conflict, provides reasonable levels of human security, does not have active policies of discrimination against minorities, manages movement for self-determination, maintains stable democratic institutions, has substantial resources and is free of serious threats from its neighbouring countries (Marshall and Gurr 2005: 8).[26] However a country is rated, there are discrepancies in the priorities between organizations that are involved in conflict prevention and resolution, humanitarian emergency aid or long-term capacity development and institution-building, leading to 'recognition of the need to reconcile the fields of development and peacebuilding' (Junne and Verkoren 2005: 4). As I will explain shortly, this recognition is confirmed by the increasing use of the concept of human security. Indeed, some argue that the only way to move from marginalization to the integration of women in peacebuilding is through gendering human security (Karamé 2001). Human security initiatives make 'human beings and their communities, rather than states' their point of reference and focus on protection of the most vulnerable (Hunt and Posa 2001: 1).

Desmond Tutu says that 'human security privileges people over states, reconciliation over revenge, diplomacy over deterrence, and multilateral engagement over coercive unilateralism' (in Mack 2005: iii). While human security and national security should be mutually reinforcing, 'secure states do not automatically mean secure peoples' (Mack 2005: viii). This is because old analytic frameworks based on wars between states are 'largely irrelevant to violent conflicts *within* states. The latter now make up more than 95 per cent of armed conflicts' (Mack 2005: viii). Enloe's point on this focus of security is valid, that 'because feminists start from the conditions of women's lives, and because they see how many forms violence and oppression can take, they are more likely to define peace as women's achievement of control over their own lives' (1993: 65). (I extend arguments on security shortly.) I have explained the difference between peace, peace processes and post-conflict reconstruction. I have indicated how others are beginning to broaden an understanding of peacebuilding, by linking it to human security. In the next section, I build this case further by showing the limitations of narrow concepts of peacebuilding.

Moving beyond post-conflict reconstruction

I argue that a typical usage of peacebuilding as located solely or even predominantly in the post-conflict reconstruction stage after peace accords is limiting. Others argue this. John Paul Lederach maintains that post-conflict is 'the greatest oxymoron of them all' (2005: 43). He also states that peacebuilding is more than post-accord reconstruction; it is a 'comprehensive concept' that 'involves a wide range of activities and functions that both precede and follow formal peace accords' (2004: 20). Lederach emphasizes that such a conceptualization is a dynamic 'process of *building*' (2004: 20; emphasis in original). My contribution explains how women build these processes.

I suggest that in terms of gender inclusivity, there are three significant consequences of a limited understanding of peacebuilding: problematic perceptions of what constitutes 'post-conflict'; ignoring grass roots peace work; and providing excuses for not including women in peace negotiations. I explore each of these three dilemmas. First, as explained, while 'peacebuilding' is understood increasingly as practically multifaceted, generally, it is referred to in the post-conflict reconstruction stage, after ceasefires or peace accords. What is wrong with positioning peacebuilding in the post-conflict stage? Specifically, what are its ramifications for women? The very notion of 'post-conflict' may be problematic. Often the term is used in a context of 'negative peace' where widespread violence has ended. The term '"post-conflict" generally refers to a period when predominantly male combatants have ceased to engage in "official" war' (Handrahan 2004: 429). However, insecurity continues in so-called 'post-conflict' periods. While the guns are silent or the machetes temporarily laid aside, cultural, domestic and structural violence remain (Vlachová and Biason 2005). While 'the forms and locations of gendered violence change at the cessation of active conflict, women's relations with war-traumatized children, family members or fighters will place gendered demands upon them' (Chinkin 2003: 11) in renegotiating relationships. Gender identities shift during war, but newly discovered self-confidence can be smashed with one reminder of aggression.

Lori Handrahan claims that, with the exception of Cockburn and Zarkov's (2002) work, 'little feminist academic work has examined gender in post-conflict environments' (2004: 430). It is mainly feminist practitioners in NGOs or UNIFEM, DAW, UN OSAGI or NGOWG who are producing reports on gender and post-conflict. The post-conflict environment is acutely concerned with male power systems, struggles and identity formation and a 'postwar moment' is 'part of a continuum of conflict' (Cockburn and Zarkov 2002: 10). 'Postwar' seems more realistic than 'post-conflict'. Within post war society, militarization 'serves to re-entrench the privileging of masculinity' (Enloe 2002: 22). As Christine Chinkin (2003) argues, not only is the use of post-conflict problematic, so too the notion of 'reconstruction' may be a misnomer for women (and other marginalized groups) in implying the restoration of a previously existing position which did not exist prior to the violence. The goal for peacebuilders is not to reconstruct a time before conflict, but to reach 'an enhanced social position that accords full citizenship, social justice and empowerment based upon respect for standards of women's human dignity and human rights' (Chinkin 2003: 11). Many civil society groups do not emerge solely in post-conflict spaces, but are present in nascent forms during conflict. Such groups have a strong concept of 'positive peace' that means more than the absence of violence, but includes all the processes that facilitate social justice and gender equity. The goal for peacebuilding activists is to create and support sustainable relationships 'and structures that are tolerant, respectful, and constructively respond to the root causes and symptoms of conflict over the long-term' (Fast and Neufeldt 2005: 25).

Chris Corrin distinguishes usefully between short-term peacebuilding, which involves the international community in 'disarmament, weapons destruction, refugee repatriation, security force training, elections monitoring and institutional reform', and longer-term peacebuilding undertaken by local people and NGOs across civil society with 'linkage across political, economic, humanitarian and social spheres' (2004: 8). I concur with Corrin in arguing that 'conventional peacebuilding methods do not capture the full range of areas across which women work toward regenerating their communities' (2004: 26). As Cynthia Enloe expresses it, the ending of any war is a complicated process. It is not an event: the signing of a peace accord, the decommissioning of a missile. It is a long series of steps, with each step shaping the steps that follow.

(1993: 13)

(Examples of such steps are given in following chapters.) Many development and relief workers and conflict resolution specialists view social transformation, humanitarian concerns, social justice and the need to nurture civil society 'before, during and after violent conflict' (Goodhand and Hulme 1999: 16) as integral to sustainable peace. Peacebuilding 'embraces immediate, short, and longer-term policy approaches to laying the foundation upon which peace can thrive' (Knight 2004: 356).

First, my criticism of the idea of post-conflict reconstruction is that it does not make sense for many women, thereby problematizing its constant use. Sometimes the exclusions and forms of oppression that stimulated violence are reproduced through the jostling for privileged positions in restructuring post war societies. When the extremity of violence ceases and peace agreements are being negotiated, there are crucial moments of opportunity. Feminist theorists ask the question, 'is it thinkable that the postwar moment be used as an opportunity to turn a society towards gender equality' (Zarkov and Cockburn 2002: 11) as part of the lasting peace process?

Second, restricting peacebuilding to 'post-conflict' misses the practical, infor-mal work that women (and men) do to build peace in grass roots groups, communities, villages, tribal groups, clans and families. Because women univer-sally are the prime nurturers in relationships, they have huge stakes in community stability, and this nurturing role is often the prime motivator for peacebuilding in all stages of conflict. Many women play crucial roles in unofficial, ad hoc peace-building. As we will see in Chapter 3, often these roles emerge from the experience of oppression and exclusion and in seeking an inclusive society. Some women are non-violent activists, mediators, trauma-healing therapists, gender pol-icymakers, educators or humanitarian aid workers. Others facilitate dialogue between warring factions, tribes, clans or ethnic groups. In the Solomon Islands, an effective strategy is to maximize the respect for women in island cultures: 'The women visited the camps of the militias engaged in the conflict and appealed, as mothers speaking to their sons, to end the violence' (Wake 2004: 109). Women often bridge divides across traditional ethnic, religious and cultural divisions, uniting on matters of commonality which generally revolve around the practicali-ties of prime nurturing – such as providing food, water, shelter, health care, educa-tion, childcare and economic welfare. Often, peacebuilding emerges at the peak of violence instigated by members of communities who are the most violated and thus have so much to gain in securing a just security. 'It is a lost opportunity not to build on the changed roles that women have adopted through war as the recovery phase can be a period of positive transformation for gender relations' (UNDP 2003: 2). As I will expand in forthcoming chapters, women's central role in famil-ies and communities is a prime motivator in seeking peaceful strategies for dealing with inter-communal violence. When women are excluded from official conflict prevention, their potential impact on political decisions is limited. My further criticism of a restriction of peacebuilding to 'post-conflict' is that it fails to recognize much of the wonderful work that happens in local communities.

Third, narrow notions of peacebuilding provide excuses for not including women at negotiating tables. Some qualifiers are needed. In many contexts, women find it difficult to build the necessary coalitions to enable them to come to the negotiation table and represent 'women's interests'. Some women are not motivated to represent 'women's interests'. Particularly in India, Indonesia and the Philippines, women are in formal negotiations as family members of powerful males but not necessarily representing other women. Certainly, as previously mentioned, some women are combatants or supportive of paramilitary or terrorist organizations. Between 1990 and 2002, girl soldiers were among fighting forces in at least 54 countries and fought in 36 conflicts (Mazurana *et al.* 2002: 97). Dyan Mazurana (2004) provides insight from in-depth discussions with 32 women leaders from 18 armed opposition groups currently engaged in armed conflict from Aceh/Indonesia, Burundi, Iran, Kurdistan/Iraq, Nagaland/India, the Philippines, Somalia, Sri Lanka, Sudan and Turkey and those recently engaged in armed conflict in Colombia, El Salvador, Ecuador, Guatemala, Kosovo and Northern Ireland. Her insight provides nuanced understandings as to why women enter armed opposition groups. Many do so to further justice by taking up arms. Most of the women joined armed opposition groups as a means to empowerment, particularly 'to shield themselves from further violations of their physical and mental integrity by state actors' (Mazurana 2004: 3). While none of these women joined these groups with women's rights in mind, 'half of the women are working within their groups to include some women's rights in their political platforms' (Mazurana 2004: 4). In Nepal, about one-third of the Maoist fighters are women, with figures as high as 50 per cent in some districts (NGOWG 2006: 25). Many of these women combatants cite economic survival as the reason for joining the Maoists. Being a combatant gives a sense of security to these women. Thus I make no assumptions as to female natural peacefulness or that all women want to be present at peace negotiations to represent women.

Generally speaking, there is a failure to grant women due recognition for their active mediation at all stages of peace processes and hence women are appallingly absent in formal Track 1 peace processes. Sanam Naraghi Anderlini and Victoria Stanski (2004: 22) suggest that there are a range of excuses typically used to rationalize women's exclusion from negotiating tables, such as locally embedded gender inequality, and the fact that fewer women are involved in fighting is assumed to mean that fewer women need to be involved in peacemaking. Other excuses are the notion that peace accords are gender neutral or liberation precedes gender equality. Women often feel insecure about their political skills and they receive insufficient support in developing their underutilized capacities. As I will demonstrate more substantially in subsequent chapters, where they are present, there is ample evidence that they initiate different issues related to human security and well-being, feeling safe and being inclusive and the practical needs of food, health, education or economic livelihood. My contention is that women are involved already to varying degrees in peace processes, albeit generally in informal ways, but they need to be included in formal peace structures in order to establish meaningful gender equality and to place on the agenda not just issues that help violence to cease, but matters that affect human well-being and sustain peace. An expanded notion of peacebuilding does not necessarily draw women in, but it ought to recognize the work that women are doing, and direct resources accordingly.

Peacebuilding as process

In this section, I explain how feminist researchers and local grass roots groups understand peacebuilding to encompass both formal and informal processes. Many agencies resolving conflict and engaged in relief and development work also understand peacebuilding broadly to mean any activity that prevents, alleviates or resolves violent conflict. Broad understandings of peacebuilding are not unique to women's groups. What is unique, as Dyan Mazurana and Susan McKay found, is that women in many different cultures understand their peacebuilding activities as being 'intertwined with issues of gender justice, demilitarization, the promotion of non-violence, reconciliation, the rebuilding of relationships, gender equality, women's human rights, the building of and participation in democratic institutions, and sustaining the environment' (2002: 75). While none of these issues on their own constitute peacebuilding, each issue is linked to women's strategies for peace and creating the conditions through which peace becomes meaningful. For example, when equal civil, political, economic and social rights are promoted with 'gender-sensitive' strategies (Spees 2004: 9), gender justice is affirmed. This is crucial, because 'if women do not participate in the decision-making structures of a society, they are unlikely to become involved in decisions about the conflict or the peace process that follows' (UN Secretary-General 2002b: 1). Given that 'one key measure to achieve justice is the increased participation of women in politics' (Corrin 2004), particular attention must be given to this dimension of justice.

Peacebuilding processes that encourage participation empower people to foster relationships. Lisa Schirch and Manjrika Sewak suggest that such networks 'form an architecture of peacebuilding networks or "platforms" that allow people to cooperate, coordinate and form connecting spaces for collaboration' (2005a: 4–5). (This idea of 'connecting spaces' crops up throughout the book.) Schirch and Sewak suggest that the cycle of peacebuilding has four components (2005a: 5). First, waging conflict non-violently involves monitoring and advocacy, direct action and civilian-based defence. Second, reducing direct violence involves the legal and justice systems, humanitarian assistance, peacekeeping, military intervention, ceasefire agreements, peace zones and early warning programmes. Third, building capacity involves training and education, development, military conversion, research and evaluation. Fourth, transforming relationships involves trauma-healing, conflict transformation such as dialogue, negotiation, mediation, restorative justice, transitional justice, governance and policymaking. Understood in this fashion, peacebuilding is a comprehensive process with an emphasis on networks of relationships.

It is important to maintain a distinction between the immediate short-term demands of peacebuilding that are essential after violence has ceased and peace settlements are signed, and longer-term peacebuilding undertaken by local people and NGOs across civil society in all political, economic, humanitarian, legal and social spheres. While many definitions of peacebuilding focus attention on the reconciliation of diverse relationships, 'it is the grass roots women's groups that emphasize the centrality of addressing psychosocial and human needs in the peacebuilding work – far more than do governmental organizations, NGOs, or the UN' (Mazurana and McKay 1999: 8). For example, Mary Abu-Saba (1999) interviewed Lebanese women, finding that they described their peacebuilding as building bridges between factions involved in the Lebanese civil war. In a report on the Akobo Peace Conference in South Sudan, Nuer women said that 'making peace means figuring out how to meet the material, social, and spiritual requirements of life as conditions necessary for peace in any meaningful sense' (Duany, in Mazurana and McKay 1999: 12). Similarly, Susanne Thurfjell says that in her experience with women in Somalia, 'peace is not seen as a matter of discussion, but as a way of living, of security and food for your family, of a future for your children' (in Mazurana and McKay 1999: 13). Caral Bluntschli writes from Haiti of the effect of economic injustice on women's roles 'and how that affects their cultural capacities to build peace', linking the priority of feeding one's children with peacebuilding (in Mazurana and McKay 1999: 13). Rehn and Johnson-Sirleaf found that in Sierra Leone, building peace can mean taking in the children of neighbours, friends or family members who were killed in the war, whereas in Kosovo, peace work meant rebuilding damaged houses as well as friendships with former neighbours (2002: 76–77). Despite different strategies, women's peacebuilding activities revolve around similar processes that contribute to the healing of relationships and meeting everyday needs.

Peacebuilding includes all processes that promote non-violence and foster equality, justice and human rights. The meanings and practices of peacebuilding are culturally specific. To build peace requires culturally meaningful dialogue and reflection on what constitutes peace and security within different cultures, nationalities, ethnicities and for different groups of people, including men and women. I agree with Donna Pankhurst that, in order to promote a peace that meets everyday needs, social, political and economic structures as well as relationships need transformation and thus the process of peacebuilding encompasses democratic principles of participation, rights, social justice and equality (1999a: 4). (These principles and the practices they lead to, are expanded in the following chapters.) The importance of processes such as mediation, dialogue, advocacy, conflict management and reconciliation cannot be overstated in building peace. For relief and development workers, humanitarian issues, sustainable development and social justice are paramount to their vital tasks, therefore they too nurture civil constituencies for peace. A broadened understanding of peace-building processes has huge implications for the UN, donor agencies, inter-national NGOs and the World Bank. My vision of peacebuilding is broad. I argue that peacebuilding involves all processes that build positive relation-ships, heal wounds, reconcile antagonistic differences, restore esteem, respect rights, meet basic needs, enhance equality, instil feelings of security, empower moral agency and are democratic, inclusive and just.

Security in feeling included in peace processes

How does this broad understanding of peacebuilding fit with contemporary security dilemmas? The end of the Cold War signalled a shift from international to predominantly intra-state ethnic, religious and political conflicts. In such a context, conflict prevention associated with military intervention challenges state sovereignty. The 9/11 terrorist attacks on America and subsequent attacks on westerners in Bali, Egypt, London and Madrid demonstrate the need to address the root causes of conflict as early as possible and tackle the threat of global ter-rorism before it escalates uncontrollably. We have noted already that until recently, a gender perspective was largely absent from conflict analyses and reconciliation processes and additionally, it 'is completely lacking from conflict early warning and preventive response systems' (Schmeidl and Piza-Lopez 2002: 2). Yet, Rose Mukankomeje, Rwanda MP, writes that there were no real surprises with the genocide: 'when we reflected on the early warning signals and the preceding events, we could see that the patriotic forces had actually prepared for this strategy' (in International Alert and Women Waging Peace, 1999: 37). Early warning is proactive and 'it is argued that engendering early warning will improve conflict prevention' by considering the concerns of men and women (Schmeidl and Piza-Lopez 2002: 4). A gender analysis on the root causes and effects of conflict can reveal nuanced understandings of inequalities, injustices and levels of oppression which are characteristic of societies embroiled in conflict (Tickner 1999) and may prevent further conflict. Studies in places such as Guatemala, Liberia and Northern Ireland suggest that women included in peace processes introduce issues of education, health care, employment, human rights and land rights as integral to debates on 'peace and security' primarily because of their intimate connections within families, tribes, clans, informal networks and community groups (Online Working Group on Women and Armed Conflict 1999: 4).[27] Mainstreaming a gender analysis at an early stage may lead to a more comprehensive understanding of the realities of conflict. For peacebuilding to occur 'a reasonable level of physical security' is a prerequisite (UN Secretary-General 2004b: 2). Creating the conditions for this security varies; sometimes it is achieved by dialogue or negotiation between warring parties, in other places, a stabilization force with robust engagement is necessary. Security does not rest on military might and economic power. A prime example of the need to expand the concept of security is evident in places where there is peacekeeping, where secur-ity should be experienced. While Sierra Leone has high numbers of peacekeepers, the women of Sierra Leone do not feel safe, and until they do and there is systematic monitoring and reporting on violations against women, rebuilding cannot begin in earnest.

Redefining national and human security

In post-Cold war terms, intra-state civil wars are the biggest obstacle to peace. The battlefields are the marketplaces, the villages and small towns where women, children, the elderly, ill and disabled remain when men go to war. 'Security' can be no longer solely defined in military terms, neither can we see the sovereign state as a guarantor of security. 'Human security' ushers a 'paradigm shift from security studies to peace studies' (Galtung 2004b: 6), where people's needs are central to international security. Security studies explore problems of violence, counterviolence and threats. 'Peace studies tend to see violence as the consequence of untransformed conflict and dehumanization, and solutions in terms of conflict transformation and depolarization *before violence gets started*' (Galtung 2004b: 6; emphasis in original). To explain the importance of a new concept such as human security, Galtung uses the examples of Rwanda in 1994 as the mistake of doing nothing, Bosnia (Srebrenica) in 1995 as giving UN-led peacekeeping a bad name, and the US-led NATO war against Serbia in 1999 to protect the Kosovans of giving humanitarian assistance a bad name. In 2001, a UN Commission on Human Security was launched, shifting attention from state security to human security.

The underlying principle to human security is an understanding that to reduce potential risks to society, the root causes of insecurity need to be tackled, including the violation of human rights, gender-based violence, all forms of inequality and injustice, women's lack of access to land and property, poverty, disease, organized crime, sexual trafficking, political corruption, environmental degradation and terrorism. A further underlying principle is that individuals and communities know what is needed for their safety and security; hence empowerment is fundamental to the realization of human security. In these senses, it overlaps in many ways with the human needs and human development traditions because security restores human dignity. Additionally (as I expand in the following chapter), the concept of human security implies a global humanitarian responsibility for human welfare. Such a concept has given advocates of marginalized groups a way to highlight the particular vulnerabilities of those who suffer state violence and the grounds on which to argue for securing human rights. In particular, the reconceptualization of security is 'based on the assumption that social justice, including gender justice, is necessary for an enduring peace' (Tickner 1992: 129). Further, 'rethinking security means recognizing the common humanity and worth of all human beings' (Steans 1998: 105). Throughout the book, I argue strongly for this recognition of our common humanity and the importance of restoration of human dignity as fundamental to peacebuilding.

During the war in the former Yugoslavia, western agencies went to Croatia and Bosnia-Herzegovina to counsel women who had been raped. Those who listened to the women learned that what was foremost for some women was to gain news through radios of the whereabouts of their husbands, or how to get medical care or milk for their babies. 'Access to basic nutrition and services for their children raised some women's sense of security as a provider' (UN Secretary-General 2002a: 22). For women who have been uprooted and find themselves as refugees, there are manifold security issues, particularly if there is a militarized presence in or around the camp. Many displaced women are forced into providing sexual services to secure safe passage for themselves and their families or to gain necessary documentation, or once they are in the camps, they are often subject to sexualized violence. Security for women often means 'ensuring security of livelihoods, access to economic activities and training in survival skills, health issues, leadership, and conflict resolution ... to ensure their sense of dignity and self-esteem' (UN Secretary-General 2002a: 28).

While there are feminist accounts of security, (Schirch and Sewak 2005b; Blanchard 2003; Tickner 2001, 1992; Pettman 1996; Enloe 1993, 1990, 1988; Reardon 1993; Elshtain 1987) the specific feminist peace and security agenda is emerging.[28] The agenda maintains:

> That in the intricate tapestry of what constitutes real peace and security, women were clearly identifying social justice, domestic reform, women's rights, co-existence, tolerance, participatory democracy, transparency and non-violent dialogue as necessary ingredients for addressing social differences and building sustainable peace.
>
> (International Alert and Women Waging Peace, 1999: 16)

All forms of discrimination or oppression that impede the freedom necessary to exercise social, political, cultural and economic choices undermine human security. 'When societal tolerance of gendered violence is supported and legitimized by structural violence, women's security ceases to exist' (Caprioli 2004: 413). Maria Stern utilizes an open-ended definition of insecurity which 'has to do with danger, threat, harm, and the peril involved with change and openness. The security of someone/thing refers to its safety, its well-being as well as to its limitation, its stability in order to ensure its safety' (2005: 65). How is this (in) security experienced?

A project, Women in Security, Conflict Management and Peace (WISCOMP) adopts a gender lens and feminist perspectives to examine security concerns in South Asia through positing non-traditional approaches to security. Meenakshi Gopinath and Sumona DasGupta maintain that their case studies from Bangladesh on how people experience security 'show how "national" security discourses actually undermine security and create conditions of insecurity and fear for women' (2006: 199). Instead, 'freedom from fear' and 'freedom from want' are the main concerns of people and thus there is a need for a 'new vocabulary of a different security discourse' that takes seriously 'issues of life, livelihood, human dignity' (2006: 192). They problematize the concept of security and suggest that we need to ask: 'security for whom, security for which values, and security from what threats?' (2006: 193). Such a reconceptualization of security reflects feminist ethics (which I explain in Chapter 2 and develop throughout the book). Feminist ethics emphasizes a relationally defined existence, values everyday life and the importance of connectedness with others. When we view security through a gender lens, 'issues of livelihood, development, globalization and human rights have everything to do with security, since they are integral to issues of conflict and violence in all its manifestations – economic, political, cultural and phys-ical' (Gopinath and DasGupta 2006: 204). Human security focuses on the sources of people's insecurity and links everyday life with broader political processes such as the role of the state, global governance structures as well as non-state actors (Hudson 2005). As we will see throughout this book, such a focus on everyday life includes attention on 'bodily and psychic pain, on anger and silences' (Pettman 1996: 105).

Security in feeling included

Exclusion exacerbates insecurity. Inclusion fosters security. In formal peace processes, women are almost completely absent from political negotiating tables. The signing of peace agreements[29] may be the start of significant progress, but there are many different stages of transition that include security, political democratization, economic transformation, capacity-building, legislative changes, rebuilding social structures and the healing and social reconciliation that is necessary after protracted conflict. Formal peace negotiations do not always consolidate these factors:

- there were no Bosnian women in the Dayton talks in 1995 but one woman signatory;
- the rights of women were overlooked in the 1996 Sierra Leone peace accord;
- there were two women in Northern Ireland elected to multiparty peace negotiations from the NIWC in 1996;[30]
- in Tajikistan there was one woman on the 26-person national Reconciliation Commission in 1997;
- at the first Arusha peace talks on Burundi in 1998, two of the 126 delegates were women and six had observer status in the next round;
- in 1999 there was one Kosovan woman at the Rambouillet negotiations;
- in Columbia in 1999, in the pre-ceasefire agreements, there were four women from 40 delegates at the National Peace Council;
- in Guatemala, from 1991 to 1996, there was one woman member of the peace negotiations in the delegation of Guatemalan National Revolutionary Unity;
- in 1999, the Consultative Council of Timorese Resistance had two women representatives from 15;
- in 2001, there were three Afghani women out of 36 delegates to the Bonn negotiations;

- eight women from the Liberia Chapter of the Mano River Women's Peace Network (MARWOPNET) participated as observers in the Liberia peace talks of 2003;
- few women participated in the 2003 meeting in Iraq where delegates discussed an interim government – three women were nominated to the interim Iraqi Governing Council, but Aqila al-Hashimi was murdered. Women were not included in committees working on constitutional reform. In June 2004, six Iraqi women were part of the 30 member transitional Cabinet and in the 2005 elections, women made up 31 per cent of the new National Assembly, drafting the constitution.

Typically, women are overwhelmingly absent in formal peace processes as defined previously. Earlier, in dissecting post-conflict reconstruction, I cited Anderlini and Stanski's (2004: 22) explanation of the excuses typically used to justify women's exclusion from negotiating tables. These authors suggest that obstacles can be overcome and they provide helpful examples (2004: 23–24). In South Africa, women worked together across the political spectrum to establish a common agenda for women. In Northern Ireland, the NIWC won two seats at the formal peace table and mediated between extremist parties. In Burundi, when the women were barred from formal negotiation, they lobbied parties and international supporters and an all-party conference developed recommendations that were included in the 2000 peace accord. In Guatemala, Luz Méndez drew on the women's rights movement to integrate gender perspectives into the final agreement.

Does it really matter if women are not included in all stages of peace processes? Much of the argument in this book addresses this question, and my answer is that it does matter (Porter 2003a, 2005b). There are three prongs to this argument. First, women are affected by conflict and thus by the consequences of a peace agreement and its terms. The peace settlement is not merely about ending war, but also about establishing the conditions for a new, just polity. Inhibitive constraints on women's involvement in decision-making are particularly acute in conflict areas. As previously explained, 'violence and the threat of violence against women do not end when the peace accords are signed. The violence of a regime begets a general culture of violence' (Turshen 1998: 8). Entire communities suffer the disastrous consequences of armed conflict, but women and girls are affected differently because of their subordinate status. Yet, women must continue to care for maimed loved ones, ill or old dependents and traumatized, fearful children while dealing with their own personal hurt. Many are left as the head of households to deal with immediate crises of inadequate food and destroyed huts. Not including women in all stages of peace processes exacerbates gendered subordination, neglects women's needs and overlooks their capacities to 'broker agreements in their own neighbourhoods' and 'predict the acceptance of peace initiatives' (Hunt and Posa 2001: 2). Exclusions undermine the content and implementation of agreements. Exclusion supports insecurity.

Second, and relatedly, women's inclusion in all stages of peace processes is crucial for the realization of inclusive social justice. The symbolism in coming to the table is rich; it involves far more than signing an agreement. It involves having a contribution, a voice in establishing the foundations of a reconstructed society based on equality, rights and justice and articulating what this might mean in concrete terms for different groups. Certainly, the belief is strong that those who take up arms must be present at the negotiation of a resolution of conflict. Such a resolution might halt violent hostilities but does not necessarily provide the framework for reconciliation. Further, peace that 'is supported and consolidated at the grass roots level' is more likely to be sustained than one negotiated among elites (Karam 2001: 12).

Third, the presence of women makes a difference to the sorts of issues brought to formal peace processes. There are worldwide testimonies that where women are present at negotiating tables, they bring 'an understanding of the root causes of conflict' and focus on 'practical issues related to quality of life and human security' (Anderlini and Stanski 2004: 25). Women tend to prioritize education, health, nutrition, childcare and human welfare and security needs. To talk of 'women's concerns' does not assume feminine essentialism. It is simply because women universally are the prime carers, so they often negotiate via their family identities. For example, in Guatemala, one woman's participation at the negotiating table resulted in specific commitments to women on housing, credit and land, attempts to locate children and orphans, penalizing sexual harassment and the creation of the National Women's Forum. In South Africa, women across all parties agreed that each party should have one-third female representation in each negotiating team for the constitutional process. Accordingly, the South African Constitution includes a comprehensive Bill of Rights with relevant gains for women on reproduction, property rights, health care, education and culture. However, the presence of women does not guarantee that gender issues will be on the peace agenda. In El Salvador one-third of the negotiators were women, but the eventual agreement included discriminatory bars to women's involvement in the reconstruction (Näslund 1999: 30). As Azza Karam writes, women's involvement should not be tokenistic or seen as a favour or a matter of condescension, 'rather, it is an issue of being *integrated* in the entire process of negotiations' so that the outcomes have a long-term basis (2001: 11).

Northern Ireland has a long history of strong women peace activists and hundreds of small women's groups and provides a useful example of women's informal and formal peacebuilding. Betty Williams and Mairead Corrigan led large demonstrations of Catholics and Protestants to protest against terrorist violence in 1976 and were awarded the Nobel Peace Prize. Throughout the Troubles, although activists in Northern Ireland have been deeply divided politically, they have come together over housing, childcare, education and job skills, agreeing not to discuss political differences. In the lead-up to the multiparty peace talks, women lobbied for the existing political parties to include women in their candidate lists. When this action was ignored and the government published its plans for the electoral system, a cluster of women formed a political grouping to contest elections. Some women's groups believed that it would be difficult to sustain a cross-communal coalition, given the extremity of political controversies. The NIWC began with women committed to civil, human and workers' rights. Equality, human rights and inclusion were adopted as the Coalition's principles.

The Coalition agreed that participants should bring their 'identity baggage' and acknowledge their differences upfront rather than a more typical reaction in Northern Ireland: keep silent or fight about contentious differences. An explicit discussion of differences, divisions, discord and political dissonance is necessary to move beyond intolerance of others' views and sectarian attitudes and practices (Porter 1998, 2000). In 1996, the NIWC secured two seats in the multi-party peace negotiations on the future of Northern Ireland that led to the April 1998 Belfast Agreement. The Coalition put on the agenda victims' rights, reconciliation and the need for a civic forum. Monica McWilliams, the leader, was aware that its 'role at the peace talks is used as an example of women's central role in conflict prevention, peacekeeping and peacebuilding' (2002: 1). She talked of the dangers of sectarianism as 'seeing the world exclusively in terms of the interest of your "own" side as against the other side' (2002: 2). She spoke also of the importance of 'working with, not burying, our differences' (2002: 7). The Coalition made a difference to the face of electoral politics, with two members in the Legislative Assembly and outspoken party members. Sadly, in the current political stalemate, there are few visible visionary women. While the Coalition occupied a presence, they reminded the electorate of their manifestos, where they had more to say about health and children's issues than all the other parties combined. They also lobbied for the early release and reintegration of political prisoners and made a case for a comprehensive review of the police service. When the parties became bogged down with insults and the bigoted past, the NIWC talked about loss, bereavement, their children and hopes for the future, reminding participants of the centrality of human security. What we learn about the Coalition's success and demise is the necessity for women to participate in decision-making structures for social inclusion, equity and justice. Many women in conflict zones bypass formal electoral politics or formal representation in peace processes and make their voices heard through community events (Association 1000 Women for the Nobel Peace Prize 2005).

Thelma Arimiebi Ekiyor, writing in the West-African context, reiterates the importance of human security in shifting the emphasis from the states to the people; re-emphasizing state obligations to ensure citizen security; recognizing borders and boundaries and non-state actors; requiring accountability for violations of human rights and humanitarian law; and acknowledging the need for multifaceted responses to human security (2004: 4). She suggests that even this broad description of human security omits specific issues affecting women's security. Hence, in order to address gender equality effectively, there are five additional interrelated issues that should be incorporated into the quest for human security:

- violence against women and girls;
- gender inequality and control over resources;
- gender inequality and power and decision-making;
- women's human rights; and
- women and men as actors, not victims.

(Ekiyor 2004: 4)

As West-African states became militarized and violence raged in the 1990s, 'grass roots women's groups worked through local associations, faith-based groups and guilds to protect their families and communities' through developing efficient information networks that inform each other about attacks and safe routes (Ekiyor 2004: 5). The West Africa Network for Peacebuilding (WANEP) developed the Women in Peacebuilding Network (WIPNET) in order to advocate a cessation of physical violence during conflict and wars, and to deconstruct the structural forms of violence which exist in everyday society and express deep systemic disregard for women. Peacebuilding addresses systemic injustice and promotes social justice. The logic is clear: if structural violence, discrimination and exclusion are contributory factors to war, 'social justice and the promotion of inclusive structures will be contributory factors to peace' (Ekiyor 2004: 15).

Conclusion

To recap: most grass roots groups understand peacebuilding broadly, but do not necessarily include gender equality as part of their remit. In women's groups, notions of peacebuilding are intertwined with non-violence, positive relationships, gender justice and equality, demilitarization, human rights, participatory democracy and reconciliation. None of these issues alone constitute peacebuilding, but each is linked to women's strategies to create the conditions through which peace is meaningful. In practical terms, 'peacebuilding' shapes policies and programmes at all stages of a conflict. A clear understanding of peacebuilding is necessary to evaluate its impact, identify what works and what may be replicated elsewhere (Fast and Neufeldt 2005). Even when there is agreement on what constitutes peacebuilding, 'the provision of the necessary resources to deploy this peacebuilding consensus are rarely forthcoming' (Richmond 2004: 132). Peacebuilding is multidimensional; my focus is on Tracks 1 and 2 diplomacy.

In this chapter, I have traced the background to the historic SCR 1325 on Women, Peace and Security. I have noted positive achievements since 2000 but concluded that while women are active in informal peace activities, they remain remarkably absent from formal peace negotiations and political decision-making. I have criticized the limitations of orthodox views of peacebuilding as solely post-conflict reconstruction because of the problematic nature of determining what is actually post-conflict, of undervaluing informal work and providing excuses for excluding women from formal negotiations. Instead, I argue that peacebuilding is a process that is relevant and necessary at all stages of peace processes at pre-conflict, conflict and post-war or post-accord stages at formal and informal levels. Throughout this book, I will argue continually that peacebuilding involves all the processes that build positive relationships, heal wounds, reconcile antagonistic differences, restore esteem, respect rights, meet basic needs, enhance equality, instil feelings of security, empower moral agents and are democratic, inclusive and just. The impact of women's contributions to peacebuilding is significant across the globe, as we shall see in the next chapters.

2 Overcoming the harm of polarization

> People who display a moral imagination that rises above the cycles of violence in which they live also rise above dualistic polarities. That is, the moral imagination is built on a quality of interaction with reality that respects complexity and refuses to fall into forced containers of dualism and either-or categories.
>
> (Lederach 2005: 35–36)

The harm of dualism

Exclusion is often a root cause of violent insecurity. Being included in all activities and groups that are personally meaningful enhances one's feelings of security. In this chapter, I explain this root cause of insecurity through scrutinizing the harm of polarization;[1] in particular, the harm of the either/or, them/us and excluded/included mentality. Such a mentality is always present in some form where there is violent conflict. Violence often begins because of the notions of the 'other', the 'traitor' the 'enemy', the 'infidel'. These terms are part of dualistic thinking and practice and I begin by explaining their moral harm. In particular, I explain the ramifications of prevailing dichotomies within IR in terms of othering, its impact on ethnic hatred and the exclusion that results. I then defend feminist ethics as a way to overcome the harm of polarization. Feminist ethics incorporates both a universalistic defence of personhood, justice, equality and rights, and a particularized practice of care that is directed toward meeting the specific needs of individuals – in this case, those who are seeking to build peace or recover from war trauma. My intention is to demonstrate that it is possible for IR theory to move beyond seemingly irreconcilable, optional or contradictory dualisms that presuppose either/or decisions. My reason for doing so is that such decisions limit the possibilities of Lederach's (2005) 'moral imagination' outlined in the Introduction and the quotation above. This imagination enables us to think creatively and move outside of polarized logic to embrace complex relationships. My aim is to demonstrate the positive benefits of inclusionary politics that counter the harm of dualism through valuing differences, incorporating principles of justice and practising care.

A dualism is an extreme opposite.[2] Historically, from Plato's division between the intellect and matter and between the soul and the body, one side of a dualism is valued more highly than the other. In fact, one side is needed to transcend the perceived shortcomings of its opposite, or the perceived dangers in being pulled to the other side of the dualism.[3] Traditional philosophical dualisms include maleness/femaleness, men/women, reason/passion, political/personal, public/private, objectivity/subjectivity and logic/intuition. What operates is 'the conceptual alignment of maleness with superiority, femaleness with inferiority' (Lloyd 1984: 32). Within IR, dualisms include idealism/realism, international order/national security, internal/external, public/private, civil society/barbarism, cosmopolitanism/particularism, global politics/nation-state, intervention/sovereignty, hero/victim and peace/war. Indeed, realists perceive the nation-state as a conceptual boundary 'for understanding relations between self (citizen) and other (foreigner), between inside (order) and outside (anarchy)' (Steans 1998: 7). A dualistic framework is stark, it allows for no intermediate positions. One is either a rational, objective, political, public man capable of warmaking, protecting the weak and negotiating at the peace table, or one is an irrational, subjective, impulsive woman suited to subordination and the domestic sphere. While such a dualistic framework still exists in some form in many people's mindset in the West, particularly in traditional families or conservative or fundamentalist communities,[4] it persists strongly in areas of conflict where patriarchal society is the norm. It is such a narrow framework that consistently works against women (and other marginalized groups) being fully included in all aspects of social and public life.

President Bush's dualistic ultimatum, 'if you're not with us, you're against us' has profoundly affected the thinking and practices of post-9/11 global politics. This dualism provokes a harmful mindset with significant political consequences. It is the philosophic basis to the 'coalition of the willing' and to the 'war on terrorism'. Further, it reinstated and cemented some dangerous parallels that accompany the 'with us'/'against us' dualism. Corresponding dualisms that have enormous implications for this book include us/them, inclusion/exclusion, citizen/foreigner, sameness/difference, free world/'axis of evil', Christianity/Islam, friends/enemies, insider/outsider, right/wrong and good/evil. It is difficult to think in this polarizing 'with us'/'against us' manner without also thinking of 'us' as being the 'same' in the sense of having similar values, ways of life and religious and cultural beliefs, and 'them' as necessarily being radically different and thus somehow not as good, right or deserving of privilege. Such thinking presupposes 'we' know we are 'right' and therefore 'they' must be wrong, given that our 'friends' are 'good' so our 'enemies' must be 'evil'. This mentality and the practices, policies and political decisions that ensue are not conducive to peaceful, global cooperative relationships because they invite oppositional responses. As we have witnessed across the globe, many of these responses are violent. While never justifiable, the degree to which they have been provoked must be explored.

What I need to explain now is the extreme ethical harm in divisive dualisms. I suggest there are four main interconnected reasons why dualism is harmful. First, a dualistic worldview assumes a self-righteous rightness about the dominant position. This leaves no scope for debate on contested concerns. Second, this worldview is dogmatic and closed-minded, so misses the opportunities that emerge with flexible openness which enable the inclusionary politics that I am proposing. Third, it sets up an oppositional framework that precludes dialogical relationships. Open dialogue is fundamental to peacebuilding. Fourth, a dualistic mindset is exclusivist, so in ethical terms, it works against the reconciliation of difference. A chief aim of peacebuilding is to further meaningful reconciliation. It is worth expanding on the philosophic foundation to these four harms before explaining how they are manifest in international politics and positing alternatives in the final part of this chapter. Before doing so, it is important to explain the nature of harm. The harm of dualism is a moral harm, in failing to respect the dignity of the 'other' and in working against the well-being of collaborative relationships. The harm comes when individuals, ethnic groups, tribal rivalries, religious believers or other groups feel controlled, dominated, undermined, radically misunderstood, ignored, despised, lied about, intimidated, victimized or discriminated against simply for being 'other'. This harm comes about when there has been no serious engagement with difference, no meaningful dialogue and no attempt to understand 'otherness'. The 'logic of domination' underlying these hierarchically valued, oppositional dualisms assume a power over conception of privilege (Warren and Cady 1994: 5). The moral harm lies in the demeaning nature of destructive dualistic thinking and practices that cannot avoid undermining the integrity of those who are different. As indicated in Chapter 1, the respect for dignity and our common humanity underlies the principles and practices of peacebuilding and directs my central arguments. I return now to the four reasons why dualism is harmful.

The first harm of dualism is caused through an assumption of rightness, that 'we', be it the West, the so-called civilized world of democratic liberal freedom, the US superpower, a privileged group of men or one ethnic, tribal, rebel or religious group, are uncontroversially right. The destructive nature in this harm is the assumption that anyone who is not part of 'us' – that is, is not western, liberal or Christian or part of our ethnic, tribal, rebel or religious group – is always wrong. There is such an arrogant smugness to this assumption about the moral certainty of one's position. Certainly, President Bush, former Prime Minister Blair and Prime Minister Howard adopted highly self-righteous positions about the necessity for the war in Iraq. Despite the lack of evidence of weapons of mass destruction, the failure to verify links between al-Qaida and Saddam Hussein, the deaths that are resulting from the war, the humiliation of prisoners and civil unrest created, each of these men continue to claim that the invasion was a just war.[5] Self-righteousness leads readily to a position of dominance, a triumphalism that justifies a crusading mentality.[6] With simple moral absolutes, 'there are no grey areas, no contradictions and no different "ways of seeing". From this position it becomes all too easy to slide into the prejudice of "otherness"; rejecting the "moral" definitions, decisions and actions of others' (Scraton 2002: 44). Soon, I will explain how 'otherness' underlies the spurious justification for violence.

Self-righteousness underlies the second harm of the dualistic perspective, namely, its dogmatic closed-mindedness. Dualism cements pre-existing tendencies toward extremism. Fundamentalism, whether ideological, Christian, Islamic or sectarian, has dogmatic, extremist leanings that are expressed in highly visible ways. Acts of terrorism against westerners in Bali, Egypt, London, Madrid and the USA are justified by the terrorists and their communities as 'acts of God' or in the 'will of Allah'. The West is quick to brandish such acts as Muslim extremism and uncivilized barbarism. Many are closed to the fact that within multicultural society, Muslim moderates mix harmoniously with multi-faith citizens. Yet there was explicit use of religious imagery and concepts drawn from the Christian political Right to justify the invasion of Afghanistan and the pre-emptive strike in Iraq. Fundamentalism of all religious and secular persuasions has dogmatic leanings. Dogmatic closed-mindedness misses the opportunities that could arise when there is openness to other responses to conflict, such as diplomacy, continued weapons inspection, multilateral decision-making or (as is typical with women's peacebuilding) coalitions working across radical difference to meet mutual needs. The harm of dualism exists both in the mindset that it fosters and the exclusionary practices that it encourages.

Self-righteous rightness contributes to dogmatic closed-mindedness and sets up the third moral harm of dualism, which is an oppositional framework that precludes dialogical relationships, without which there can be no development of trust, healing of wounded relationships or reconciled communities. Open dialogue is crucial to peacebuilding. As I will expand later in suggesting alternatives to dualism, dialogue presupposes openness to others. In contrast, an oppositional framework that emerges from an 'us' or 'them', friends or enemies mentality, necessarily is antagonistic. It sets up a psychological approach or a political administration that presupposes the 'other' as being so different from 'us' that we need to fear this difference. 'They' – that is, anyone who is different from 'us' – is perceived readily as 'our enemy', which is typical in all areas of violent conflict and is occurring in the West with anyone who looks Middle Eastern or wears the *hijab* or *burqa*. As Tseen Khoo puts it, writing about 'fortress Australia' post-9/11, 'the confused, binary representation of *hijab*-wearing women as both "victim" (of the Taliban regime, silenced and oppressed) and "perpetrators" (upholders of fundamental precepts, which quickly came to be perceived as sources of terrorist motives)' (2004: 585) creates a false opposition. When such rigid stereotypes become fixed in citizens' minds, there is little motivation to discover more about different cultures, religions or ethnic backgrounds. The idea of talking with those whom we have come to believe are so different from 'us' appears frightening, or to many, even unnecessary. The idea of a stereotype itself is an artificial barrier that presupposes characteristics about social groups. 'We' do not need to know about 'them' because 'they' are foreign, alien, wrong and therefore necessarily evil. Now, 'there is no simple enemy, like the Soviet Union. Enemies have pluralized. They are now everywhere. Inside and outside' (Eisenstein 1996: 15). There is great harm in such a dualistic worldview – to individual identity and self-esteem, community relationships and multicultural pluralism, and certainly to blocking conflict resolution.

Given this mindset and these consequences, the fourth harm of dualism lies in its exclusivist position, which has no desire to work toward a reconciliation of differences. Exclusivist positions defend a single identity, whether it be western, American, Christian or civilized or, as in conflict societies, British Protestant or Irish Catholic, Turkish Cypriot or Greek Cypriot, Bosnian Serb, Albanian Serb or Bosnian Croat, Hutu or Tutsi, Indigenous Fijian or Indo-Fijian. Single-identity communities are strong, self-generating their own mythology and protecting those who belong. Those who differ are branded as outsiders, intruders or, invariably in conflict societies, as enemies. Those from within the community who dare to step out as dissidents, lovers or simply estranged or curious individuals, are alienated from their families. Where there is a transitional period of ceasefire and peace negotiations, there may be some tolerance of the possibility of multiple single-identity communities. However, such a positioning intensifies the segregation of groups. It has no desire to reconcile differences, that is, to make sense of the range of differences in light of one's own 'otherness' which is problematized rarely; someone else is always classed as the 'other' because this is much easier than dealing with the peculiarities and contradictions of one's own positioning. Miroslav Volf writes about the exclusion that is signified in a term such as 'ethnic cleansing': 'exclusion is barbarity *within* civilization, evil *among* the good, crime against the other *right within the walls of the self*' (1996: 60; emphasis in original). Ethnic cleansing 'suggests atrocity, purification, homogenization, elimination, expulsion and ritual violence' (Humphrey 2002: 73). Volf suggests that an adequate reflection on exclusion should satisfy two conditions. First, it should 'name exclusion as evil ... because it enables us to imagine nonexclusionary boundaries that map nonexclusionary identities' and second, 'it must not dull our ability to detect the exclusionary tendencies in our own judgments and practices' (Volf 1996: 64). (I return to this issue of evil in Chapter 6.)

Forms of inclusion and exclusion are responses to difference. 'Experiencing differences, or even just seeing them, challenges and uproots certainty about the self' (Eisenstein 1996: 25). It encourages critical self-reflection. In conflict zones where sectarianism or ethnic hatred divides groups, often one simple, effective way of disrupting typical stereotypes is to take people out of their mundane contexts into workshops in different locations, international exchanges or youth camps where people engage with the 'other' for the first time and, surprisingly, discover that they are 'normal' human beings. It is impossible for many to picture themselves as someone else's enemy. For example, Australia has rested comfortably on its relaxed reputation in international politics as a country with easy-going, 'she'll-be-right mate' tolerant citizens and finds the Bali bombings of 2002 that killed 202, including 88 Australians and injured 350 others, and the Bali bombing again in 2005 as an unsettling experience, not just in obvious terms of the deaths of Australians, but also in being perceived as someone's enemy.[7]

To summarize, dualism fosters a sanctimonious sense of rightness, dogmatic closed-mindedness and an oppositional framework that necessarily contributes to exclusivity. All of these aspects lessen the possibility of an inclusionary politics. Challenges to dichotomies are essential to minimize potential harm. Repeated cycles of violence are often stirred by polarized interpretations of complex histories.

> We are right. They are wrong. We were violated. They are the violators. We are liberators. They are oppressors. Our intentions are good. Theirs are bad. History and the truth of history is most fully comprehended by our view. Their view of history is biased, incomplete, maliciously untruthful, and ideologically driven. You are with us or against us.
>
> (Lederach 2005: 36–37)

The moral imagination that Lederach talks about, and which I am developing in my own way, refuses to reduce life to one-dimensional or oppositional frameworks, but accepts the fundamental need to hold multiple, complex, often paradoxical perspectives simultaneously. All sorts of possibilities open.

'Othering'

An important reason to challenge dichotomies in IR is their impact on relationships: specifically, how they impact on our understandings of 'otherness'. Some form of 'otherness' is necessary to affirm self-identity and to recognize that identity emerges in relation to others who are different from us. When difference is accepted unproblematically as part of life's rich tapestry, there need be no harm in this 'otherness'. Where difference is seen as inferior, strange, weird or is the justification for violence, the difference of 'othering' is harmful. Harmful 'othering' is based on hierarchically valued dichotomies which are not simple opposites, 'but rather mask the power of one side of the binary to control the other' (Bell 2002: 433), categorizing others as us/them, citizen/foreigner and good/evil. One of the most significant harms of dualism is the effect of 'othering' that undermines, demoralizes and potentially fuels tensions that escalate into violence. As we will see in subsequent chapters, this form of 'othering' drives war rape, ethnic cleansing and genocide where people are not treated as humans worthy of respectful dignity, but as conquests or beasts to be destroyed. As noted previously, the orthodox security approach thrives in a culture of dualism, particularly with absolutist readings of 'Good/God/Christ versus Evil/Satan/AntiChrist, with an Armageddon type battle as the final arbiter' (Galtung 2004a: 2). Such an approach requires a 'construction of the other as evil' who exists only to be exterminated, crushed, contained or converted (Galtung 2004a: 2). Cultures where this approach dominates have vertical social codes, demarcated by ascribed categories of gender, generation, race/ethnicity, class/caste, tribe, nation and state. As explained in the early parts of this chapter, since 9/11, many of the gains in multicultural liberal democracies seem to be under threat. There is movement away from a tolerance of difference to danger-ous expressions that entail rigid dichotomies based on an 'othering', where this is understood as a stereotyping of those considered different from 'us'. Abso-lutist dichotomies are blind to the pain of those who are excluded by those stereotypes and those most in need of protection. They make people feel vulner-able and at risk simply for looking different, holding a different faith or having different political values.

Johan Galtung (2004) suggests there are two diametrically opposed dis-courses about violence: the security discourse and the peace discourse.

> The Security Approach is based on four components: an evil party, with strong capability and evil intention; a clear and recent danger of violence, real or potential; strength, to defeat or deter the evil party; in turn producing security, which is also the best approach to 'peace'.
>
> (Galtung 2004a: 1)

In contrast:

> The Peace Approach is also based on four components: a conflict, which has not been resolved/transformed; a danger of violence to 'settle the con-flict'; conflict transformation, empathetic–creative–non-violent; producing peace, which is the best approach to 'security'.
>
> (Galtung 2004a: 2)

Galtung explains the diverse foundations to his 'Peace Approach'. He suggests that it has roots in abrahamitic and African (*ubuntu*)[8] religions, Hinduism, Bud-dhism and Daoism, women's focus on compassion and 'the secularism of *liberté, egalité, fraternité*' (Galtung 2004a: 3). In such cultures where this approach exists, diversity is a source of mutual enrichment and inequality and the exclusion that arises from dualism is accepted as mutual impoverishment. I have always found Julia Kristeva's reaction to xenophobia and nationalist movements in France to be illuminating. Kristeva writes:

> I am convinced that, in the long run, only a thorough investigation of our remarkable relationship with both the *other* and *strangeness within our-selves* can lead people to give up hunting for the scapegoat outside their group.
>
> (1993: 51; emphasis in original)

Her interest is not only in a personal interrogation of 'otherness', but in the dia-logic practice of the 'speaking subject' (an issue discussed in more detail in Chapters 3 and 5). Suffice to say here that 'talking face-to-face contradicts the destructive "othering" processes, allowing alternatives to develop' (Corrin 2004).

An example of such an alternative is pertinent. Take Somali society, which is organized according to clans and sub-clans and women are not considered full members of clans. This clan structure excludes women from forums where decisions to make war are taken and simultaneously denies Somali women the ability to join forums where peace agreements are negotiated or political structures are discussed. Elisabeth Rehn and Ellen Johnson-Sirleaf (2002) provide the instance of 2 May 2000 where 92 Somali women stood outside the military tent in Arta, Djibouti waiting for the Somali National Peace Conference to begin. This was the fourteenth attempt since 1991 to find a peaceful solution to the civil war. These women were chosen to be part of delegations representing traditional clans, but their goal was to break out of clan-based allegiances. In terms of the critique of this chapter, such allegiances rely on antagonistic differences, exclusivist, oppositional dichotomies and the exclusion that is explicit in derogatory 'othering'. One delegate affirmed that peace 'would come from cross-clan reconciliation, not official negotiations among warlords and faction leaders. ... So we care for the wounded and build schools in communities regardless of clan, ethnic and political affiliations' (in Rehn and Johnson-Sirleaf 2002: 78). While the women themselves came from four major clans and coalitions of minor ones, they presented themselves at the conference as a 'sixth clan' reaching beyond the constructions of ethnicity, as Asha Hagi Elmi, leader of the Sixth Clan Coalition said, toward a 'vision of gender equality' (in Rehn and Johnson-Sirleaf 2002: 78). Women lobbied for quotas for women in the future legislature, and while only 25 seats in the 245 member Transitional National Assembly were guaranteed, the women also ensured protection of the human rights of women, children and minorities. The message to be learned from this example is that the negativity of 'othering' can be overcome through rising above either/or categories.

Ethnic hatred

Harmful othering and ethnic hatred are allies. Ethnic hatred and racism are intertwined. Racism involves behaviour and attitudes that are based on the belief that one race is superior to another. Racial groups are defined on the basis of shared physical criteria, such as hair colour and texture, slant of eyes, facial features and body size. Racism leads to racial discrimination. Ethnicity involves the shared set of cultural characteristics that derive from membership of a particular national origin and includes a sense of belonging and identification. Ethnic groups are defined on the basis of cultural criteria, such as language, religious beliefs and practice of cultural rituals, dress and art. Ethnic stratification is a structured inequality whereby social positions are allocated on the basis of ethnicity. In places where this stratification is extreme, this leads to feelings of ethnic inferiority and superiority, which spur ethnic hatred and violence.

Zillah Eisenstein posits some powerful thoughts on this subject. She writes that 'the racializing of difference – be it "the" Jew or black or girl/woman – requires that we look through and in between the horrors of hatred' (1996: 13). She explains how hatred is written onto bodies that are shackled, beaten, tattooed, starved, castrated, raped, tortured, macheted, decapitated and 'locate the borders for hate while nations are reconfigured' (1996: 14). This space of 'psychic hate' is triggered by context and history, which means it is subject to continual flare-ups and repetition, and the reopening of old wounds.[9] Racial hatred spins in multiple spirals, often out of control.

> Hatred embodies a complex set of fears about difference and otherness. It reveals what some people fear in themselves, their own 'differences'. Hatred forms around the unknown, the difference of 'others'. … Because people grow othered by their racialized, sexualized, and engendered bodies, bodies are important to the writing of hatred on history.
>
> (Eisenstein 1996: 21)

Eisenstein's analysis is powerfully blunt, but it explains the underlying emotions that drive many atrocities in war. It focuses our attention on the physical manifestations of violence. She also reminds us that even the worse psychic hatreds are changeable. This notion of 'space' recurs throughout the book, not only in this destructive example of 'psychic hate' but more frequently in open, exploratory spaces where reconciliation might occur.

The conflict in Bosnia-Herzegovina is an example of destructive 'othering' and ethnic hatred, but also of the possibility for overcoming this hatred. The conflict 'has often been characterized as a *fratricide*, a middle-English term meaning to kill one's "countryman" who is like a brother' (Baines 2004: 98; emphasis in original). Within many communities, Bosnian Croat, Bosnian Serb and Bosnian Muslim had lived together as friends, neighbours and relatives. Erin Baines explains that while the 'othering' of the Bosnian Muslim was part of building the Serb identity, 'the diversity of Bosnian Serbs was violently denied' (2004: 103). Concepts used to develop exclusivist national identity include fear and intimidation tactics for anyone betraying a sense of difference. 'State and citizen, and protector and victim, became intertwined in a symbiotic relationship, one that mimicked traditional gender stereotypes' (Baines 2004: 104) and affirmed the type of dualism that I am suggesting is harmful. Despite the mass expulsions, murders, genocide and rape that occurred, one can find stories of how Bosnian citizens defied popular beliefs that the conflict was based solely on ethnic divisions or ancient hatreds. 'With every story of humanity – acts of everyday kindness during the war – the ethnic hatred argument falls apart' (Baines 2004: 99). What this conflict did cement was a gendered nationalism. Militant masculinism proves its masculinity and patriotism 'by exercising hyper-violence against the enemy, including rape and mass murder' (Baines 2004: 105). This provides a violent, culturally justified avenue for ethnic hatred. In contrast, nationalist women practise their nationalist obligations as reproducers of the nation, as good wives and mothers. Rape of these women becomes a political act, impregnating women becomes heroic. These conclusions about the impact of nationalism on ethnic hatred extend widely to other contexts.

Exclusion

Where there are strict dichotomies that lead to destructive 'othering' and ethnic hatred, it is hardly surprising that harassment, violence and discrimination, allied with poverty and exclusion from full participation in social life, create fertile grounds for conflict. Where cultural membership cements an ethnic nationalism, belonging 'is warmly *all-encompassing to its own* community and fiercely *unyielding to outsiders*' (Porter 1997b: 868; emphasis in original). Such intensity is to be feared because of its 'deep connection between violence and belonging. The more strongly you feel the bonds of belonging to your own group, the more hostile, the more violence will your feelings be toward outsiders' (Ignatieff 1993: 188). The implications of exclusion are real, manifest in social, political and economic disadvantages. Such disadvantage is a moral commentary on relationships of difference. Exploring the underlying rationales, constraints and implications of these relationships is imperative in order to work toward rectifying the harm of exclusionary practices and move toward inclusionary politics. Yet, Lesley Abdela writes:

> I have worked, boots on the ground, as a civilian in Kosovo, Sierra Leone, Afghanistan and Iraq, and have seen the same damaging mistakes made repeatedly by the international community because they ignore the participation and perspective of women in peace initiatives, post-conflict programs and policies.
>
> (Abdela 2005: 1)

Abdela's point is that when women are excluded from negotiations, men appoint men to power and set the agenda for formulating the treaties, transitional governments, post-conflict reconstruction planning and policymaking. Windows for gender inclusivity are closed.

Across Africa in particular, autonomous women's organizations have emerged to open these windows, promote women's leadership and involvement in politics and bring women together from all parts of the political spectrum around common interests. Aili Mari Tripp suggests that there is some irony that 'women have transformed their exclusions into autonomous bases for challenging the status quo' (2000a: 658). She maintains that it is only 'because women were outside of existing power structures and patronage networks that they so often found themselves strategically positioned to challenge these same networks' (2000a: 658–659). As noted in the discussion on 'othering', Somali women have been able at times to transcend cultural barriers that typically exclude them. Their innovation to ensure inclusivity was to create a 'woman's clan'.

Similarly, other examples defy the pain of exclusion. After the 1996 Tutsi-dominated military coup in Burundi, the neighbouring government called for a return to constitutional order. In 1998, 17 different parties met for the first round of Arusha peace talks. The violence continued and economic sanctions from neighbouring countries took their toll on civilians. From across the social and political spectrum, Hutu and Tutsi women protested against this exclusion, joining together in a quest for a place at the peace table and seeking support from regional heads of state. Imelda Nzirorera, working in the Burundian Government's Ministry of Human Rights, recalls how the women told the facilitator of the peace process, ex-Tanzanian President Julius Nyerere (since deceased), that their views were crucial 'because when there is a crisis, we as the women, pick up the pieces', only to be told 'your own brothers from Burundi will not accept your participation' (in Anderlini 2000b: 21). Observer status was negotiated. Those women who did make it to the peace table generally have had the support of both women's community groups and the international community, particularly through training and facilitating to develop skills in negotiation, strategizing and leadership.[10] A good example of this is the assistance by UNIFEM at the All-Party Burundi Women's Peace Conference in Arusha, Tanzania in July 2000. Winnie Byanyima, a Ugandan member of parliament, served as facilitator and described the significance of the meeting:

> The men who were at the negotiating didn't feel that women had any right to be there. These men felt they had a right to be there because they were fighters, or have been elected to some Parliament before the war escalated. But Burundi women who had suffered so much didn't have any legitimacy in their eyes. By bringing in women the documents have more legitimacy now. People from the grass roots have made their input to the future. The conference created a space that was necessary but lacking, not only between women in political parties and women working for peace and reconciliation at the grass roots level, but also between international facilitators and women.
>
> (in Rehn and Johnson-Sirleaf 2002: 80)

Since then, the support has been replicated by UNIFEM in other parts of the Great Lakes region and elsewhere. These examples of defying exclusion come with support by the international community and intense lobbying by grass roots groups. Women rarely are included as equals in formal negotiations. Even when they have had roles as combatants and political leaders in national liberation movements, their organizing efforts are ignored. Colombia is a good example. As many as 30 per cent of the fighters of the Revolutionary Armed Forces of Colombia (FARC) are women, but FARC included only one woman, Mariana Paez,[11] among its representatives to the official negotiations in 2000 with the government (Rehn and Johnson-Sirleaf 2002: 79). According to Inonge Mbikusita Lewanika, President of the Federation of African Women's Peace Networks (FERFAP) based in Kigali, Rwanda, women's credibility as peacemakers is established at the grass roots, so 'making it from the grass mat to the peace table has nothing to do with their qualifications as peacemakers', but once the foreign mediators arrive and official negotiations start, 'you have to be able to sit at the table, and speak their language. Often women are not trained or given the chance' (in Rehn and Johnson-Sirleaf 2002: 79).

Obstacles to inclusion are formidable. In many cultures it is taboo for women to sit among the elders or traditional or religious leaders. In such cultures, men 'find it embarrassing to have women represent them at peace talks' (Zeitlin 2005: 31). One of the most difficult impediments to the inclusion of women in peace processes and in post-accord governments are traditional beliefs and cultural practices concerning what is appropriate for women to do. (I analyse the reasons for this in Chapter 4.) It is important here to remind ourselves why it is important that women are not excluded.

> When women are there, the nature of the dialogue changes. Women's concerns come not merely out of their own experiences, but of the rootedness in their communities. They represent different constituencies: those in need of education, of health care, of jobs and of land. They have a different experience of war from male fighters and politicians.
>
> (Rehn and Johnson-Sirleaf 2002: 79)

Quotas are important to bring women into the political process, as has occurred in Mozambique, Rwanda, Somalia and South Africa. East Timor provides an interesting example. Women's groups supported quotas for national election but the DPA did not and threatened to pull out if there was an insistence on quotas. While there were no quotas, UNIFEM gave training for 260 potential women candidates for the Constituent Assembly and 24 women were elected from 88 members. However, the political parties which decided that a woman could not represent their interests subsequently replaced some of these women. Exclusions prevent equality and undermine human dignity.

Cultural clashes

Gender-based exclusions cement cultural stereotypes, such as the idea that men are suited to the public realm, are dominant in the household and valued and that women can only operate in the domestic sphere, are naturally subordinate and inferior. The stereotypical dichotomies are major stumbling blocks to empowering women and encouraging their capacities to flourish. Such dichotomies justify the priority given in many cultures to boys' health and education over girls' and remain, in my view, the biggest obstruction to why women's grass roots peacebuilding does not translate to a greater presence of women around formal negotiating tables. Binaries value one side while disparaging the other. Anna, a Liberian president of a women's development association, reports how 'the fighters had a common saying, "What is a woman? A woman is nothing. We can step on women"' (in Bennett *et al.* 1995: 47). Whether the fighters were mercenaries, foreign fighters or Liberians is irrelevant to this point – the comment is demeaning and indicative of the harm of cultural gender-based dichotomies.

Here we unavoidably enter the turbulent waters of cultural notions of gender roles, equality and rights. CEDAW defines discrimination but acknowledges the impact of cultural and religious differences on notions of equality. Christine Chinkin (1999) cautions against the assumption that the equal participation of women in all aspects of decision-making enhances substantive equality, because we cannot assume gender awareness or good governance in each cultural context. However, rights discourse is 'a framework for challenging situations in which the rights of women are compromised for the benefit of cultural traditions which institutionalize and reproduce patriarchal hegemony' (Obiora, 1997: 381). As Mary Midgley puts it so well, when we talk about rights, we 'talk directly about the people who need relief. ... It makes it harder to say "this is none of my business"' (1999: 167). While the Beijing PFA and the Beijing +5 and +10 reviews spurred international legal reforms, particularly the removal of blatantly discriminatory practices, there are no sanctions or censures against failing to satisfy commitments. Cultural prejudices about women underlie discriminatory practices, such as their exclusion from political decision-making. Many women as well as men hold culturally accepted views which translate to demeaning practices. Attention to cultural specificity respects cultural traditions, but it should not be at the expense of universal human rights. I argue that 'when there is a conflict between universal rights to equality and culturally specific subjection of women, rights to equality should take normative priority' (Porter 2003a: 251–252). This prioritizing need not disregard differences, and it is worth noting here that the valuation of difference by western feminists, writers on queer theory and diverse sexualities and post-colonial theorists contrasts with the despising of difference in divided societies such as Northern Ireland, the former Yugoslavia, or Israel and Palestine, 'where difference has mattered "too much"' (Tripp 2000a: 649). In such instances (as we shall see in the next chapter), the challenge is to find commonalities that minimize potentially antagonistic differences leading to conflict in order to build coalitions.

Within cultures, gender is tied intricately to other aspects of identity such as 'race', ethnicity, class and religion. Tripp argues for 'a recognition that the world is not divided into the west versus "the rest" when it comes to women's rights and that women the world over share common struggles that take varying forms' (2000b: 5). Our common humanity ties us together in our problems and capacities to solve dilemmas in culturally meaningful ways. An allied argument is that equality requires attention to difference because universal principles of equality and rights require particular application to culture, context and embodied practices in order to be realized. 'The recognition of difference and particularity must not signal a descent into moral relativism ... but rather it must encourage a commitment to tackle the ways in which difference is assigned and oppression and exclusion justified' (Robinson 1999: 82). (I begin to develop this argument in the next section and extend it more substantially in Chapter 4.)

In this first section, I have outlined the harm of polarized attitudes and practices, stressing the harm of exclusion from full participation in peace negotiations and political decision-making. I have reiterated how destructive 'othering' and ethnic hatred are tied closely and create triggers for conflict. In the next section, I posit feminist ethics as a way to overcome gender-based dichotomies, counter the harm of dualism and enable women and men to be part of inclusionary democratic practices. The outline of feminist ethics forms the basis for the forthcoming chapters, where I argue that it is possible to have recognition and inclusion, justice and compassion, memory and truth, apology and forgiveness and reconciliation across differences.

Feminist ethics: justice and care

Throughout this book, I argue that feminist ethics helps to break gender-based dichotomies. Feminist ethics has three main features.[12] First, its starting point is women's lives in their full myriad of variety – in the case of this book, women living in war zones, conflict areas, divided societies and transitional societies, women peacebuilders, women in grass roots groups, women campaigning against violence, women struggling to participate in negotiations and those in NGOs, government, academia, peace groups or the UN striving to realize the aspirations of SCR 1325. Specifically, feminist ethics addresses gender inequalities. Second, feminist ethics interrogates the male privileging of what constitutes security and insecurity, what the conditions are for sustainable peace and how to overcome women's exclusion from negotiating tables. Feminist ethics 'asks questions, queries double standards, contradicts oppositional assumptions and stubbornly refuses to slot women in as if they are second-class citizens' (Porter 1999: x). Third, it proposes alternatives that emphasize personal experience, relationships, context and nurture. It adopts a social ontology of what Carol Gould calls a 'socially understood *individuals-in-relations*' (2004: 4; emphasis in original). It stresses agency, that women and men are empowered to make informed decisions about matters that affect them and also that 'emotions of care and sympathy lie at the heart of the ethical life' (Nussbaum 1999: 14). Feminist ethics provides a framework to break down dualistic perspectives. Part of the linkage between feminism and peace is about breaking down the logic of domination. In particular, 'value-hierarchical thinking' attributes high value, status and prestige to whatever is deemed of value; power is seen as 'power-over'; and 'a logic of domination' is harmful in that it 'presumes that superiority justifies subordination' (Warren and Cady 1994: 5).

I wish to clarify right from the start that I am not drawing specifically on an 'ethic of care' as outlined originally by Gilligan (1983) and developed substantially by a host of important theorists.[13] The reason for this is that most versions of an 'ethic of care' apply to particular, personal relationships,[14] whereas the subject matter discussed in this book includes individuals, groups, communities, tribes, NGOs and intergovernmental organizations that are part of global politics. However, this is not to say that an ethic of care has no bearing on feminist ethics. To the contrary, it has influenced the development of feminist ethics. In Gilligan's research (1983) she explored how women approached moral dilemmas and discovered a 'different voice' that expressed a priority on responsibility to others, not harming others, the web of relationships and taking into account the full particulars of a dilemma before making a moral decision. Her findings relate to a general tendency for women to have a relational identity and to draw typically on a responsibility-based care perspective rather than an abstract individualist perspective. Fiona Robinson uses 'a care ethic' to talk of a moral orientation that 'relies on a relational moral ontology, and leads us to consider different values in terms of human flourishing' (2006: 5).

Why feminist ethics?

Feminist ethics draws on *both* a justice perspective derived from liberal theories of individualist entitlement and a care perspective derived from ethic of care theorists.[15] The characteristics of a justice perspective are generalized, universal and formal, and with a care perspective, they are contextualized, particular and informal. The priorities for a justice perspective are formal abstraction, individual rights and the generalized 'other', whereas for a care perspective, they are contextualized content, social responsibilities and the concrete 'other'. The justice perspective is concerned with equality and fairness, thus balancing competing claims of entitlement in order to come to a rational resolution and fulfil obligations. The care perspective is concerned with equity and need in order to be inclusive and fulfil responsibilities in a compassionate way. The central norms of feminist moral discourse are equality, openness and inclusiveness (Jaggar 1998). Gilligan maintained that justice and care are a complementary relationship of 'two cross-cutting perspectives' (Gilligan 1987: 25) where on some occasions, principles of justice come into play, and on other occasions, personalized care takes priority. Yet, 'understood fully, the ethic of justice and the ethic of care both require contextual details and general principles' (Porter 1999: 17).

I defend the need to synthesize both perspectives as a way of overcoming the harm of polarization. Justice and care are 'mutually interdependent' (Clement 1996: 109). Uma Narayan (1995) provides a pertinent example of the need to integrate justice and care. In India, there is a fatal neglect of girls in terms of education, health care and nutrition. Cultural notions of justice diminish the levels of care considered appropriate for girls. Narayan argues that, without changes to the idea of justice which alters cultural values affecting daughters, the failure of satisfactory care for girls means that they do not have the opportunity to grow up to become adults bearing rights. Justice without care may be harsh. Care without justice may be oppressive. However, each ethic provides 'enabling conditions' for the other ethic (Narayan 1995: 139) within a 'dialectical interplay' (Porter 1991: 50). Such interplay allows for a politics of compassion that is based on our shared humanity, our vulnerability to risk and the urgency to maintain or restore human dignity. (This interplay between universal principles of justice and a particularized care and politics of compassion is developed fully in Chapter 4.)

Gould explains this interplay as a form of 'mutuality', which she suggests 'goes beyond the recognition of the equal freedom, needs, and worth of others to an active concern with enhancing their well-being' (2004: 42). To this end, justice and care have explicit implications for the politics of peace. For care to be meaningful, it has to translate practically and respond to the particular needs of individuals or groups at the emotional, economic, social, political and cultural levels. Gould suggests that there are three key features of feminist ethics that can be generalized to democratic communities. First, a concern for the specific individuality of the other leads to a 'social reciprocity or the reciprocity of respect' with 'an empathic understanding of the perspective, feelings, and needs of the other' (2004: 45). (This concern is in stark contrast to the 'othering' analysed in the first section of this chapter.) Second, concern for each other's participation and concern for responsibilities for joint undertakings lead to a 'cooperative reciprocity' (2004: 45). Third, it demonstrates concern for the vulnerable. (I remind the reader that I am developing normative ideals worth striving towards. Obviously, translating these features in practice in violent communities provides additional dilemmas to which Gould is not referring.)

Sara Ruddick's work on the relationship between 'maternal thinking' and peace politics is influential in adding further substance to these features. She argues that mothering depends on birth, providing shelter and sustenance, protecting, attending, healing and maintaining connections whereby 'maternal "peacefulness" is not a sweet, appeasing gentleness but a way of living in which people demand a great deal of each other' (1992: 142). She maintains that it is the '*commitment* to care for rather than assault or abandon children' (1992: 143; emphasis in original) that fosters the struggle to live non-violently. Ruddick rightly corrects any notion that mothers are necessarily peaceful; they support soldiers and often are fierce fighters themselves, supporting a 'maternal militarism' (1992: 147). She distinguishes 'maternal thinking' as a part of the 'rationality of care' (1992: 143). That is, 'the attentive love of mothering requires concrete cognition, tolerance for ambivalence and ambiguity, receptiveness to change, and recognition of the limits of control' (1992: 145). Being attentive to particular 'others' make one less ready to kill, more likely to protect.

One of the underlying arguments to this book is that justice is not possible without care and that care without justice is oppressive.[16] Truth Commissions are a good example of the practical ramifications of this argument. In telling one's story of pain, anguish and loss and in being listened to, there is an attentiveness that is fundamental to a feminist ethic of care. However, where the victim has to confront a perpetrator or see the perpetrator receive amnesty or communal forgiveness without appearing to be apologetic, or demonstrating remorse, some victims may feel that truth does not necessarily coincide with justice. (These are massive issues and dealt with more substantially in Chapters 5 and 6.) It is important to state that 'the idea of "globalizing care" is rarely explicitly addressed' (Robinson 1999: 43) and that 'feminist approaches to ethics in the context of world politics remain barely visible' (Robinson 2001: 69). The bringing together of ethics, feminism and IR has 'traditionally been seen as inappropriate' (Hutchings 2001: 194). Joan Tronto argues that we 'cannot understand an ethic of care until we place such an ethic in its full moral and political context' (1993: 125), also that 'care is not solely private or parochial, it can concern institutions, societies, even global levels of thinking' (1995: 145). Certainly, she maintains that practices of care resemble those qualities that are necessary for democratic citizens to live together in a just, pluralistic, flourishing society. Tronto lists the four ethical elements of care as 'attentiveness, respon- sibility, competence, and responsiveness' (1993: 127). I am trying to make care explicit in applying these ethical elements to political issues within IR and specifically to the issues of security or insecurity that affect women's ability or inability to flourish as active citizens.

In order to respond practically to the need for human security which, as we have seen in the previous chapter, often means simply to feel safe, free from coercion and violence, there needs to be different ways to conceptualize (in) security and different forms of politics to realize gender-inclusive sustainable peace. Norma Nemeh uses the language explicitly when she says that:

> It is time to allow for a 'different voice' to be incorporated in the discourse on security. With the threat of terrorism prominent throughout the world today, the need to consider the human factor in the voices of women in the overall security equation has never been more imperative.
>
> (Nemeh 2001: 4)

Nemeh defines human security as that which rectifies the inequalities and injus- tices of existing social systems and power structures in order to address the security needs of a population. In incorporating justice and care, feminist ethics offers a significant alternative to orthodox approaches to international politics.

Fiona Robinson extends this alternative. She argues that the political priority typically placed on autonomy, independence, non-interference, self-determination, fairness and rights means that liberal ethics are dominant in IR. Robinson argues further that this 'has resulted in the creation of a global "culture of neglect" through a systematic devaluing of notions of interdependence, relatedness, and positive involvement in the lives of distant others' (1999: 7). Robinson's emphasis on 'a critical politicized ethics of care' (1999: 47) overlaps with my emphasis in this chapter and throughout the book, that the distinctiveness of feminist ethics lies in its emphasis on particular 'others' in relation to each other. Such an emphasis is as relevant to relationships between individuals within communities, tribes, clans and villages as it is between territories, nations and states. It enables us to have both an empathetic imaginative response to situations of suffering and the critical scrutiny of structures of power differentials, insecurity and injustices which have led to the exclusions described previously. It places international peace 'within an ethics of care that privileges our human, emotional connected- ness and social interdependence' (Allison 2001: 207), given the premium on pre- serving and maintaining relationships. In grass roots women's collective gatherings, sharing personal narratives is a priority. This includes reflecting on the effect of militarization and war's destruction on personal and family life.

Some examples are useful. Deborah Mindry, writing on the diversity of women's transnational networks, 'suggests that a moral politics, a politics of virtue, is at work in these global networks' (2001: 1193). That is, women often articulate their relationships to one another in terms such as 'the global family'. Mindry suggests that 'this global family signals a moral commitment, often expressed in terms of feminized and naturalized obligations, "to help one another"' (2001: 1193). Through drawing on her research with black South African, Indian and women of colour as well as white South African women working in NGOs, Mindry found that these women 'frequently expressed the belief that they brought compassion and understanding regarding the shared humanity to their relationships' (2001: 1198). This meant that they felt close to the everyday lives of people and felt the struggles of other women and their families and communities. In interviews, Mindry found that women's special contribution to politics lay in a closeness to the grass roots, that is, at a local level; their face-to-face interaction meant that they knew how to meet the practical needs of different groups. She argues that the grass roots is a 'moral terrain', a site of need where local struggles become connected to the global (2001: 1202). This does not assume that grass roots women's groups are 'morally pure' or apolitical, rather it shows how these groups do not form for political reasons, but because of the urgency to meet basic needs and overcome immediate crises of insecurity. In the process of doing so, they become politicized, aware of solidarity with other groups and power struggles to obtain resources. Mindry also suggests that 'women frequently invoked their capacities for caring by claiming they were best suited to ensure that promised democratic transformations would actually take place in communities' (2001: 1200). A different but related example is given by Biljana Kašić, who suggests that the Women in Black, who exhibit their bodies every Wednesday in the City Square in Belgrade, have chosen a 'bodily resistance to war' as 'a ritual of disobedience' (1997: 9). Kašić writes that the political 'is expressed as a search for public responsibility for peace as an unquestionable value, an ethical imperative and the only alternative' to violence (1997: 7).

Feminist challenges to dichotomies in international relations

Feminist ethics does not sit comfortably within IR. I seek to demonstrate its importance in challenging dichotomies. In Cynthia Enloe's early work (1988) she looked at key issues of war, militarism and security, explicating how they all depended on gendered notions of the masculine warrior subject as protector, conqueror or exploiter of the protected, conquered, submissive feminine object or 'other'. An important part of this chapter is to penetrate deeply behind the mythology that depicts war and conflict in these gendered terms in order to reveal their significance. In feminist challenges to these terms, 'conventional categories and dichotomies are not taken for granted but problematized' (Peterson 2000: 206). As already alluded to, classic gendered dichotomies include public/private, production/reproduction, culture/nature and soldier/protectee, and these dichotomies underpin so much about global politics and security studies. In addition, there are other significant binary categories of white 'other', victims/perpetrators, colonized/colonizers, dominated/dominators and us/them that are not necessarily gendered but have major implications for understanding the root causes of violent conflict and the need for peacebuilding. I suggest that all binary categories need to be deconstructed. But I also suggest that there are specific feminist challenges to critiquing dichotomies in IR.

Within IR theory, methodologically conventional realist scholars have 'an ontology based on unitary states operating in an asocial, anarchical international environment' (Tickner 1997: 616). Such traditional notions of security mark strong dichotomies, because they rely on rigid distinctions between an inside and an outside, where borders are tight in order to keep strangers out and ensure the safety of those who are within. 'Borders define and differentiate an inside from an outside. They are constituted through a construct of difference that is singular and exclusionary' (Eisenstein 1996: 29). The state assumedly acts as protector. It is easy, then, to blame the 'stranger' for any instance of insecurity.[17] Borders are symbolic: 'Borders signify friendship and acceptance or suspicion and aggression. They foster or discourage citizen belonging. They demarcate inclusions and exclusions' (Porter 2003b: 8). Within hegemonic national security policies, 'the naming of the enemy (and therewith naming the self under threat) is also crucial for clarifying the particular nexus of sovereignty and the attendant understandings of in/security' (Stern 2005: 27). Such boundaries are markers of difference between ethnic, religious and cultural groups which know who they are distinct from – that is, they have a clear concept of the 'other'. I have already suggested that this is not a concept of the 'other' as equal, but as different, where difference is seen as wrong, inferior or justification for exclusion. In violent societies, the 'other' is 'enemy', a justification for violence.

Nationalism is predicated on a sense of border, unity, likeness, belonging and loyalty, characteristics which have the potential to be good. However, problems arise where 'shared commonness is privileged against diversity, which is problematized as disorderly. Why? Because diversity means difference, and difference means conflict, and conflict is disorderly' (Eisenstein 1996: 46). Nationalism also has the potential to create divisions: 'Nationalism constructs "the people", simultaneously including/excluding us/them. The nation is a form of identity and difference. It creates the outsider, the other, the stranger' (Pettman 1996: 46). Ann Tickner explains the importance of breaking down dualisms in terms of different approaches to national security and insecurity (concepts explained in the previous chapter). She suggests that realist scholars 'define security in political or military terms, as the protection of the boundaries and integrity of the state and its values against the dangers of a hostile international environment' (Tickner 1997: 64). On these terms, states are seen as unitary actors and military power is crucial. In the 1980s, peace researchers and environmentalists began to broaden this understanding and introduce economic and environmental considerations into definitions of security.

Additionally, IR feminists define security even more broadly, beginning with individuals or communities rather than states or the international system. In particular (as already suggested in the previous chapter), security is elusive and depends on people's contexts. As explained, feminist ethics is grounded in an ontology where social relations of self-identity with constitutive others are central and where there is a commitment to emancipatory goals, such as the achievement of justice and peace through eliminating unequal, unjust gendered relations.[18] Within a feminist epistemology, the knowledge basis is grounded in everyday lives, thus the subjectivity, identity and security of women as agents is the crucial starting point of analysis. Jan Jindy Pettman explains a feminist revisioning of security in this way:

> [T]aking women's own experiences of violence and security seriously means focusing on everyday life, on bodily and psychic pain, on anger and silences within regrouping war surviving families and relationships, on coping with and loving 'enemy' children.
>
> (1996: 105)

Accordingly, feminist definitions of insecurity and security and the parameters of IR emerge from the centrality of social relationships rather than state sovereignty, global anarchy or superpower aspirations. Feminists challenge state-centred structural analyses and 'question realist boundaries between anarchy and danger on the outside and order and security on the inside' in order to concentrate on 'the interrelation of insecurity across levels of analysis' (Tickner 1997: 625). Vulnerable groups do not assume that the state will provide security, even though it should. Indeed, as the examples throughout this book demonstrate, the military often threaten women's security, not acting as a protector; local state agents threaten security; and even some peacekeepers violate women's sexual dignity. It is hardly surprising, then, that feminists challenge orthodox understandings of security, insecurity and international relations. Views of security which scrutinize what and who threaten people disrupt traditional notions of national security.

Throughout the rest of the book, I will rely on feminist ethics as an enabling framework to think through ways to overcome seemingly irreconcilable options. I argue strongly for the necessity of justice and care in order to achieve a peace with justice and security. In particular, I endorse Christine Sylvester's idea of 'empathetic cooperation', which she explains as 'a feminist method for managing, working with, respecting, and surpassing rigid standpoints, positions, and issues without snuffing out difference' (2002: 244). The crucial aspect to this idea is that of listening to the voice of the 'other'. Hence I fully support Sylvester's explanation of empathetic cooperation as a 'research gaze'.

> It is a process of positional slippage that occurs when one listens seriously to the concerns, fears, and agendas of those one is unaccustomed to heeding when building social theory, taking on board rather than dismissing, finding in the concerns of others borderlands of one's own concerns and fears.
>
> (Sylvester 2002: 247)

In Chapter 4, I develop my defence of a politics of compassion. I believe that such a politics is a matter of assessing all aspects of national and international security in relation to their effect on human security, and being prepared to adjust political decisions that have a negative impact on human well-being. I appreciate that this position is unashamedly idealistic. As such, it is an aspiration worth striving for.

Beyond irreconcilable options

I began this chapter by explaining the harm of polarization, and outlined feminist ethics as a way to counter some of the harm. In particular, I argue in support of a peace with justice and care. This chapter concludes with further positive suggestions on how to move beyond seemingly irreconcilable options to counter the harm of dualism and to value differences in inclusionary politics. Emily Schroeder *et al.* (2005) report on work on gender, small arms and light weapons and DDR.[19] They note how many of their contributors struggle with contradictions and ambiguities. These researchers suggest 'the need to explore stereotypes and question readily accepted concepts and definitions', listing pertinent dichotomies as:

- conflict/post-conflict;
- war/peace;
- public spaces/private spaces;
- human security/state security;
- real security/perceived security;
- small arms as protection/as threat;
- imposed solutions/local or indigenous solutions;
- women as peacemakers/as fighters or inciters of violence; and
- men as powerful/as threatened.

(2005: 4)

They rightly stress that 'exclusionary stereotypes make it more difficult to find, and celebrate, alternative understandings and expressions of masculinity and femininity that contribute to the success of peacebuilding and other human security initiatives' (2005: 4). In this chapter, I suggest that it is imperative to move beyond these exclusionary stereotypes. I seek to minimize the harm of dualism and to overcome the limitations of seemingly irreconcilable either/or options in order to create scope for inclusionary, holistic notions of interdependent peacebuilding. To this end, overcoming the harm of polarization is as pertinent for men as it is for women.

Countering the harm of dualism

In countering the harm of dualism outlined in the first part of the chapter, particularly the rigidity of dichotomies that lead to destructive 'othering', ethnic hatred and exclusion, I posit four responses:[20] humility, openness, dialogue and reconciliation, as ways to move beyond irreconcilable, optional or contradictory concepts and practices. First, an attitude of humility counters the arrogant smugness of a self-assured self-righteousness. Those who are humble accept that at times we are wrong, make bad decisions or act in ways that hurt others. Humility is the state of mind that is open to learning from others. In doing so, and in acknowledging the new understanding that we gain from others, we break down the distance of the 'other' and validate others as important persons who are worthy of respect. Thus humility is not a passive virtue, it is part of active peacebuilding.

Second, in being open to others, the dangers of dogmatic closed-mindedness are avoided. Being open to others does not mean having to accept as true, right or worthy everything that others tell us, but it does involve being willing to consider whether the claims being made might be true, right or worthy of consideration, rather than dismissing others' views as irrelevant. Openness, like closedness, is a mindset with consequences. Openness allows for the questions, uncertainties, doubts, ambiguities and middle positions that dualism disallows because it assumes rightness or superiority. Such openness allows for deliberation, reflection and the possibility of being persuaded to change one's view. Such openness is integral to conflict resolution, peacemaking, mediation, negotiations of a peace accord and ongoing peacebuilding. Openness permits new relational spaces to form.

Third and relatedly, open dialogue is the avenue through which we listen to the voice of the 'other'. Without mutual dialogue, the presuppositions we hold about others may be unfounded, our knowledge misinformed and our conclusions simply naive. Take, for example, the 'war on terrorism' as a response to 9/11. Persons in the US Administration were quick to talk about the terrorists as those who did not love freedom. However, the actual motivations of those who commit acts of terrorism are complex and sometimes indicate stories of suffering, dispossession, frustration at political stagnancy, desperation and anger at 'the other side' as well as being blinded by promises of religious martyrdom. These motivations do not excuse terrorism – all acts of terrorism are wrong because they harm others. Yet, in the post-9/11 global context of the Afghanistan and Iraq wars, more countries that are part of the 'coalition of the willing' are vulnerable to terrorism. Rather than aggressively lashing out (as with the war in Iraq), concerned people need to try to understand the reasons for terrorism in order to address the underlying political and structural reasons which could minimize future acts of terrorism. There is also the need, where appropriate, for world leaders and politicians to admit to political culpability for aggravating terrorism. I am not suggesting that these responses are easy or all that is required.

What I am suggesting is that in all situations of conflict, whether domestic, communal, inter-ethnic, ideological, religious or international, dialogue is the key to mutual understanding and peaceful conflict resolution. Even where there is massive dissent, as is to be expected even in democracies, dialogue is imperative for all forms of cooperation. Dialogue involves listening and talking, establishing the basis for building the trust that strengthens relationships. Listening is as important as talking. With careful listening, we begin to hear the voice of the other. Dialogue 'repudiates the safe dogmatism of one's own position or being ignorant of another's views' (Porter 1998: 55). Indeed, in listening carefully, the 'other' loses the abstract distancing of 'othering' to become a 'subject', a real person, a moral agent in their own right. The strange 'otherness' dissipates, albeit tentatively, with caution, stepping slowly around issues of contestation, vulnerability, power inequality, historical myths and personal exposure. The stories we hear may be troubling: stories of hurt, pain, torture, suffering, oppression, exclusion, humiliation, anger and discrimination. However, we have a moral duty to listen and to make sure that diverse voices are heard and – as long as the demands do not undermine respect for others – heeded. These features underlie a politics of compassion.

Further, implicit in the liberal foundations to western democracy is the inclusive tolerance of difference. In learning to trust those who we have feared, despised or, minimally, tolerated, we begin to take seriously our differences and begin the process whereby the possibility of common ground can be explored. This is where creative moral imagination permits an empathetic crossing into unknown spaces, the unfamiliar territory of the world of others. Such creative imagining allows for a stutter and then a flow of alternative ideas and practices that dualism prevents. For groups who have been kept apart through apartheid, racism, ethnic segregation, sectarianism or religious persecution, it is often a moment of illumination to realize that what they *share* with those they had classified as 'the enemy' may be greater than what divides them, at least in terms of common aspirations for livable housing, welfare, education, health, jobs, free expression of language, culture and religious beliefs in a peaceful, just society. Clearly, groups with long histories of antagonism differ on how to achieve these shared goals, but coming to realize that the aspirations overlap can be groundbreaking in peacebuilding processes. Usually this understanding emerges in informal settings, over the kitchen table, in the café or pub, or under a tree, inside a hut or in a bustling marketplace. It is a mistake to assume that commonality always leads to agreement. A respectful agreement to differ can assist peaceful coexistence. This can only occur where there is equivalence in difference, that is, an equality of respect for difference, assuming that the differences are respectful and do no harm to others.

Fourth, reconciliation of differences is inclusive and challenges the exclusivism of dualism (an argument developed more fully in Chapter 6). Social exclusion is a moral state in undermining people's integrity. Social exclusion thus requires moral responses. A reconciliation of differences between previously opposed groups is one such response which creates a community space in order to value those differences that are mutually respectful. Any expression of difference that harms others, such as with sectarianism, racism, sexism and ethnic cleansing, is morally unacceptable. However, those differences of belief, culture, gender, sexuality and ethnic practice that are not discriminatory and do not harm others, highlight the richness of being human. An inclusive society values the demonstration of those differences that nurture the mutual well-being of diversity. A society that takes reconciliation seriously does more than tolerate other differences or is satisfied with a peaceful but benign coexistence. It is a society that is keen on healing the divisions between, for example, Tutsis and Hutus, British Protestants, unionists, and loyalists and Irish Catholics, nationalists and republicans, Indonesians and East Timorese, Indians, Pakistanis and Kashmiris, indigenous peoples and colonizers, and between moderate religious believers of all faiths who despise all forms of religious extremism. It is a society that cherishes respectful differences, and delights in the deeper understanding of the rich complexity in being human. It is possible not just to coexist in peace with diverse groups, but also to flourish together in community. An inclusive peace with justice embraces our common humanity and respects plural differences. The harm of dualism can be overcome.

Valuing differences in inclusionary politics

The valuing of differences that I am suggesting is a crucial counter to the harm of dualism warrants further attention, because it is the reluctance to embrace diversity that often triggers violence or is the stumbling block to reconciliation (the focus of Chapter 6). Elise Boulding (2002) writes of the need to develop a peace culture. What lies at the core of a peace culture is not a culture without conflict, for such a society would not change and progress, but the creative protection of differences. Boulding defines a peace culture 'as a mosaic of identities, attitudes, values, beliefs, and patterns that lead people to live nurturingly with one another and the earth' (2002: 8). Robinson also encourages us to focus on caring about others in ways that make us rethink 'our own attitudes about difference and exclusion by locating that difference within relationships, thus dispelling the claim that any one person or groups of persons is naturally and objectively "different"' (1999: 164–165). Vivienne Jabri, also intent on moving debates in IR beyond dualistic confines, stresses the importance of taking difference 'into account as the formative moment of a late modern subjectivity that is responsive to its constitutive other' (2001: 162). This is an ontological argument based around moral agency as a 'situated self' (MacIntyre 1981), constituted by communities, families, neighbourhoods, tribes or ethnic groupings, which forms the setting for individual moral judgements. It is also an epistemological debate in the sense of being a morality with its foundations in reasons, often in the case of war, of religious, ethnic or tribal-based rationales.

Undoubtedly, one of the pressing issues of the times we live in is how to value differences of religious beliefs. Azizah al-Hibri discusses the importance of civility in the project of finding common ground between people of faith and secular humanists, and suggests that 'despite their different worldviews, they share a commitment to democracy, egalitarianism, and mutual respect that should make their conversations meaningful' (2001: 84), resolving difficulties through mediation and principled compromise. Too often, secularists and fanatic religionists have difficulties in communicating because of their fanaticism. Central to a concept of civility is a respect for human dignity, a respect that is undermined by stereotypes, oppressive hierarchies or any form of crushing humiliation. Incivility occurs whenever we treat 'another as an inferior "other"' (al-Hibri 2001: 85). The choices are between conflict and domination or cooperation and community. But (as I demonstrate in forthcoming chapters), cooperation around common needs can occur without political agreement and difference need not lead to conflict. Violence emerges when there is an anti-hermeneutic stance toward 'otherness', a reluctance to be self-critical about one's own 'otherness' and interpret others with an open mind. Violence also begins when 'otherness' is seen as a threat to identity. As we shall see in the next chapter, in countries where the politicization of difference has resulted in violent conflict based on ethnic, racial, religious and cultural differences, the challenge for women's groups is to find ways to minimize differences that aggravate antagonism and to seek commonalities among women that foster coalitions.

Valuing differences is a crucial part of developing a compassionate society. Compassion is not charity or condescension toward others. Compassion is grounded in a response to the equal worth and value of every person's humanity and our equal vulnerability to suffering. The fundamental value in each person can be expressed in multiple ways, so we must recognize common humanity by also recognizing the importance of differences. As we will see in Chapter 6, this is crucial for the reconciliation of differences and the humanization of 'the enemy'. In this chapter, I have explained the harm of polarization, particularly in presenting either/or scenarios that cement a them/us dualism which sees the other as enemy. I have maintained that feminist ethics strives toward realizing justice and care, overcoming exclusionary strategies and valuing respectful differences. I have argued that in being freed from the rigidity of dualistic constraints, spaces open to expand interactive possibilities. In the next chapter, I apply these ideas to the inclusive recognition of differences.

3　Recognition and inclusion

Increasing and enhancing the participation of women around the peace table, *as well* as ensuring an engendered discussion at the peace table, stands to secure a more inclusive settlement to the conflict, as well as lay the groundwork for rebuilding a just and equitable post-conflict society.

(Gopinath and DasGupta 2006: 202)

Identity and recognition

What do recognition and inclusion mean and why are they important to peace-builders? Many violent conflicts erupt when feelings of antagonism, rivalries, bitterness and fear which have deep historical roots affect people in personal ways, so that their identities feel challenged. In such societies, individuals and groups feel unrecognized, unappreciated, discriminated against, marginalized and angry. These people rarely are included in any meaningful way in peace processes. When uniqueness of self-identity, collective identity and national identity is not recognized by others and not affirmed, emotions of rage, disappointment and bitterness associated with exclusion can erupt into aggressive reactions. An explosion of violence may be based on stereotypical distorted views of the enemy or the ethnically hated and are a potent force for social exclusion. The recognition and affirmation of identities and the inclusion of different groups in all aspects of peacebuilding is crucial, to minimize and ultimately suppress such negative feelings and the violent responses that they provoke. This chapter has four main aims. First, it builds a case for the importance of recognition of identity in peacebuilding work. Second, it explains the strengths and limitations of liberal democratic paradigms of tolerance, coexistence and pluralism as strategies for inclusion. Third, it explains some of the principles underlying coalition-building. Fourth, it provides examples of ways in which women peacebuilders have formed coalitions as strategies for inclusion in peace processes.

Let me expand these aims a little before developing them in full to indicate the direction of my argument. First, identity is crucial both to self-awareness and a communal sense of belonging. Identity only becomes a problem or a site of contention when it clashes with a dominant group, the majority or rival identity for whatever reason. A clash of competing identities often leads to violence. 'In situations of armed conflict, people seek security by identifying with something close to their experience and over which they have some control' (Lederach 2004: 13) and this could be clan, ethnicity, religion or regional affiliation. However, having the freedom to express self-identity is important because it determines differing relevant claims, needs and demands that are requisite to fulfilling one's capabilities and aspirations. When women and other marginalized groups are silenced, their identities are not acknowledged, their needs are not heeded, there is no recognition of particularity and thus dignity is undermined. Hence there is urgency in theorizing on peacebuilding to include an understanding that differences of identity and the lack of recognition of identity have the potential to spark conflict. The more inclusive a society, the more it accepts the legitimacy of differences, and therefore the less it is likely to resort to violence based on a clash of identities. Recognizing different identities is important in knowing how to attend to particular needs. Does this mean that we should tolerate all differences?

The answer to this question comes in the second section, where I explore liberal democratic paradigms that operate within a multicultural framework where tolerance toward ethnic, cultural and religious groups needs to occur minimally for coexistence, or ideally for the mutual recognition of multiple identities and respect of plural differences. In this chapter, I defend the importance of pluralism, mutual recognition and mutual respect of differences as fundamental to peacebuilding. However, violent conflict disrupts the full appreciation of difference, precisely because difference and identity are often the root causes of violence, with different identity clashes revolving around religion, culture, ethnicity, language and power differences between different identity groups. When women are not aware of their human rights or their intrinsic capabilities, they are not likely to seek recognition of their particularity or specific needs or try to be included in decision-making bodies.

The third and fourth aims overlap. Despite enormous personal and political obstacles that obstruct differing conflicting sides from coming together, there are significant instances of women peacebuilders who build coalitions across differences. In doing so, they are aware of the potentially volatile nature of such differences given their clashing identities, but through dialogue, confidence-building measures and organizing across borders, many women build amazing coalitions on the basis of shared needs and what they hold in common. Through coalition-building, women demonstrate practices of recognition of difference and commonality in order to insist on inclusion in negotiation, decision-making and peacebuilding processes.

Recognizing identities

Why is it important to recognize identities? One's identity is not merely individualistic, it is shared in some ways with other members of various communities. Identity is a marker of similarity and difference. Identity marks those aspects we share with other members of our tribe, ethnic group, religious heritage, culture or nationality. It also marks individual differences within these collectivities. The need for recognition of individual and shared identity 'is one of the driving forces behind nationalist movements in politics' (Taylor 1992: 25). Charles Taylor suggests 'that our identity is partly shaped by recognition or its absence, often by the *misrecognition* of others. ... Nonrecognition or misrecognition can inflict harm' (1992: 25; emphasis in original). There are many instances of such misrecognition in global politics: the need for Palestinians to have their own land and state; Kurds spread over Armenia, Iraq, Iran, Syria and Turkey living without a separate Kurdistan; indigenous rights; the recognition of suffering and poverty that might arise simply because of one's place of birth; gender; sexuality; or having given birth to a child of the 'wrong ethnicity'. Instead of misrecognition, 'the possibility of just practices depends instead on fuller recognition of our multiplicities, mutuality, and antagonism, and the often tangled and bloody histories' (Flax 1998: 152–153). In this chapter, I make the case for recognition; in the next chapter I explain the significance of justice in moving conflict beyond its complicated mess.

An apt example of misrecognition is when women internalize cultural notions of inferiority (as referred to briefly in the previous chapter). Nancy Fraser calls this misrecognition '*social subordination* in the sense of being prevented from *participating as a peer* in social life' (2002: 24; emphasis in original). To redress this injustice, Fraser does not look to identity politics to affirm recognition of identity, which is a typical response for many marginalized groups, but she looks for other ways to judge recognition claims. She suggests that 'participative parity is the proper standard for warranting claims' (2002: 35) because it is 'only by looking to integrative approaches that unite redistribution and recognition can we meet the requirements of justice for all' (2002: 38). Thus claims for recognition can be considered contextually as remedies for particular injustices and justified recognition claims are those that promote participatory parity as a 'radical democratic interpretation of equal autonomy' (Fraser 2003: 229).[1] These claims are readily applicable in rectifying the injustice of women's exclusion from all stages of political negotiation and decision-making. This is not a glib statement. Rectifying the injustice of women's exclusion is a massive task. Understanding the theoretical basis to participative parity provides the grounds to work towards the practical realization of these ideals.

Misrecognition, oppression, domination and injustice are linked. For women, two aspects of injustice prevail, what Iris Marion Young suggests are 'oppression, the institutional constraint on self-development, and domination, the institutional constraint on self-determination' (1990: 37). Oppression is a central political category for a wide variety of groups including women because it defines the social, shared experience of identification.[2] Oppressed people do not experience oppression in exactly the same way, but all oppressed people suffer common constraints in their capacity to realize full self-development. Young (1990) talks usefully of the five faces of oppression:

- exploitation involves a systematic, unreciprocated transfer of power over someone who feels dominated;
- marginalization occurs when people are banished from meaningful participation in social life and are subject to severe material deprivation;
- powerlessness results when people have limited opportunity to exercise autonomy in their everyday life because they lack status, authority or a positive sense of self;
- cultural imperialism establishes one dominant culture as the norm; and
- violence is a feature of the lives of many groups and humiliates or harms people.

Young maintains that the five faces of oppression 'function as a criterion for determining whether individuals and groups are oppressed. ... The presence of any of these five conditions is sufficient for calling a group oppressed' (1990: 64). On these grounds, many groups including women in many different nation-states are oppressed. This claim does not homogenize women's group identity, for the experience of women is vastly different between and within nations. But for those women who are oppressed there are both commonalities of oppression and significant differences. We examine issues of justice more closely in the next chapter. Now, it is pertinent to note that sometimes, despite Fraser's caution, identity politics seems to be a spur for moving groups toward integrative, inclusive approaches.

Politics of identity

The politics of identity arises when individuals organize collectively around identity issues such as religion, gender, sexuality, culture, ethnicity or nationalism, or indeed, the interrelationship between aspects of these identity issues. Understanding the peculiarities of national distinctiveness means that we have to try to understand more than traditional binary oppositional identities, such as between Catholic nationalist and Protestant unionist in Northern Ireland, Greek and Turkish Cypriots or Muslim, Hindu and Christian Indonesians. Individual and group positions within all identity formations are complex, and there are overlapping relationships between gender, class, race, ethnicity, religion and national identification. Such relationships change with inter-marriage, education and personal contact with the 'other', for whom there are many cultural stereotypes and mythical constructs. In conflict societies, a clash can be between combinations of these overlapping relationships. Given the close proximity of differing conflicting groups in neighbouring villages or between close sub-clans, people seek security in narrow groups, identifying with those who share similar experiences. Violent conflict is spurred by clashes between rival ethnic, religious or tribal affiliation. Thus, in worst-case scenarios, tightening of identity occurs with roots 'in long-standing distrust, fear, and paranoia, which are reinforced by the immediate experience of violence, division, and atrocities' (Lederach 2004: 13). A vicious cycle often ensues. The slightest spark of hatred can ignite wild flames of violence.

The politics of identity makes political demands on public spaces. When one's identity is threatened, one's security, safety or feeling of belonging is in danger and it makes political sense to register collective protest against these threats. As I will outline later, forming coalitions between those who feel the threat of insecurity is not easy: it requires compromises, often with some aspect of identity being suppressed in order not to threaten others who do not share the same identity characteristics. 'Taken to the extreme, the focus on identity may make it politically impossible to build coalitions because all oppressions are seen as equal, therefore constantly requiring similar attention' (Tripp 2000a: 652). Identity politics is central to most violent conflicts because nationalism, ethnicity, religious divisions or territorial claims are often premised on who is included and who is excluded. Ethnic conflicts can be defined as conflicts 'in which the goals of at least one conflict party are defined in (exclusively) ethnic terms, and in which the primary fault line of confrontation is one of ethnic distinctions' (Wolff 2006: 2). Examples of such conflicts include Cyprus, Israeli–Palestinian disputes, Kashmir and Sri Lanka, Kosovo, Northern Ireland, the civil war in Democratic Republic of Congo and the genocide in Rwanda. For example, being a Hutu or Tutsi was so significant to the 1994 Rwandan genocide that long afterwards, the dilemma remains 'that to be a Hutu in contemporary Rwanda is presumed to be a perpetrator' (Mamdani 2001: 266). Stefan Wolff presents a powerful argument about people's willingness 'to kill and to die because they see themselves as ethnically different from others' (2006: 23). He explains further that 'ethnic conflicts are stories about deliberate choices made by human beings about action or inaction. Above all, however, they are stories of human suffering' (2006: 24). When threatened, people seek security with their own identity groups, giving false courage in allowing ethnic hatred to mount.

Another stark example of the impact of conflict on identity is war rape. Rape is a military strategy and

> as an ethno-nationalist 'policy' expresses deep inter-ethnic hatred and manifests itself in the kind of mass rape that happened in Bosnia and Herzegovina in the early 1990s. It is meant to humiliate, demoralize, and eventually destroy an ethnic group.
>
> (Wolff 2006: 103)

Rape attacks not merely an individual girl or woman and her family, but also the identity of the village, town or ethnic group from which she originates. 'From Bosnia to Rwanda, rape victims have been shunned by their own families and communities for dishonouring their communal identity' (Anderlini 2000a: 8). Once-integrated communities crumble under these pressures of civil conflict and 'wars that manipulate identity make the task of assuring cultural continuity, of handing on a sense of communal identity to future generations, more difficult for women and challenge the foundations of their place in society' (Turshen 1998: 9). In assisting these women, it is imperative to incorporate those who can identify with victims and survivors. For example, 'having Kosovar women activists in camps with refugees enabled them to help Kosovar Albanian rape victims at earlier stages than was the case in Bosnia' (Corrin 2004: 26). In many African countries, women who identify themselves as rape victims are ostra- cized from families. In north-east Congo, where violent, ethnically driven con- flict has raged for much of the past decade, and where women are at risk when fetching water and wood, women community leaders urge rape victims to come forward for counsel, provide opportunities for work such as gardening and baking and help to reintegrate women into the community, thereby rebuilding self-esteem. Providing assistance to the victim's husbands and families is a crucial part of this reintegration. These jobs often are the family's only source of income and this helps men to become sensitized to the trauma of rape and the recovery process.

Maria Stern offers an interesting example of 'Mayan women's security nar- ratives' (2005: 5) as an instance of the importance of recognizing particular identities. During 30 years of armed conflict, Guatemalan national security policy 'silenced Mayan women's voices, sanctioned the axe which threatened them, and skewered relations of power which placed them in marginalized positions within many different and interfacing systems of domination' (Stern 2005: 7). From the early 1990s, many Mayan women began to express pub- licly their feelings of insecurity as women, as part of an oppressed ethnic group and as members of the struggling socio-economic class. Many also felt threatened by Guatemalan nationalism and the sexualized violence of military tactics. That is, there were overlapping relationships that impacted on iden- tities. 'Many Mayan women therefore, represented their security and insecu- rity as contingent and multiple – even hybrid' (Stern 2005: 5). The narratives as 'Mayan, women, and poor' (2005: 7) reveal a fusion of identities, a variable notion of both insecurity and security and a cry for recognition of potential and actual agency. Stern writes that in making claims for security and identity, these women knew who threatened them, so in 'negotiating their struggles in simultaneous sites of subjugation and resistance', they altered unequal power relations to forge a vision of a secure existence (2005: 5). The significance in self-redefining lies in affirming their active agency as Mayan women, rather than remaining in passivity or victimhood. Orthodox concepts of security rarely heed specific identities.[3] Further, cultural traditions present obstacles to women flourishing and sometimes, 'the traditions have become so deeply internalized that they seem to record what is "right" and "natural", and women themselves endorse their own second-class status' (Nussbaum 1999: 29). I agree entirely with Stern 'that *who (we say) we are* matters in how we con- ceive of, strive for, and practice security' (2005: 7; emphasis in original). As explained in Chapter 1, there are gendered implications to security. Further, how we understand security and name particular threats, dangers, feelings of safety and well-being expresses our personal situations and therefore reflects our identities.

For women from ethnic and racial groups who have suffered 'a lifetime of feeling inferior, subordinate and oppressed, to name and to claim an identity as one's own is extremely liberating' (Porter 1997a: 86). There is an empowering nature in asserting a once-suppressed identity. Also, identity politics has the potential for alliances. For example, during the violent times in Northern Ireland, women across divides from working-class areas, who suffered the deprivation of poverty, realized that there were overlapping socio-economic needs that they shared in common, regardless of holding different identity allegiances. Despite having enormously dissimilar political, often sectarian, views of each other, local community groups emerged from segregated housing estates to form alliances that agreed to avoid political conflict in order to concentrate on the needs of childcare, housing, safe play spaces and vocational skills. The connections between structural violence, the violence of exploitation, inequality and poverty and the violence of war are linked. The connections make it possible for cross-community groups, such as the women's centres in Belfast or Derry, to focus on the similarities of women suffering from poverty and paramilitarism on both sides of the conflict.

However, there can be some seriously negative dimensions to identity politics. By definition, identity politics has an exclusionary dimension. 'The cost of a "home" in any identity is the exercise of power to include the chosen and exclude the other' (Aziz 1992: 304). When groups with overriding identities retreat to their tribal territories, clans, clubs and communities, they include those who share their identity but ostracize and exclude those who do not. As noted in the previous chapter, ethnic nationalism plays a powerful identity role in many countries where there is violent conflict, and where 'ethnicity, religion, and politics are soldered together into identities so total that it takes a defiant individual to escape their clutches' (Ignatieff 1993: 164). We cannot be blind 'to the volcano of interethnic negative passions that hisses everywhere' (Yovel 1998: 899), and provide spurious reasons to justify violence. When cultural membership is tied to ethnic nationalism, belonging and identification, it affirms the identity of community members and alienates others. Such intensity is a concern because it links belonging with violence. Strong protective bonds to insiders can prompt hostile, aggressive responses towards outsiders (Ignatieff 1993: 188). Such extreme nationalism is an example of the absolutist identity criticized in the previous chapter for being exclusive and hostile to others. Recognizing particular identities is important, but not at the expense of valuing and including other equally valid identities. Yet, Cynthia Enloe offers some useful reminders of the fact that 'nationalism has provided millions of women with the space to be international actors' (1990: 61). That is, national consciousness has encouraged many women to feel confident in public organization and debate. 'Furthermore, nationalism, more than many other ideologies, has a vision that includes women, for no nation can survive without culture being transmitted and children being born and nurtured' (Enloe 1990: 61).

As is repeatedly the story in this book, for many local women peacebuilders, it is their responsibility as mother or nurturer which fundamentally defines their prime identity and motivation to move away from communal violence. Many women from the Democratic Republic of Congo, Kenya, Liberia, the Pacific Islands, Rwanda, Somalia, South Africa, Sudan and Sri Lanka draw on the moral authority that their societies confer as a result of being mothers or upholders of communal stability to call for an end to armed conflict. The important factor is that 'the concerns these groups have about their children give them a social legitimacy and a linkage with women from different sides of the conflict' (UN Secretary-General 2002: 55). As outlined later, this common linkage breaks the crippling bind of exclusive identity politics, which can be so narrow that 'outsiders' are not included in group activities.

Including differences

Valuing diversity is fundamental to an inclusionary politics. It is part of breaking down dualisms and is crucial to facilitating the inclusion of women in all aspects of peace processes. Inclusionary politics 'requires the creative integration of diversity and commonality, particularity and universality, individualism and pluralism' (Porter 1997a: 83–84). It is important to keep reiterating that:

> The principles of gender equality and inclusion are fundamental values on which every attempt at democracy and peacebuilding must be based. This means that women must be central to and participants in any peace process. Building peace from the grass roots level is an important aspect of women's participation. Even as they hold their families together in war and post-war conditions, women are creating and sustaining peace at the community level.
>
> (Machel 1996: 45)[4]

I return to the example of Somalia to make a different point. A woman's networks typically span several lines of clans because they can travel from the clan of marriage to the clan of origin, and women are well positioned to establish a communication bridge between warring clans. 'Thus traditionally it is men, the elders, who have the means to make peace a reality and women who have a significant role in making it a possibility' (Gardner with Warsame 2004: 163). Traditionally, only men represent the clan. When a small cross-clan group of women came to the talks in 2002 they were denied a platform, as they were not official clan representatives. The women responded by demanding a place in the negotiations as a clan of women, as representatives of Somalia's sixth clan. This reached beyond the limitations of ethnicity to a vision of gender equality. The women were able to get a quota in the final resolution of women in government.[5] While women's facilitatory role here is crucial, it does not fulfil the gender equality and inclusion that Graça Machel refers to above. John Paul Lederach pays tribute to the 'innovative, constructive and transformative role in peacebuilding' of Somalian women in comparison to the formal peace conferences of militia leaders (2005: 100). Lederach explains that:

> [T]he women of Wajir did not set out to stop a war. They just wanted to make sure they could get food for their families. The initial idea was simple enough: Make sure that the market is safe for anyone to buy and sell.
>
> (2005: 10)

The significance of this simple goal is that it includes women of all clan backgrounds who seek to make the market a zone of peace, fulfilling a complex goal. The Wajir Women's Association for Peace formed. Given the women's ability to slide from clan of marriage to clan of origin, they were well situated to foster social change among strategic groups, helping to create the space for clan elders to meet.

As suggested, an inclusive society is less likely to resort to force as a method of conflict resolution. Inclusivity includes prevention measures. The point of trying to include gender-sensitive intervening factors is to include women and men as equals in the hope that this will decrease the likelihood of conflict and draw on local prevention initiatives. The factors include NGOs that address the special needs of men and women, regional initiatives that engage and encourage women in peace negotiations and peace activities, gender-sensitive international assistance and the long-term empowerment of women alongside an empowerment of communities (Schmeidl and Piza-Lopez 2002: 17). Local prevention initiatives are imperative, but often require support from major international bodies to raise awareness of the potential of galvanizing local women across a region. 'Despite growing awareness of the roles women play in conflict prevention and peacebuilding, resistance to the intentional inclusion of women is still widespread' (Schirch and Sewak 2005b: 99). Many peace activists and women's advocates spend a lot of time simply explaining to others why it is essential for women to be involved in these processes. The importance of women's involvement in peacebuilding is crucial for so many different reasons. Lisa Schirch and Manjrika Sewak (2005b: 99–100) suggest six main reasons. First, women are more or less half of every community, thus their skills are necessary. Second, as chief caretakers of their families, everyone suffers when women are oppressed, victimized and excluded from conflict prevention and peacebuilding. Third, women are socialized into fostering relationships and avoiding violence. Fourth, women and men have different experiences of both violence and peace, hence women must be encouraged to bring their insights to peace processes. Fifth, women's empowerment challenges sexism which, along with racism, classism and ethnic and religious discrimination, all stem from the same sort of belief that others are inferior or superior. Sixth, women continue to prove themselves to be successful peacebuilders because of their firm belief in the principles of inclusivity and collaboration, which allows for strategizing across differences and understanding the importance of multi-track peacebuilding. Schirch and Sewak emphasize the importance of building a discourse on peace and security that includes the perspectives of men and women, and stress that 'infusing a gender analysis into peacebuilding requires concrete action' (2005b: 102) in planning, implementing and evaluating all conflict prevention and peacebuilding programmes. The ideals I am defending will remain only a nice idea, unless they are translated into concrete, culturally sensitive strategies for transformative change.

I reiterate that attention to differences is an important part of inclusionary politics. Without such attention, women (and other marginalized groups) are routinely ignored, marginalized or deliberately excluded. However, are there differences we should not recognize and thus not include in peace processes? I argue that there are, thus it is important to develop principled positions to defend what types of differences or assertions of a politics of identity can be accepted. There are differences that in my view do not warrant support and cannot be justified ethically. Examples include political, nationalist or religious allegiances that refuse to condemn bombings that kill or maim civilians and result in infrastructure damage, or any form of separatism that is so exclusive that it fails to respect others, or any political majority that does not grant reciprocal esteem to other significant political communities. A principled politics of difference respects those differences that do not harm, undermine, humiliate or threaten another. The right to express differences corresponds to the responsibility to respect others' differences. I suggest that there are three main requirements to an accommodation of identity and difference that is mutually respectful of human dignity, namely, 'a disassociation of inequality from difference; an openness to difference; and a readiness to face the otherness of the other' as well as the otherness within one's self (Porter 2000: 169). Difference often means inequality or privilege. Difference marks those who are deprived from those who are given access to full citizen rights. The possibility of just practices arbitrates against unjustified discrimination of differences so as to recognize the antagonisms across identities. We shall see in subsequent chapters how the place of memory is crucial in recognizing how identities are constituted historically. Only once the equal worth of differences that do not harm others is accepted can there be an openness to mutually respectful differences and readiness to face the realities of 'otherness', including appreciating ourselves as an 'other'. Without this readiness, there is a lack of mutual recognition of selfhood, which dehumanizes and contributes to much of the ethno-nationalist violence which dominates the current security agenda.

While in the main it is reasonable to argue that women's access to power and decision-making is critical to gender equality and altering power structures in households, Srilatha Batliwala suggests that in India, it is particularly frightening to see 'the way in which fundamentalist parties have mobilized and fostered women's political participation to advance their own agenda' (in Zeitlin 2005: 12). The answer to the question of what differences we should recognize and include in peace processes must avoid the pitfalls of ethnocentrism, moral self-righteousness and the dogmatic narrow-mindedness of religious and political fundamentalism. The benchmark of what to avoid is that which harms or undermines others' dignity or restricts human rights and capabilities (such as with all fundamentalist orientations). Before expanding on the ways that women bridge the divides across differences to form coalitions that empower women's inclusion in peacebuilding, I examine tolerance and coexistence as providing some of the underlying framework to this empowerment.

Beyond tolerance and coexistence to mutual respect

Tolerance

Intolerance stirs conflict and works against peaceful coexistence. Michael Walzer defends toleration because it aids peaceful coexistence but suggests that this 'is not to argue that every actual or imaginable difference should be tolerated' (1997: 6). In the previous section, I outlined my principled politics of difference; I now extend Walzer's views as they relate to peace. He suggests that toleration has five different degrees:

- a resigned acceptance of difference for the sake of peace;
- a benign indifference that it takes all sorts to make a diverse society;
- a moral stoicism that others have rights, even if the exercise of them is unattractive;
- an openness to the other, a curiosity, possible respect, willingness to listen and learn; and
- an endorsement of difference.

(Walzer 1997: 10–11)

A significant benefit of these degrees of toleration is that it legitimates many previously repressed voices. 'Toleration makes difference possible; difference makes toleration necessary' (Walzer 1997: xii). Again, it is important to keep restating the idea of principled difference. If we adopt a qualifier of difference only in terms of those differences that respect human dignity and do not harm, some cultural practices toward women should not be tolerated, such as *sati*,[6] female genital mutilation (FGM), femocide and prioritizing boys' education over girls'.

Further, it is crucial to ask what we are doing when we tolerate, because it suggests a condescension, that it is from a position of power that one tolerates the seemingly intolerable or the undesirable. Amy Gutmann suggests that while 'toleration extends to the widest range of views, ... respect is far more discriminating. Although we need not agree with a position to respect it, we must understand it as reflecting a moral point' (1992: 22). The ideal of mutual respect is, in my view, important to maintain – it is essential to my argument of principled difference. Ideally, within multicultural societies, there are 'a wide range of such respectable moral disagreements, which offer us the opportunity to defend our views before morally serious people with whom we disagree and thereby learn from our difference' (Gutmann 1992: 22). So Gutmann suggests that those views which disregard the interests of others, do not take a moral position, make implausible claims or refuse to treat people as equals, are 'undeserving of respect' (1992: 22–23), and all forms of sexism and racial and ethnic hatred fall into this category. Yet, on the other hand, decent moral disagreements require deliberation, not denunciation, so there needs to be a willingness to articulate disagreement and 'be open to changing our minds when faced with well-reasoned criticism' (Gutmann 1992: 24). Many examples of where this willingness is needed come to mind, particularly with regards to different faiths, differing cultural values and disputes over boundaries, territories, rights and lucrative natural resources.

As Charles Taylor puts it, 'we define our identity always in dialogue with, sometimes in struggle against, the things our significant others want to see in us' (1992: 32–33), as dialogical beings. Taylor also suggests that 'the struggle for recognition can find only one satisfactory solution, and that is a regime of reciprocal recognition among equals' (1992: 50), to confirm both equal dignity of humanity and particular authenticity of individuality. All forms of inequality, injustice, powerlessness or oppressive relationships that lie at the root of much violent conflict work against equal recognition and equal valuing of differences, whether these are gender, ethnic groups, racial groups, tribes, rival rebels or cultural differences. The confirmation of equal dignity of humanity which underlies respectful recognition of others is fundamental to reconstructing the moral and social basis in societies emerging from conflict, which is why a toleration of difference that leads to mutual respect assists the efficacy of peacebuilders.

The idea of a tolerant society that values cultural pluralism appears very attractive, given the radical and often violent clashes of values that spark ethnic conflict. Tolerance and multiculturalism are closely aligned.[7] However, dualisms still prevail and as Ghassan Hage (1998) points out, tolerance/prejudice, racial/social harmony and multiculturalism/ethnic inequalities can coexist. Hage asks the question, 'what does one do when one tolerates'? (1998: 88) and suggests that those who are 'tolerated' are 'positioned' (1998: 90): they are allocated a space in which they should not trespass or a stereotype which should not be defied. This space is rigid, there is no chance to transgress its boundaries. Those who engage in practices of intolerance are not necessarily uncommitted to tolerance, but 'feel that someone has exceeded their own threshold of tolerance and that they are entitled to put them back where they belong, within the limits and boundaries of tolerance they have set for them' (Hage 1998: 93), especially when 'they' are not like 'we' are. The consequence is misrecognition that harms dignity. Tolerance, then, has the air of condescension, reluctant accommodation or patronizing acceptance and does not assist the move toward reconciliation of differences.

This is very different to what Yirmiyahu Yovel terms 'tolerance as the capability to recognize humanness. ... The human in others as echoing and responding to the human in ourselves' (1998: 901). Importantly, Yovel stresses that this recognition need not imply sympathy or goodwill, but often starts with conflict and ill-will where others appear as a threat to one's identity, tribe or nation. This tolerance can form the basis on which power-sharing arrangements between former enemies can begin. The hope of reconciliation explored in Chapter 6 is that moral recognition of the humanness of the other grows, as former opponents or enemies learn to appreciate something about each other's concrete humanity.

However, it is not appropriate to develop debates on multicultural tolerance fully here because they presuppose the valuation of cultural differences and an equality of respect that is absent in situations of violent conflict. It is important, though, to flag the issues of diversity and tolerance as basic preconditions to the ideal of mutual respect that is necessary in order for marginalized groups to be encouraged to participate in all aspects of negotiated processes.

> At the opposite end of the table, the other side acquires face, allowing for listening to take place, and for the development of an understanding of the motives and/or grievances of the other party. Even so-called enemies will be seen to possess a humanity, making it possible to identify common ground.
>
> (Garcia 2004: 35)

The face of humanity differs but is reflected in the shared basis of common humanity, an equal dignity.

Coexistence

In many ways, the practice of coexistence overlaps with some of the limitations of tolerance outlined above. Coexistence implies some acceptance of the need to live with fundamental differences between individuals, groups and nation-states.[8] In coexistence work, peacebuilders encourage antagonistic groups to avoid confrontation and seek compromises that permit groups to overcome crises and live together despite conflicts of interest or irreconcilable differences. All forms of face-to-face dialogue potentially help to break down hostility and prepare the way for acceptable compromise. In a situation of compromise where groups accept that they have to get on with each other, political, social and economic arrangements can begin to address longstanding grievances in tackling the inequities and root causes of conflict. Coexistence work is based on the belief that it is paving the way toward consensus and cooperation, and if reconciliation does not eventuate, at least extreme brutal conflict will have been prevented. Coexistence responds to the 'alien other', the 'enemy' and accepts their right to exist. Coexistence

> [f]unctions as a check and restraint on totalistic visions that seek the annihilation of an enemy viewed as the incarnation of evil. Once people are willing to agree to coexist, they begin to embrace a less toxic vision, one that may settle for something other than a complete victory over the enemy.
>
> (Weiner 2000: 15)

Eugene Weiner suggests that without the concept of coexistence, there is only dedicated struggle, victory or defeat: 'coexistence work is a way to get through the day – alive' (2000: 20). Weiner suggests that while coexistence is minimalist, often simply allowing antagonists to live in the same locality, 'it can be a prelude to a durable peace' (2000: 15). He defends the usefulness of coexistence work, particularly in ferocious conflicts between ethnic groups such as in Lebanon, Nigeria, Pakistan and Sudan. As we shall see later, coexistence work is most successful when it begins to cultivate the virtues of listening to alternative views and where there is an attention to the common good of shared goals.

Across the globe, seemingly intractable conflicts are of high concern, particularly where adversaries identify in terms of powerful identities of ethnicity, language, religion or tribe.[9] Along with the violence between opposing identity groups comes a dehumanization of the other. In such intractable conflicts, particularly after ceasefires or when peace talks begin, it is imperative to find an accommodation of differences that permits some form of coexistence. Finding accommodative ways of relating between adversaries is tricky. Moving beyond destructive relationships requires a propensity 'to push aside feelings of hate, fear, and loathing, to discard views of the other as dangerous and subhuman, and to abandon the desire for revenge and retribution' (Kriesberg 2000: 184). While we look at reconciliation in more detail in Chapter 6, and dealing with the past in Chapter 5, it is pertinent to our understanding of this chapter to state that the open recognition of injuries suffered and losses experienced by victims of civil war and violent conflict is fundamental to beginning the process of reconciliation. Ideally, former adversaries look to a future where the mutual respect of differences can occur within a context of security with high levels of integration.

Sadako Ogata, as the UN High Commissioner for Refugees (1991–2000), saw people who had 'fled the cruellest of human inhumanity' (2003: xi) and in Bosnia, East Timor, Kosovo, Rwanda and Sierra Leone, were returning home to societies rent into fragments. 'Home was where your neighbour had killed your husband with a machete or had firebombed your house or had raped your daughter' (Ogata 2003: xi). Simmering hatred, distrust and palpable tension hovers after the gunfire subsides or the axe is laid aside. As explained in Chapter 1, 'post-conflict' might not mean 'no conflict'. The 'Imagine Coexistence Project'[10] accepts that ruptured relationships must be addressed or they can erupt into violence again. In this project, members of conflicting groups begin strategic parallel or joint activities. The imagining process is linked with practical developmental concerns which can bring people together to decide on practical communal needs, such as where to build a well or a bridge. The aim is that shared experiences build some respect for others, so that once starkly divided groups can begin to imagine what it could be like to live together peacefully. Ogata links human security with making coexistence work.

As previously explained, the aims of coexistence are modest, involving some interaction between ethnically divided groups of youths, women, mixed adults, sportsmen or ex-combatants. 'The minimum concept of coexistence asks only that members of such groups live together without killing each other' (Afzali and Colleton 2003: 3). A good example of this are the prospects for coexistence in Central Africa, where ethnic animosity, extreme violence, widespread distrust and fear make the task daunting. In Rwanda, coexistence efforts are considered to be part of programmes of reconciliation, still a challenging ideal. 'The less demanding concept of coexistence denotes a spirit of getting on with life and indeed was the spirit that *appeared* to exist in Rwanda' just before the 1994 genocide occurred (Sommers and McClintock 2003: 43; emphasis in original). Coexistence programmes are varied. In Rwanda, they include programmes to bring former genocide victims and perpetrators together. Contact for women includes health education to bring all members of the community together on issues of HIV/AIDS and maternal and child health, vocational school development for both Hutu and Tutsi girls and opportunities for women to mix together in peace programmes. The aim of these programmes is to reinforce women's capacity to prevent and resolve conflict and develop coalitions.

Coexistence projects are all concerned with providing quality opportunities for direct contact with the 'other'. These projects occur while attitudes of hatred, prejudice and stereotypes about ethnic differences usually remain intact. Sara Cobb explains the importance of understanding the strength of the myths that varying sides hold about each other, 'regardless of the fact that there is little or no knowledge of the other's story' (2003: 295). These myths cement intransigent stereotypes which form the basis of identity, are resistant to change and conflict resolution. As noted, ethno-nationalist projects engage individual and collective identity and hence coexistence work has to engage all levels of participants' identity. This may be personally confronting. For example, 'in Bosnia, twelve Croat girls left the folkloric dance troupe with which they had been training for months ... rather than perform ethnic Serb dances (along with Croat, Muslim, and other Balkan dances) in public' (Chigas and Ganson 2003: 71). The forces of identity are powerful. As noted previously, until there are positive changes in perceptions toward different identities, hostility toward the 'other' remains, undermining the possibility of coexistence. Diana Chigas and Brian Ganson stress the political nature of coexistence in communicating an altered 'vision for society – a vision of shifting the social norm from one of ethno-national exclusion to one of tolerance, coexistence, cooperation, and in some cases multiethnicity' (2003: 76). Coexistence initiatives challenge all exclusionary nationalist strivings for dominance. Yet, where there is a willingness for engagement, unresolved tensions over political differences of visions hover and easily explode into conflict.

Michael Ignatieff believes that it is important to distinguish coexistence from reconciliation. He sees coexistence as crucial to further political ends: 'Coexistence cannot proceed in the absence of two conditions: a political deal between antagonists and a security deal to ensure safety on all sides (2003: 331). For example, in the South African TRC, many whites came to be reconciled to majority rule, and many black victims accepted that their desires for vengeance and revenge would not eventuate. 'This meaning of reconciliation – being reconciled to the facts – has an intimate relationship with coexistence' (Ignatieff 2003: 326). Ignatieff adopts a pragmatic approach to the fact that political enemies and historical antagonists 'can coexist' with people they 'cheerfully detest' (2003: 326). He points to the dilemmas in knowing what should be prioritized when coexistence and justice appear to collide. In the case of prosecutions for war crimes, such as in Bosnia, it is tempting to suppose that coexistence should trump justice. 'Yet there are cases where moral discussion about impunity is so strong in a victim community that it cannot coexist with the perpetrator community and less guilty individuals are punished. In such cases, doing justice works to further coexistence' (Ignatieff 2003: 327). I accept Ignatieff's points that coexistence furthers political stability and that people can be 'reconciled to the facts' underlying coexistence, but in Chapter 6, I seek to develop a solid defence of the ideal of reconciliation.

It is fitting to end this section with a positive example of coexistence.

> A workshop in Rwanda in the summer of 2002 engaged a group of Hutu and Tutsi women in a dance, matching one Hutu and one Tutsi and tying their hands together with a thread. As one moved, so the other had to, and they practice learning to move harmoniously. They performed the result gracefully and then sat back, marvelling at what they'd done.
>
> (Minow 2003: 230)

Judy El-Bushra conducted extensive fieldwork experience in African countries and in working with Rwandan women's groups, she suggests that the significance of the groups lie 'in the potential for rebuilding relationships as much as the ability to offer emotional support and share productive tasks' (El-Bushra 2000: 74). So far, I have established the importance of recognizing respectful differences of identity. I have discussed the importance and limitations of tolerance within diverse cultures. I have suggested that coexistence is a limited but crucial strategic goal in situations where intransigent hostilities overwhelm the possibility of living side-by-side without destroying each other. How then do groups who can barely coexist meet to form coalitions?

Coalition-building

Coalitions rely on common, shared interests which can be the focus of attention rather than the divisive elements that are inherent in all groups. In this section, I explain why women often draw on their common tasks as mothers and/or nurturers to build coalitions across hostile differences. I argue that there are three crucial peacebuilding characteristics that help to build coalitions: the need to foster confidence and gain the trust of those previously perceived as enemies; open engagement in dialogue across differences; and the development of listening skills that enable one to hear others' stories. We look at trust, dialogue and listening in turn. Before doing so, it is useful to note some gendered differences in coalition-building. Tamra Pearson d'Estrée and Eileen Babbitt (1998) observed the interaction styles of male and female Palestinian and Israeli participants in interactive problem-solving workshops held as a means of coalition-building. The workshops brought together individuals from communities across conflict lines. The women noted that in the women's workshops, the discussion was more constructive than in mixed-gender groups. There was more empathy, connections were nurtured and women were more prepared to confront the emotional aspects of conflict, including the tough issue of Jerusalem. D'Estrée and Babbitt conclude that given these skills, 'women may be able to make a significant contribution during the prenegotiation phase, in which the building of relationships and empathy is a key component for breaking down mistrust and polarization' (1998: 205).[11] Once negotiations have begun, this range of skills in building relationships remains important to keep the parties engaged, to provide a groundwork for successfully managing the predictable crises and breakdowns of negotiations and to promote empathy and reciprocity in creating decisions for settlement. Repeated contact with those from across conflict divides permits meaningful connections in times of crisis. For example, after a women's workshop, the women 'arrived home to find that 50 Hamas supporters had been expelled from Israel in retaliation for a terrorist attack for which Hamas took responsibility' (d'Estrée and Babbitt 1998: 204). The women were able to use their newly developed relationships to understand the 'other side' undistorted by conventional stereotypes.

Commonalities

I have noted in this chapter the importance of identity to self-esteem and how a politics of location that incorporates experience, specificity and positionality are assets that foster an acceptance of diversity. However, where difference and plurality are prioritized over commonality and coexistence, the political potential to speak for universal and specific interests for human rights and women's rights is lost. Feminist politics draws on women's perspectives, voices and experiences, accepting that women have some interests in common and many that are different. Western feminism, particularly postmodern feminists, stress differences in order to counter any assumption about essentialism. Post-colonial feminists stress differences to counter false assumptions about western arrogance. However, too often 'difference is understood in terms of inequality, distinction, or opposition, and sexual difference modelled on negative, binary, or oppositional structures' (Grosz 1994: 91). An inclusionary politics of difference must accept the differences between and within communities. Young presents strong defences of the relational concept of group difference, whereby conflict can be resolved in polities which foster 'institutions and procedures for discussing and deciding policies that all can accept' (1993: 135) and where there is specific representation of disadvantaged social groups. During periods of conflict, these safeguards are unlikely. It is only in transitional periods where divided societies are emerging from intense periods of violence that there can be any institutional resources for listening to and respecting the needs of different groups. Grass roots groups work throughout conflict and maximize the spaces between extreme violence. Young defines politics as 'public communicative engagement with others for the sake of organizing our relationships and coordinating our actions most justly' (2006: 123). This definition is particularly useful in examining women's coalitions because many women do not explicitly define their activity as political. Often what begins a dialogue is a common language born of pain and grief and coalitions form when the empathetic mutual understanding grows.

As we shall see shortly, the building of coalitions occurs in the middle, messy spaces that negotiate between radical diversity and surprising commonality, between the myriad differences within and across identity formations and when formal opponents grasp, often tentatively, whatever can become a shared basis from which to work. This middle ground is neither philosophically weak nor a pragmatic compromise. 'Rather, it is a strong position that respects diversity, makes space for different forms of individuality, and seeks grounds for commonality' (Porter 1997a: 92). Such a complex position accepts the importance of individuality and pluralism and of particularity and universalism, so that neither is sacrificed to the other. It recognizes 'the dignity of the generalized other through an acknowledgement of the moral identity of the concrete other' (Benhabib 1992: 164). Whereas responses to the 'generalized other' are governed by norms of formal equality and reciprocity and the moral categories of rights, obligation and entitlement with corresponding feelings of respect, duty, worthiness and dignity; responses to the concrete 'other' are governed by norms of equity and complimentary reciprocity with moral categories of responsibility, bonding and sharing with corresponding emotions of love, care, sympathy and solidarity (Benhabib 1992: 158–159). The ideals of complimentary reciprocity are inherent in feminist ethics and underline political relationships of mutual respect.

To recap the point made continually throughout this chapter and Chapter 2, to overcome harmful either/or dualisms, middle positions adopt principled approaches to the politics of difference in respecting those differences which do not harm others. This makes these spaces messy, troublesome and demanding. They require deep reflection on what differences should be respected. Relations of domination, violence, sectarianism and racism are not differences to be recognized as legitimate: 'all differences are not equal nor do they deserve the same political consideration' (Flax 1993: 111). I support Judith Squires' argument that 'if not all manifestations of otherness are to be celebrated and fostered, principled positions are in need of political articulation and ethical justification' (1993: 9). As already argued, there are differences that are not ethically worthy of support, political allegiances that lead to killings, maiming, economic damage, disrespectful separatism, violent destruction and victimization that leads to unspeakable traumas. I am reintroducing the idea of a principled approach to difference because it is foundational to coalitions. How, then, can groups find the space that permits work across differences to flourish and mutual respect to grow? In responding to such a question, Cynthia Cockburn identifies 'the space between the differences' with examples of ways in which women seek commonalities, listen carefully and respectfully, are sceptical of damaging labels and are 'intelligent in selecting agendas that they can work on, or setting aside issues that they cannot' (in Online Working Group on Women and Armed Conflict 1999: 24).

The basis of commonalities differs with each coalition. Peacebuilders cross the boundaries of divides to seek those common goals that build trust.

The common experience most typically used by women peacebuilders is an empowering claim of moral authority that is socially assigned to mothers, wives, daughters or older women. It is an interesting example that in South Africa, 'both ANC-supporting and apartheid-supporting women articulated their political positions in terms of maternalist imagery and loyalties' (Pettman 1996: 122). Again, it is important to repeat, it is not that all women are naturally peaceful or maternally inclined, but that generally, women are responsible for meeting everyday needs. While one can say that different ethnic groups have culturally specific practices of mothering, gender roles and family life, 'commonalities in the nature of gender relations sometimes transcend national frontiers and ethnic and "radical" specificity' (Walby 1996: 252). For example, within Northern Ireland, common factors across political divides include the importance of the family and the influence of the church in reinforcing religious fundamentalist conservative theology and practices. As we shall see in the examples given below, women's commitment to community attachments and family care is the thread that weaves through the disjunctions of violent societies. As outlined in the previous chapter, this commitment is a practical manifestation of a feminist ethics of care that is anti-dualistic in nature, defying the fragmentation that can easily occur when diverse national allegiances drive women apart despite their common identities as mothers and carers. In many conflicts, women's social status becomes a basis for organizing to pressure the authorities to investigate the disappearance of husbands, or to struggle to claim inheritance of land.

Mariam Djibrilla Maiga is founding member and President of the National Women's Movement for the Maintenance of Peace and National Unity, Mali. She writes that the mechanisms used by this movement are based upon shared social values: 'We particularly emphasized the social pacts that unify the number of communities; we emphasize the question of parenting and families, and we emphasized marriages and extended family networks' (International Alert and Women Waging Peace in Anderlini *et al.* 1999: 44). The movement identified arms proliferation as the most important problem and at a heads of states summit, organized a meeting of civil society organizations to sign a declaration to have a moratorium on arms in the region, with the majority of countries signing. This initiative brought warring parties together through non-conventional channels. In a different example, Nani Chanishvili, when a professor in Georgia, formed an NGO to campaign for the prevention of armed conflict, mobilizing women across ethnic and national divides. She says, 'the best way to make peace is to focus on common activities, common life' (in Anderlini 2000b: 22), hence the groups' focus not just on peace issues but also on culture, education, health and summer schools.

The LWI was established in 1994 in order to bring popular pressure to bear on politicians and warlords. Frustrated with stalemate in the peace process, women became involved in the Liberian peace process, maintaining a high-level presence at all the peace conferences. LWI is non-partisan and the women belong to various political parties and different walks of life. They have shared their experience with other bodies in Ghana, Nigeria and Sierra Leone.

'The strategy they adopted was to take a unified stance on issues that affected everybody' (Anderlini 2000b: 20). Like the activists of the LWI, Mu Sochua 'chose to campaign around a single issue that was of common concern: elections without violence', and in 1991 founded the first Cambodian NGO, which was called *Khemara* (Cambodian Women) (Anderlini 2000b: 25). She went on to become Head of the Ministry for Women's and Veterans' Affairs. In the Cambodian elections in 1998, the UN and women's groups went to the grass roots to explain elections and how they affect women's lives. Finding commonality is an important way to address shared needs and build workable coalitions. From a small group of ten Turkish Cypriots and ten Greek Cypriots in the 1990s, meeting in the 'Green Line' – the area which until 2003 divided Cyprus – numbers grew to 3,000 meeting regularly in women's groups. Sevgul Uludag explains that the women are given the opportunity to present their perception of the most traumatic moment in their history, usually presented as a role-play. 'Common feelings, common values and awareness of common interests emerge' (in Online Working Group on Women and Armed Conflict 1999: 13). As a way to further this mutual understanding, there is a consensus that there are basic human needs of identity, belonging to a community, security and the vitality of ethnicity. Uludag writes that how one satisfies these needs is open to discussion, but this provides space for exposure to 'find alternative solutions to the existing conflict, and this is a very creative phase' (1999: 14).

Eugénie in Kigali-Nali joined the local women's group to overcome the poverty that came from being a widow after the genocide in Rwanda. She says, 'once we understood that there is strength in unity, widows and non-widows came together to overcome our common problems – chronic poverty accentuated by war, genocide and the loss of relatives' (in Women for Women International 2004: 12). Similarly, Suzanne Ruboneka, responsible for Pro-Femmes, an umbrella organization for Rwandan women's groups started just after the genocide, acknowledged that it urged women to come together 'to build our collective on what we had in common as mothers and citizens, rather than looking at what kept us apart. This way we could rebuild the country for our children' (in Women for Women International 2004: 15). As a Rwandan woman said, 'boundaries do not separate the commonalities women face everywhere in this region such as poverty, violence against women, feeding their children and shelter' (in Baines 2001: 32). The common concerns of women form an agenda which can transcend ethnic, cultural and religious divisions.

Given the phenomenal diversity within groups that are trying to forge coalitions during and after times of violent conflict, solidarity 'should come from criss-crossing ties' which grow when people work together on any shared passion, but 'criss-crossing connections cannot grow when people do not encounter one another' (Minow 1998: 152). In conflict and transitional societies, successful alliances have to be renegotiated continually. Every time conflict erupts, relationships change as fear returns and trust is jeopardized. Janet Jakobsen maintains that alliance politics requires activity in four sites of diversity:

- *diversity among* persons and groups that give them specificity;
- *diversity within* individuals and communities that articulate the complexity of interactions;
- *différance* as the site where heterogeneity is so open that it resists simplistic binary oppositions (as critiqued in the previous chapter); and
- *diversity between* differences, that are 'lived in the interstices and intersections between axes of differentiation'.

(1998: 13)

Among these sites of diversity, alliance politics seeks common passions that permit the building of coalitions. The commonalities can involve shared concerns and needs, a common basis of suffering, as well as the shared emphasis on mothering, nurturing and meeting family and community needs.

In Northern Ireland, the NIWC is a good example of alliance politics. The Coalition was cross-community, with women from Catholic, republican and nationalist traditions and from Protestant, loyalist and unionist backgrounds as well as women who did not identify with either tradition. It was cross-class, with working-class activists and middle-class professionals. It was cross-region, incorporating women from rural and urban areas. It was cross-sector, bringing together women from all sections of life. For some women, the mere notion of having to work with people from disparate traditions involved enormous personal journeys, with occasional agreements to differ, but generally there was more emphasis on accommodation, flexibility, negotiation, process and striving to establish workable solutions. An agreement amongst diverse groups that they do share common interests and concerns is a monumental first step for individuals who are more accustomed to viewing each other as enemies. Winning each others' confidence and trust can be a stressful task – so much is at stake, including vulnerability. The input of the NIWC into the negotiations that led to the 1998 Good Friday Agreement was significant. As a result, there emerged 'an agreement whose human rights and equality commitments went well beyond addressing the "nationalist/unionist" communal divisions to address other exclusions' (Bell *et al.* 2004: 322).

I have outlined in detail the way that women peacebuilders across cultural diversity typically draw on their shared role as mothers, wives, widows or daughters to form coalitions across difference that help women to meet their families' and communities' needs for material and emotional sustenance. I now explain three characteristics of coalition-building that are as relevant to men as they are to women: building trust, engaging in dialogue and listening.

Building trust

Trust is the end product of respectful relationships. It has to be earned and can easily be lost. Before reaching trust, there are many preparatory stages. In discussing relationships between Serbs and Croats and between Palestinian and Israeli Jewish women, Nira Yuval-Davis talks of transversal politics whereby each individual participates in 'rooting' and 'shifting'. Her idea is that each participant brings with her the rooting in her own membership and identity but at the same time tries to shift in order to put herself in a situation of exchange with women who have different membership and identity.

(Yuval-Davis 1994: 192–193)

The process of shifting does not involve losing connections to one's personal roots or homogenizing the 'other', but it does involve a genuine attempt to try to understand where another person is coming from, particularly when there are extreme differences which have been the root cause of deeply held grievances. Cockburn stresses the imagination as the heart of transversal politics and maintains that 'the making and maintaining of working alliances across differences depend more than anything else on the capacity to step into another person's shoes and see the world from her position' (2004: 186–187). Where there has been deeply embedded antagonism, distrust between individuals and communities is extreme, yet often is based on an ignorance that comes from no personal contact or the misunderstanding that accompanies myths and stereotypes. Confidence-building measures are necessary to overcome blatant ignorance. Often the motivation for being prepared to take the risks that are necessary to stay 'rooted' yet also 'shift' is knowing that there is a need to find compatible strategies to work towards common goals (as discussed earlier). Perhaps the goals may differ, but similar strategies bring people together in the process of working through them. In conflict societies, the risks can be life-threatening or open old wounds. It may be distressing to feel personally vulnerable in exploring long-held myths about the 'other' or suddenly find out that the reasons for long-held bitter hatred are unwarranted, that the 'other' is an ordinary human being with shared feelings, hopes and fears similar to one's own.

In conflict societies, sharing stories about pain and fear is a typical starting point to building trust between adversaries as both sides begin to realize that there is common ground in shared pain and suffering and the desire to move on. Cockburn's work (1998) provides useful examples of building trust across risky transversal politics. Cockburn stayed with women in three organizations: the Women's Support Network in Belfast, which represents women's community centres from both Catholic and Protestant areas and focuses on poverty and peace; Bat Shalom, an alliance of Israeli Jewish and Palestinian Arab women which focuses on a peaceful settlement to the Middle East, including an end to the occupied Palestinian territories; and the Medica Women's Therapy Centre in Zenica, central Bosnia-Herzegovina, a project established by German and Muslim, Serb and Croat women to respond to the needs of those traumatized by rape and bereavement. It is interesting to note that there was no NGO sector in pre-war Bosnia-Herzegovina, it needed the introduction of a multiparty system. As Branka Rajner writes, 'in Bosnia-Herzegovina, the NGO sector, especially the peace and human rights movements, are primarily women's movements' which provide women with transferable political skills (in International Alert and Women Waging Peace, 1999: 41).

Cockburn identifies similarities in the three groups in being women-only, with a conscious blend of ethnicity, nationality and religion: 'alliances holding together differences whose negotiation is never complete and is not expected to be so' (1998: 14). Cockburn also identifies six identity processes that are common. First, they affirm differences in a positive manner. Second, rather than essentializing or assuming inevitabilities, they strive towards a 'non-closure of identity' (Cockburn 1998: 225) which allows for all sorts of self-expression. Third, the groups found ways to reduce typical polarizations by incorporating other differences, such as including Chinese youth in a Belfast programme. Fourth, there was 'an acknowledgement of injustices done in the name of differentiated identities' (1998: 226), that societies founded on terrible wrongs must face up to the realities of layers of oppression. Fifth, care was taken to identify issues with which all felt mutually safe. Sixth, group processes gave equal weight to all voices and shared decision-making was important. Cockburn concludes that the crux of risky alliances is '*a creative structuring of a relational space between collectivities marked by problematic differences*' (1998: 211; emphasis in original). The degrees of trust built over time vary and come through ongoing, meaningful dialogue across differences. This notion of a relational space is extremely useful. It is creative, flexible, can be visualized and revisualized and it repudiates oppositional extremes.

During 1999 to 2000, Cockburn worked with seven women's organizations in Bosnia-Herzegovina and writes that 'women saw women as the best hope for integrative working in these divided and embittered towns. ... The impulse to rethink enmity and recover friendships seemed to wake in women before men' (2002: 76). Cockburn also worked with women across the Green Line partitions across the Republic of Cyprus and the Turkish Republic of Northern Cyprus.[12] The line was open for the first time for 29 years on 21 April 2003. Cockburn uses the idea of the line as a simple notion of the construction of difference and 'otherness'. She asks, 'what is implied in the way we draw our lines, for inclusion and exclusion, closeness and distance, love and hate' (2004: 24)? Cockburn warns against the drawing of a line by dominant collectivities or identity groups. Rather, she talks of the strengths of transversal politics to cross imaginatively into others' positions, encouraging groups 'to forge alliances of differently-identified groups resisting racism, fundamentalism, nationalism and war' (2004: 38). Cockburn witnessed a 'Hands Across the Divide' project, demonstrating that 'when a successful dialogue takes place across difficult differences it is because the participants have come to understand the plurality of truth' (2004: 39). There is great potential for building trust when former enemies move into open, exploratory, honest relational spaces.

Engaging in dialogue

Trust comes through dialogue. The challenge of creating dialogue across differences can be enormous, particularly where deep discord and mistrust have complex historical roots and thus pain, fear of the unknown and suspicion of others prevail. Many ethnic conflicts appear to be resistant to resolution, given the strength of ethnic identity that is so fierce that the stakes are deemed to be high enough both to kill and to die for. In such contexts, how does one begin a dialogue that recognizes diversity without prompting a violent reaction? For example, there are enormous challenges in finding a common language whereby Kashmiri Hindu and Muslim women can find some common ground, or where women polarized by Sinhala-Tamil or Tamil-Muslim ethnic constructs somehow forge a coalition based on cross-cutting identities. How do women leaders in Armenia, Azerbaijan and Georgia promote cross-border networking? National coalitions for peace formed in each country, with a Coalition 1325 in Azerbaijan, Peace Coalition in Armenia and the Unity of Women for Peace Network in Georgia. These national coalitions formed a regional alliance, establishing the Southern Caucuses Regional Coalition – 'women for peace'.

Seyla Benhabib provides some guidelines on the importance of discourse ethics to communication and mutual understanding 'with others with whom I know I must finally come to some agreement' (1992: 9). After long periods of antagonistic relationships, unity or consensus is difficult to reach. There are many reasons for these difficulties. Often it is because there is such deep, long-held mistrust. Confidence-building measures that lead to mutual understanding have to be worked out through dialogue between those with very different viewpoints on issues such as the meaning and justification of borders, ownership of natural resources, concepts of the state and nationhood, the role of the international community, decommissioning of weapons, policing and security issues, political prisoners and ex-combatants, reconstruction efforts, national identity and the possibility of reconciliation between previous enemies. Benhabib's guidelines do not depend on a model of universalistic rights-bearing abstract individuals. Rather, they reflect ordinary moral conversations where people must try to come to terms with others' views and where there is some reciprocal respectful recognition of each others' differences. In conflict societies every political issue is highly contentious and rarely mutually respected, particularly when grievances have deep historical roots, as is the case in the Balkans, the Middle East and in many post-colonial nations. Appeals to particular parties, tribes or ethnic groupings alone preclude the opportunity for decisions to be made on shared concerns.

Deliberative democracy is idealistic; it aims towards a practical commitment to emancipation and liberatory relationships and structures. The starting point for these ideals is 'the idea that each of us must be given access to and heard at the bar of informed ethical and political debate' (Frazer and Lacey 1993: 203), defending a moral urgency to attend to difference. The sort of difference that leads to violence is not the inconvenience of minor disagreements, but differences deemed to be so fundamental that they are sufficient to escalate into conflict. Deliberative democracy helps to sort through these quandaries. A political goal in transitional societies is to move toward a deliberative and communicative democracy where 'political engagement can change initial statements of preference and interest' (Phillips 1995: 149). Through discussion, new positions can be formulated. This is of crucial importance in political stalemates when ceasefires break down or peace accords are not carried out. Careful deliberation can expose possible resolutions to conflict that were seemingly impossible before dialogue took place. What makes this interaction possible, even when between adversaries, is not friendships, consensus or even trust, but 'a quality of *attention* inherent in the very practice of deliberation' (Bickford 1996: 25; emphasis in original). Such attention to others is integral to feminist ethics. Sometimes this attention is merely 'strategic or grudging' (Bickford 1996: 41), but such attention keeps the conflict political rather than personally defensive. For example, sometimes, ex-paramilitaries or political prisoners learn to redirect their attention and realize during their imprisonment that democratic processes are preferable to violence. From inside prison and when released they play a pivotal role in persuading their communities to keep the guns silent, or to 'bury the hatchet'.

Young argues that deliberative models of democracy promote reason over power. That is, it is not just those with the powerful voices who should be heard, but 'democracy requires an equal voice for all citizens to press their claims, regardless of social position or power' (Young 1997: 62). She stresses that these claims need to include expressions of anger, hurt and passion, all emotions that hover close to the surface of ethnic conflict and peacebuilding measures. After protracted conflict, this is the type of democracy worth working towards. Kevin Clements underlines the importance 'that no one or no group is assumed to be unreachable or incapable of conversation, and where – given the right conditions – everyone is capable of engaging in positive transactions' (2005: 81). He reiterates the importance of the humanist enterprise, that the world is not divided into natural dualisms of good/evil, save/unsaved and blessed/cursed, but as we talk, we also should listen. Deliberation offers the best hope for conversations 'free of fear, superstition and prejudice' (Kaldor 2003: 160).

Listening

Open spaces for conversations of trust require listening engagement. We often hear about talking, deliberation and dialogue, but less about listening. However, without listening and, indeed, without trying to understand others' positions, it would be impossible to gain an understanding that might lead to mutual respect of someone we fear, dislike or have grown up to see as 'the enemy'. While we can never fully understand somebody else's experiences, the more we try to understand their motivations, the more we can engage with their stated needs. In stable societies, we can talk of 'a deliberative disagreement' as 'one in which citizens continue to differ about basic moral principles even though they seek a resolution that is mutually justifiable' (Gutmann and Thompson 1996: 73), but this is dependent on principles of accommodation and mutual respect of respect-ful differences. What prevents these attitudes from being widely accepted in conflict societies are interrelated factors such as misunderstandings, entrenched controversies, a 'win/lose' culture, malicious lies, contempt, continual blaming of others, bitterness and a refusal to release the bind of the past.

Listening 'requires an uncomfortable, shifting vision' (Flax 1998: 151). Lis-tening is necessarily relational, it applies 'the insights of "connection" to the exercise of democratic persuasion' (Mansbridge 1996: 126) and thus opens politics to difference. Deliberative communication and listening acknowledge 'a difference that may be the source of conflict, *and at the same time* foregrounds the possibility of bridging that gap by devising a means of relatedness' (Bickford 1996: 5; emphasis in original). Listening in this way is never passive; rather it is constitutive in the active process of figuring out in the face of conflict, what seems best to do. Listening and speaking should engage mutual agency and situatedness, the rooting and shifting of transversal politics, a shifting back and forth, speaking and listening as equal participants of difference whose identities need to be recognized in all their fullness and complexity. Those speaking need to be reflective, careful of how they refer to the 'other side' and try to avoid offence. Listeners too should be self-critical, taking responsibility for responding appropriately to what they hear. An example of this importance of speaking and listening across tense differences can be found in a women's cooperative in Rwanda called *Dusohenye* (Mourning Together). It is comprised of both Hutu and Tutsi women, many who are widows. They ritualize shared suffering. 'They adopted positions as narrators, telling their stories; as listeners, as others told of suffering; and as characters, in the reciprocal stories that were told about community life, before and after the genocide' (Cobb 2003: 296). Into these stories they built accounts of uncertainty, fear and acknowledgement of how much had been learned just by listening to others. Such listening enables bridges to be built across borders, physical and psychological. Listening opens once-silent spaces.

Building bridges across borders

Borders are not merely territorial or national demarcations of land. They are cultural, ethnic, religious, gendered, sexualized and personal. Organizing across borders requires defiance of accepted norms and in conflict zones, high risks. Countless examples of women's courage across borders can be given. At the Security Council meeting on 'Women, Peace and Security', Kofi Annan acknowledged women's role 'in building bridges rather than walls' (2000: 1). Women's organizations at the grass roots level foster confidence to organize across borders both regionally and internationally. Most women's organizations do not have political affiliations and thus are able to provide supportive assistance, aid, trauma counselling, education and rights awareness campaigns to people regardless of ethnic or political differences. That is, their motive for engagement draws on an attention to care for the needs of suffering people to which political considerations are often secondary. In Afghanistan, women's networks work with Hazara, Pushtun, Tajik and Uzbek women regardless of their ethnic background. This does not deny the importance of ethnic affiliation; rather it stresses the importance of building across bridges. While West Africa experiences internal crises, most of these have cross-border implications. MAR-WOPNET has members from Guinea, Liberia and Sierra Leone. The network 'brings together high-level women from established political networks as well as grass roots women, all searching for a way to end the fighting that has debilitated their three countries' (Rehn and Johnson-Sirleaf 2002: 77–78).

The group Women in Black was founded in 1988, a year after the Palestinian *intifada*, an uprising in protest of the Israeli occupation of the Gaza Strip and West Bank, and is a grass roots Israeli and Palestinian movement. Israeli and Jewish women began to stand in weekly public vigils, initially in Jerusalem, then branching out to other parts of Israel and other parts of the world. It has become a model for cross-border organizing. Groups have sprung up all around the world, taking on the political context of the country in which its silent vigils are held and creating an international network of women prepared to demonstrate peacefully. Lepa Mladjenovic, a counsellor from Belgrade, explains the significance of silence: 'It is a very loud silence. It mocks the silence that is imposed on women. And because our silence is so loud, it is a rebellion against the way that women are politically and socially silenced' (in Prince-Gibson 2005). (I will return to the profound significance of silence in Chapters 5 and 6.) The wearing of black expresses grief for all victims. In Germany, the women protest against neo-Nazism and racism against foreign workers. In India, women focus on ending the ill-treatment of women by religious fundamentalists. Support from the network provides solidarity for members from diverse countries who confront militarization and aggressive regimes. Stasa Zajovic from the Serbian Peace group, Women in Black, reiterates the importance of networks of solidarity which combine feminism and anti-militarism (in Rehn and Johnson Sirleaf 2002: 76). Across Australia, Women in Black meet on the steps of Parliament House in different states to protest against the war in Iraq.

Accounts of other positive coalitions are reassuring. Conflict occurs where adversaries refuse to engage with each other and where the 'other' is dehumanized and feared. Yet, there are examples of Hindu, Muslim and Sikh women crossing the 'enemy lines' in Kashmir to initiate projects on trauma healing and reconciliation. Kashmir is one of the most militarized regions in the world. In the conflict between Pakistan and India, groups such as WISCOMP (Women in Security, Conflict Management and Peace) and WIPSA (Women's Initiative for Peace in South Asia) facilitate communication between women's groups. Even when Track-1 diplomacy is 'caught in war rhetoric and political jingoism and civil society dialogue has been irregular and limited', WISCOMP and WIPSA have been consistent in facilitating dialogue (Schirch and Sewak 2005a: 7). Sometimes there are good reasons why coalitions do not form. For example, in the Kashmiri conflict, Rita Manchanda writes, 'the only women's groups to emerge have been fundamentalist', and while there is the possibility to build alliances with mainstream Indian women's groups, 'since this is a pro-separatist identity struggle, women's groups in India are very reluctant to get involved' (in International Alert and Women Waging Peace, 1999: 31). Conflict resolution often begins simply by getting people together in order to restore some form of communication. For example, in strife-torn Kashmir, the project called *Athwaas* (A Warm Handshake) is breaking through the barriers of mistrust and suspicion by first talking to Hindu, Muslim and Sikh women about their experiences, and then creating safe spaces called *Samanbals* where meetings, dialogue and joint activities can take place that bridge the divide and facilitate reconciliation (van Tongeren *et al.* 2005: 87). Despite starkly different political convictions, women engage in safe spaces to search for common ground. The initiative is part of WISCOMP. The women share stories of exploitation, torture, exile, escape, custodial deaths and horror. As we will see more fully in Chapter 5, the stories reveal that there is no one truth about conflict and affliction.

> Pain, loss, and suffering interspersed with profiles of courage and determination in the face of adversity were the common thread that united women across diverse communities. The *Athwaas* members were able to understand first-hand how women negotiated the space between victimhood and agency and how in many cases boundaries between the two categories get blurred.
>
> (DasGupta and Gopinath 2005: 114)

The inclusive nature of this network of Kashmiri women is crucial in transcending those differences that serve as barriers, enabling the listening to the voice of the 'other' and supplanting the need for vengeance with the urge for reconciliation.

Practices of inclusive recognition

Many women peace activists, intent on developing shared spaces where open and respectful dialogue can take place, excel in the acceptance of diversity and constructing creative ways of inclusion. Anna Snyder (2006) conducted a study of how informal coalitions of women's peace organizations built a political agenda in the NGO Forum 1995 which ran parallel to the UN Conference. She concludes that WILPF, the NGO which led the Beijing peace activities, used informal and consensual decision-making processes such as inclusivity, empowerment and non-hierarchy. 'Unfortunately, the consensus process facilitated the suppression of conflict and difference and reinforced the power of the northern organizers' (Snyder 2006: 36) and this left off the agenda contentious issues that some women wanted to talk about, such as decolonization from women in the South Pacific and self-determination for Palestinian women. Recognition of what is most important in peoples' lives is imperative for attentive listening and meaningful inclusivity.

When we return the discussion to women's inclusion in all stages of peace processes, inclusive recognition is paramount. Examples abound: the Center for Women in Bujumbura, Burundi opened in 1996, with assistance from Search for Common Ground, Washington[13] and the US Agency for International Development. For a long time, the Center was the only safe place in Burundi where Hutu and Tutsi women could meet openly and safely to talk and exchange information. Between 1998 and 1999, International Alert and Women Waging Peace and UNIFEM worked with women leaders on both sides of a conflict in Burundi that spun from decades of ethnic and political violence to train nearly 3,000 women leaders on conflict resolution and mediation skills. For the first time, women of all ethnic groups sat together and discussed peace and security. Through open dialogue, perceptions of each other's ethnic group have been rehumanized. The women at the All-Party Burundi Women's Peace Conference held at Arusha, 17–20 July 2000, knew that in large measure it was their efforts that sustained Burundian communities, and this fact should be acknowledged, rewarded and supported.

There are many other examples of inclusive recognition. Joyce Seroke was an anti-apartheid activist who had been tortured and served several terms in prison. She explains that the inclusion of women at the negotiation table did not come easily and male participants at the negotiations had to realize the huge contribution that women made.

> There was no way that they could simply forget all of that and wipe out the years of sacrifice: balancing our roles in the home – motherhood on the one hand, and demands of leadership in the political arena on the other. We absolutely had to be included, not just the numbers, but we wanted to be taken seriously. And they did. Look at our Constitution now.
>
> (Seroke in Gobodo-Madikizela 2005: 7)

SCR 1325 recognizes that where there is

> an understanding of the impact of armed conflict on women and girls, effective institutional arrangements to guarantee their protection as full participation in the peace process can significantly contribute to the maintenance and promotion of international peace and security.
>
> (S/RES/1325 2000)

In December 2005, a Gender Expert Support Team from Darfur supported the ongoing Inter-Sudanese peace talks. The all-women team included economists, lawyers, health workers, parliamentarians, educationists, ministers, academics and grass roots women workers. UNIFEM supported this group in order to make women's participation in the peace talks possible. The African Union is facilitating the negotiations between the government and the rebel groups. Participation of women in these peace talks is historic and include Mariam Abdalla Omar, once a commander in the Sudan Liberation Movement/Army, now a campaigner for peace. Issues of wealth, power-sharing and security affect women and men. On International Women's Day 2006, the women delegates to the Darfur peace talks made some crucial statements acknowledging the increase in women participating in the talks as women in their own right and across party affiliations. They reminded the parties in the talks that when negotiating and implementing the Peace Agreement, they need to include provisions for:

- the protection of women and girls against gender-based violence;
- the special needs of women and girls during repatriation, rehabilitation, reintegration and reconstruction;

- supporting local women's peace initiatives and indigenous processes for conflict resolution;
- respect for the human rights of women and girls;
- building the capacity of women delegates to engage effectively with the negotiation process;
- generating support for women's priorities;
- special measures to ensure women's equal, effective participation in governance at all levels; and
- equal benefit from the Special Reconstruction Fund to ensure economic and social security.

(Statement by Women Delegates to Darfur Peace Talks 2006)

East Timor is often cited as one of the UN's success stories. While the involvement of the UN was crucial, Emily Roynestad stresses that 'the process was nonetheless driven by East Timorese women themselves, without whose determination and persistence, progress would have been less far-reaching' (2003: 2). She points out also that the majority of women in East Timor are illiterate and rural, living in an overwhelmingly patriarchal society influenced by indigenous culture, the gendered impact of Portuguese colonialism and Catholicism. The case of East Timor strengthens the feminist analysis, which suggests that where women are involved during conflict, in peacemaking initiatives and in formal negotiations, they are more likely to be included in reconstruction. In pointing to significant milestones, Roynestad firmly stresses 'the necessity of women *of the nationality in question themselves* being prepared to fight the battles to mainstream gender' (2003: 3). Milestones include an attempt in the early 1990s for East Timorese women to break into the peace negotiations. REDE,[14] the East Timorese Women's Network, was formed at the first Congress of Women of Timor Loro Sae, the first post-conflict gathering of representatives of women's organizations. They articulated a Platform of Action to which the United Nations Transitional Administration in East Timor (UNTAET) responded by incorporating it into the workplan of Gender Affairs. The Gender Affairs Unit was part of the original organizational structure then was deemed unnecessary, and then subsequently put back in place but without a budget. Sherrill Whittington, head of the Unit, says that this is a lesson learned that 'should never happen again to any unit established in a UN peacekeeping mission' (2003: 48).

Leading up to the first free elections for the Constituent Assembly, REDE argued for a quota of at least 30 per cent of women in the Assembly. While the proposal was defeated, East Timorese women restrategized and a women's caucus established an effective network to increase women registering as candidates. The Gender Affairs Unit, in conjunction with UNIFEM, held training workshops on democracy and political decision-making. UNTAET also held workshops for district gender focal points as well as internal UNTAET gender focal points in order to build their capacity to develop gender action plans. There was success in 'that 26 per cent of candidates elected to the Constituent Assembly turned out to be women' (Roynestad 2003: 5). Of the Constitutional

Commission established to consult with the East Timorese people 40 per cent, were women. Consequently, a Women's Charter of Rights in East Timor was established. Peace support operations are not just peacekeeping missions, they steer the redevelopment of society. 'Gender mainstreaming in post-conflict reconstruction has to be backed by commitment and resources by all parties concerned, not by a Gender Unit alone' (Whittington 2003: 51).

Many of the women elected to parliament floundered, not only because of the need to toe the dominant Fretilin party line, but also due to lack of experience, lack of confidence and limited understanding of gender concepts, which make them susceptible to male domination. Exploring why this is so is important. 'East Timorese women have been effective at countering cultural relativist arguments that gender equity is a foreign imposition. They have pursued a rights based approach' (Roynestad 2003: 9). The resurgence of violence in 2006 between defence forces and rebel militia groups led to numbers exceeding 135,000 displaced persons. Temporary shelter had to be constructed near Dili National Hospital to care for women in late stages of pregnancy. Women in East Timor have the highest fertility rates in the world as well as the highest rates of child mortality.[15] (One lesson to be learned from the resurgence of violence is the importance of the international community in sustaining long-term assistance. I return to East Timor in the book's conclusion.)

Similarly, the Office of Gender Affairs at the United Nations Mission in Kosovo (UNMIK), focused on the priority areas of increasing the representation of women in decision-making in reconstruction and peacebuilding processes; addressing the issues of violence against women; and integrating women into the economic recovery of Kosovo. Internally, the Office ensured a gender perspective across mission policies by being part of high-level meetings. The Kosovo Transitional Council, which began as the highest consultative body, was expanded to include Kosovan woman representatives of political parties and NGOs. UNMIK also initiated a Kosovo Transitional Council Gender Policy Working Group to review legislation and policy training of potential women candidates for the elections. There was also training for gender focal points in different regions and municipalities as well as programmes that included strategies for literacy, higher education, legal protection for women in the labour force, social assistance for low-income women heads of households and widows, and referral systems for women subject to violence (NGOWG 2001).

Elsewhere, strategic transnational activism led to donor reaction to the plight of Rwandan women post-genocide. The Rwanda Women's Initiative (RWI) was established with women's committees interlinking local areas, districts and national levels of governance based on similar principles to the Bosnia Women's Initiative and Guatemalan experiences. Since 1996, the Bosnia Women's Initiative became a significant part of the UNHCR programme in Bosnia-Herzegovina. It developed small-scale projects that could be implemented by local women's associations and NGOs and focused on empowering women through improving their social and economic skills. Projects focused on educational and vocational training, income generation and contributing to community development. The coalition-building within the RWI involves the umbrella of UNHCR implementing partners, NGOs and local women's associations. Projects include practical issues of land and agricultural projects and paralegal training sessions, but also create safe havens to talk about violence against women and the common loss of relatives in the geno-cide. 'Given the national scope of the project, RWI projects promoted collect-ive action and provided a space for communication across differences. ... This is not reconciliation, but it is working across differences' (Baines 2004: 146) where common gender discrimination occurs across ethnic difference.

In this chapter, I have argued that misrecognition of identity aggravates antagonism, but recognition and affirmation of identity encourage inclusive practices. I have shown that sometimes, conflict societies are grateful for coexis-tence, a lull allowing people to live alongside those who are very different. I argued that we should respect differences that are mutually respectful and do not harm others. I gave examples of gaining trust, engaging in dialogue and lis-tening across differences. The building of bridges across difference entails hard work. Right across the world, what stops women from being included fully in politics, public decision-making and negotiations for peace are similar factors – the cultural constraints against women's activity, high illiteracy rates, poverty and powerlessness in knowing where to begin. Within coalitions, fresh relational spaces open and mutual respect grows.

4　Justice and compassion

> Justice cannot only be measured by judgments. It must be reached through a
> process that is fair and that upholds the rights and dignity of those who come
> before it. This is particularly of concern for international justice mechanisms that
> seek to provide redress to conflict-affected victims who have been degraded,
> demeaned and dehumanized.
>
> (Nowrojee 2005: 20)

An important part of peacebuilding lies in dealing with the past, in creating
space for the truth to emerge about the past and for accountability to occur.
Democratization processes that abound since the 1990s inevitably are tied with
questions of how to deal with the past, in terms of attending to gross violations
of human rights, the prosecution of perpetrators, victims and debates about truth.
As Tuomas Forsberg expresses it, 'these questions have always been around in
one way or another; but what is new is the context of a normative democratic
ethos' (2003: 65). Forsberg correctly reminds us that while questions of the past
are particularly pertinent in societies emerging from violent atrocities, 'the issue
of how we should deal with the past is always with us, and only in its most
urgent sense does it concern transitional societies' (2003: 67). Where societies
have been characterized by violence, polarization, segregation, ethnic conflict,
caste and clan division, the link between justice and reconciliation is critical in
times of transition from an oppressive discriminatory regime to a more democratic form of government where human rights are respected.

In this chapter, I make four substantive arguments. First, I make a case for a
politics of compassion as an ethical response to political issues of justice that are
outside of our immediate everyday relationships. Second, I argue that both
justice and peace are necessary in societies going through a transitional period,
that is, the option of peace or justice is based on a false dichotomy. Third, given
the particularity of the injustice, inequality and denial of rights for women in
conflict zones, attention must be given in peacebuilding efforts both to the universality of human rights and the particularity of gender rights in different cultural contexts. While there are different notions of justice and equality, the
inclusion of gender justice and gender equality in peacebuilding are important

considerations. Fourth, for transitional justice to be meaningful, victims' needs must be addressed. I explore the merit of restorative justice in restoring the dignity of victims and offenders.

A politics of compassion

In Chapter 2, I explained the importance of feminist ethics. I now develop this further and defend the possibility of a politics of compassion.[1] Care ethics and a politics of compassion are committed to the particular, contextualized characteristics of care, including the moral requirement of compassion. Whereas care ethics typically is directed towards a known person, a politics of compassion extends the domain in which it is even possible to imagine that compassion might operate. It includes those examples where we do not personally know people who require care, such as many of the women who are the focus in this book; woman who are refugees or displaced, women who have been raped in war; traumatized civilians whose families have been killed by the 'smart bombs' of the insidious 'war on terrorism'. My argument is that while the 'ethics of care' has broadened over time into a 'politics of care', a politics of compassion extends these debates so that in situations where there is a lack of previous history and everyday relationship, the role of compassion enlarges to adopt an important feature in the relationship. 'A politics of compassion links the universal and the particular in that it assumes a shared humanity of interconnected, vulnerable people and requires emotions and practical, particular responses to different expressions of vulnerability' (Porter 2006a: 99). Within IR theory, national and international security, conflict analysis and decisions about war are perceived as part of the hard world of politics. Yet, they have an immediate bearing on human security and well-being. Indeed, particularly in a post-9/11 context, it is important to avoid an oversimplification of soft or hard politics because all decisions about territory and national and international security have a profound effect on people's lives. I suggest that to ignore this is to ignore the human dimension to security. I seek to demonstrate that security and political compassion are compatible and necessary for justice to be realized.

What, then, is compassion? Most theorists understand compassion as incorporating in some way feelings, empathy and co-suffering. First, compassion involves a feeling with another person, an emotional identification with the pain, anguish, misery, grief, distress, despair, hardship, adversity, destitution, affliction, agony, hardship and suffering that someone else is enduring. Often this feeling of compassion comes through trying to imagine what our reactions would be if our daughter was raped in war, our brother was bullied simply because he looks Arab, or our village was ransacked just because it was close to an oil field or diamond mine.

Second, if we understand compassion as the capacity to feel for others and, to some extent, share their emotions and enter into their predicament, there is controversy as to the extent to which one can empathize with others.

> Empathy taps the ability and willingness to enter into the feeling or spirit of something and appreciate it fully in a subjectively-moving way. It is to take on board the struggles of others by listening to what they have to say in a conversational style that does not push, direct, or break through.
>
> (Sylvester 2002: 256)

Seyla Benhabib supports an egalitarian reciprocity that recognizes 'the dignity of the generalized other through an acknowledgement of the moral identity of the concrete other' (1992: 164). To this end, as we seek to identify with another, we increase the likelihood of being able to understand some of this person's deep needs and pain. Without putting ourselves in the position of others we fail to grasp the nature of our differences, and 'we fail to risk the vulnerability of being truly open to others' (Porter 2000: 175). It is important to recognize that in doing so we actually may be repulsed by our differences. They may expose religious beliefs, cultural practices, political commitments and personal idiosyncrasies that leave us flummoxed or morally outraged. Also, there are limits to how fully we can identify with others. Those who have first-hand knowledge of people's pain are more likely to be able to empathize more directly than those who feel the pain from afar. However, it is also true that sometimes aid workers, health specialists and those working directly with those suffering in war or in refugee camps have to develop some emotional distancing in order to cope with the constant distress of what they face, otherwise, they would never be able to complete their practical support. Compassion is grounded in the universality of human vulnerability and it requires an avoidance of presumptuous paternalism in order to respond meaningfully to particularity.

Third, there are crucial differences between merely having sympathy for someone and co-feeling or what some writers refer to as co-suffering. Whereas with empathy someone tries to identify similar emotions in order to understand sympathetically how the person is feeling, co-feeling implies attachment 'as identifying with and feeling the suffering of others' (Arendt 1973: 81). Empathy is important, it sympathetically identifies with others' emotions, but compassion takes this further – it feels some of the pain and importantly responds accordingly. As Sara Ruddick puts it, in 'imaginatively apprehending another's pain as painful', the compassionate person is 'pained by the other's pain, and ... acts to relieve the *other's* suffering' (1992: 152; emphasis in original). For Ruddick, compassion is different from pity, empathy and co-feeling; it is not that the compassionate person actually shares in the other's suffering, for such appropriation leads to misunderstanding and the romantic or mystifying identification that can never fully appreciate the extent of someone else's grief. As Martha Nussbaum adds the important qualification, compassion involves empathetic identification where 'one is always aware of one's own *separateness* from the sufferer' (1996: 35; emphasis in original). The compassionate person is pained by another person's distinct pain and acts to relieve it.

Compassionate co-suffering presumes a sense of shared humanity. In other words, somebody else's suffering is based on the sort of pain that could happen to anyone, including ourselves. There is inequality of suffering and some people in some areas endure far more than others, but we are all vulnerable to suffering. Thus, respect for the equal worth of each person's humanity is absolutely crucial to this understanding of compassionate co-suffering. Without the respect and recognition that I have outlined in the previous chapter, we cannot be truly attentive to people's needs. It is too easy for us to impose our own small-mindedness or western, patronizing, unrealistic solutions or offer what has worked for us. This is not to say there are not important lessons that cannot be learned by our experiences. However, peacebuilders know only too well of the difference that peace makes when it springs from the grass roots, local context. Compassion presupposes our shared humanity and is an emotional and practical response to the particularity of suffering. The compassionate person, after careful consideration of context and listening to the specific nature of the suffering, makes a reasoned judgement about the specific needs of a person, group or socio-political concern. We are human. Sometimes we misjudge. Realistically, there are many issues we cannot care for directly because of distance, limited resources, ignorance or because it just would not be appropriate for an outsider to intervene. In a politics of compassion, the universal and particular considerations maintain a taut balance, as we shall see in the examples that follow.

To summarize, I suggest that compassion involves feeling pain, empathizing with others' needs and co-suffering. There is a process of compassion. The compassionate person feels some of the pain of another and, in experiencing some distress, becomes a co-sufferer. The compassionate person tries to identify imaginatively with the sufferer in order to understand the sufferer's viewpoint and what might relieve the pain. In this context, the sufferer is not a passive victim but knows their own interests and needs.[2] The compassionate person thus attends to the sufferer's interests through listening, heeding and judging perceptively in order to discern how best to respond to the sufferer's needs. This involves sensitivities to the victim's sense of personhood and what is needed to restore dignity, so that a victim becomes a survivor. The practical wisdom required for a politics of compassion is in the Aristotelian sense of *phronesis*, where there is an understanding of appropriate feelings, careful deliberation, scrutiny of available options and then carrying out good intentions through effective, reasoned choices.

> I suggest that political compassion can occur with a combination of three central features: first, attentiveness to the suffering of vulnerable people who are experiencing pain, marginalization, belittlement, and loss of citizen rights; second, active listening to the voices of sufferers in order to discern their needs; and third, compassionate, appropriate, wise responses to particular needs.
>
> (Porter 2006a: 111)

I expand these three features. First, attentiveness to suffering is needed because we are fragile humans who all face vulnerability to suffering. Nussbaum suggests that compassion comes into play when suffering is serious and 'the suffering was not caused primarily by the person's own culpable actions' (1996: 31). This is suffering caused through war, bombs, missiles, genocide, tribal spearings, axing of limbs, war rape, terrorist attacks and all the reasons why peacebuilders are necessary. Nussbaum suggests that 'judgment' which does not utilize the 'intelligence of compassion in coming to grips with the significance of human suffering is blind and incomplete' (1996: 49). This judgement is crucial for trying to understand the conditions that give rise to harm or pain in injury and which can prompt the wise responses needed to address such harms. Such judgement requires responses to people that affirm their human dignity. Yet, it is difficult to humanize the experience of others when that experience is just horrific, such as occurs in torture, war rape, sexual trafficking or surviving in a refugee camp. Attentiveness to the plight of others affirms dignity as a concerned responsiveness to people struggling in despair.

Second, to be attentive requires careful, sensitive listening to sufferers' voices in order to discern needs. Listening (as explained in the previous chapter) involves a willingness to be attentive. As we shall see in the next chapter, truth is hard to digest. Particularly in conflict societies where truth exposes so much hurt from the past, listening to stories about pain and fear exposes excruciating insults on human dignity. The duty to listen includes being exposed to stories of torture and suffering that are almost too distressing to absorb. I am using the idea of listening liberally; the listening attention can come also through books, films, art and the internet.

Third, to demonstrate compassion, the duty to listen also requires the duty to respond. Many women's coalitions and all peacebuilders rely on compassionate listening in order to build trust. Listening affirms peoples' agency. In addition to attentiveness and listening, compassionate responses are necessary. For those people who live in areas of armed conflict, violently divided societies or in occupied territories, everyday life is full of terror, fear, uncertainty, violence, shootings, bombings and daily exposure to tragedy. The work of peacebuilders as articulated in this book demonstrates examples of compassionate politics. How, then, does a politics of compassion translate to justice with peace?

Justice and peace

All throughout this book, I argue that there are harms in dualisms. The question of whether peace or justice is a priority is a dichotomy that often 'is presented along more sophisticated lines: peace now, and justice some other time' (Bassiouni 1997: 12).[3] This dichotomy is 'deceptive', in that the choice is 'fallacious' because 'the attainment of peace is not necessarily to the exclusion of justice, because justice is frequently necessary to attain peace' (Bassiouni 1997: 12). For example, amnesties granted by governments are a form of forgiveness and thus may facilitate peace, however, the lack of accountability for crimes committed prevents the sense of justice for aggrieved parties. Alex Bouraine, who was Vice-Chairperson of the South African TRC, writes that 'not only is it impossible to prosecute all offenders, but an over-zealous focus on punishment can make securing sustainable peace and stability more difficult' (2005: 335). I agree with Bouraine's holistic position that in making states work, 'transitional justice ought to be considered as embracing accountability, truth-seeking and truth-telling, reconciliation, institutional reform and reparations' (2005: 319). Reparations may take the form of restitution, compensation, rehabilitation or guarantees that similar crimes will not be committed, and are important for achieving justice.

In addressing the direct link between peace and justice, Richard Goldstone suggests five positive contributions which justice can achieve. First, 'exposure of the truth can help to individualize guilt and thus avoid the imposition of collective guilt on an ethnic, religious, or other group' (Goldstone 1996: 488). Goldstone speaks of his personal experience as a former prosecutor for the Yugoslav Tribunal and how he was astounded in Belgrade at the Serbs who were consumed by their historic hatred of the Croats, and equally astounded in Zagreb, Sarajevo at the collective guilt ascribed to Serbs or Muslims. Second, 'justice brings public and official acknowledgement to the victims' (1996: 489). Third, public exposure of the truth is the 'only effective way of ensuring that history is recorded more accurately and more faithfully' (1996: 489). Fourth, good policing must ensure effective criminal justice. Fifth, the exposure of human rights violations often reveal a systematic pattern of violation: 'The public and official exposure of the truth is itself a form of justice' (1996: 491). What, then, can justice achieve?

> One must not expect too much from justice, for justice is merely one aspect of a many-faceted approach needed to secure enduring peace in the transitional society. The merit in securing justice, however, is that it provides a procedure for exposing the truth, ... enables a society to move beyond the pain and horror of the past.
>
> (Goldstone 1996: 486)[4]

This chapter on justice and compassion and justice and peace links to the following two chapters on memory and truth, and reconciliation and difference, which includes the examination of forgiveness and apology. Inevitably, the themes are interrelated. For example, it is very difficult to talk about truth without also explaining its connections with justice. Indeed, some even argue 'that the relationship between truth and justice is essential, whereas that between truth and reconciliation is contingent' (Forsberg 2003: 72). Others argue that 'truth complements justice; justice can reveal the truth' (Hamber 2003b: 170). It is difficult to analyse the importance of forgiveness without seeing its connections to reconciliation. To deal effectively with the past, debates need to be opened about all the aspects that trouble people – truth, justice, reparation, memory and selective forgetting.

John Paul Lederach provides a useful example of these interconnections between values of peacebuilding. During the 1980s, he was working in a conciliation team that mediated negotiations between the Sandinista government and the Yatama, the indigenous resistance movement of the Nicaraguan east coast. The conciliation team accompanied the Yatama leaders as they returned from exile to their home area to explain the agreement that had been reached with the Sandinistas. At the start of each village meeting, the Nicaraguan concili-ators read Psalm 85: 10 which, in the Spanish translation, is 'Truth and mercy have met together; peace and justice have kissed' (Lederach 2004: 28). At a training workshop later, Lederach asked the conciliators more about this text. They said that while truth requires 'honesty, revelation, clarity, open account-ability, and vulnerability' (2004: 28), alone it is insufficient. With mercy, images emerged of 'compassion, forgiveness, acceptance, and a new start' yet alone, it covers up, it moves on too quickly without attending to the importance of justice, 'of making things right, creating equal opportunity, rectifying the wrong, and restitution' (2004: 28). With peace came images of unity and well-being and feelings of respect and security that are a farce if only of benefit to some. On asking the participants what to call 'the place where Truth and Mercy, Justice and Peace meet', one answered, 'That *place* is reconciliation' (2004: 29; emphasis in original). Lederach stresses the significance of this conceptualiza-tion as being the social space where people come together in a spirit of reconcili-ation. He summarizes the interrelationships accordingly:

> *Truth* is the longing for acknowledgement of wrong and validation of painful loss and experiences, but it is coupled with *Mercy*, which articulates the need for acceptance, letting go, and a new beginning. *Justice* represents the search for individual and group rights, for social restructuring, and for restitution, but it is linked with *Peace*, which underscores the need for inter-dependence, well-being, and security.
>
> (Lederach 2004: 29; emphasis in original)

Each different conflict will see and experience differing, sometimes contra-dictory, tensions between the urgency for truth, the occasional gracious act of mercy, the passionate need for justice and the daily desire for peace. Sometimes, women approach these seeming contradictions in different ways to the norm, and I shall highlight these alternative ways of seeing the relationship between justice and peace. In El Salvador and Guatemala, there have been tensions between truth commissions and amnesty programmes when truth has not led directly to justice. I endorse Lederach's position that resolving such tensions involves finding, indeed creating, 'the social space where both truth and forgive-ness are validated and joined together' (2004: 29). (In the next chapter, I explore truth commissions in more detail. In this chapter, I am making a case for a polit-ics of compassion that permits when appropriate, a just mercy.)

Justice and mercy are seen as logically opposed: one can have justice or mercy, not both. It is assumed that justice implies determining the truth and pun-ishing the guilty party. To prosecute and punish the guilty, mercy involves leniency in sentencing, but this rarely results in restitution or reconciliation and thus justice is questionable on the terms that we are using here. In Argentina and Chile, women have been extremely vocal in insisting that reconciliation should not be at the cost of ignoring human rights abuses. There are sound reasons for this protest. Nussbaum explains that for the Greeks, equitable judgement and mercy are treated as closely linked in the moral term *epieikeia*. Nussbaum explains that *epieikeia* is 'a gentle art of particular perception, a temper of mind that refuses to demand retribution without understanding the whole story' (1999: 159). The ability to judge injustices and respond with sensitivity to all the particular details of a person's situation requires 'leniency in punishing', not at the expense of justice, rather to fulfil 'equity, and mercy' (Nussbaum 1999: 156). Such an approach is temperate and resists harsh punishment. It listens to the particular details of the whole story in order to have a sympathetic understanding. Mercy as a form of clemency 'is opposed at one and the same time both to strictness in exacting penalties and also to retributive anger' (Nussbaum 1999: 166). Within retributive notions of justice, there are no intrinsic reasons to treat people in a caring manner. A politics of compassion attends to individual stories, listens and responds wisely. The just responses thus will vary according to different needs.

Justice, equality and rights

In the previous section, I have begun to set the scene to argue that both justice and peace are necessary for sustainable peace. This argument is valid for men and women. However, the particularity of injustice, inequality and the denial of rights that women in conflict zones and in transitional societies face, suggests that attention to difference is an important part of attending to justice. Despite important UN resolutions and international conventions that protect women's rights,[5] difficulties in implementation recur constantly, and difficulties are readily justified in the name of history, culture or patriarchal tradition. Shortly, I will elaborate the dialectic between universality and particularity, but before doing so, I need to build more of the case that demonstrates women's specific needs for justice, equality and human rights. I do so because formal, procedural notions of justice can insist too readily on rules, methods and formal procedures to adhere to the letter of the law while discounting the social relationships of those affected by injustice, consequently failing to recognize the impact of pain, loss of self-dignity or suffering. There is a human face to injustice. Attending to the human narrative is intrinsic to realizing a politics of compassion.

In this section, I will argue that the conceptual framework that enables us to understand and practically tackle the interrelationship between justice, equality and rights has three components. First, it lies in defending universal principles which have particular adaptability. Second, we have a moral obligation to help restore dignity. Third, security is fundamental to peace with justice. Before developing these arguments, I explore what constitutes gender (in)justice, (in)equality and the denial or fulfilment of rights.

Gender injustice and justice

The recognition of injustice, inequality and the denial of rights is a crucial acknowledgement, a first step in restoring lost dignity. Gender injustice occurs when girls and women do not receive what they are due – their dignity – and they are treated unfairly and are discriminated against on the basis of their sex. This discrimination takes many forms. Sometimes it is explicit: the choice is made to prioritize boys and men in education, jobs and even food; at other times it is more subtle and arises because of the lack of opportunities to develop human capacities. 'Injustice is not just a *consequence* of conflict, but is also a *symptom* and *cause* of conflict' (Mani 2005: 25; emphasis in original). There are many obstacles that prevent women from seeking justice. Poverty and insufficient resources prevent the pursuit of legal avenues, there is often the inability to leave families and the intimidation many feel in facing the criminal justice system. In many cultures, women are not taken seriously as witnesses or complainants. Indeed, women often are blamed for the crime of rape committed against them and thus there is shame and stigma attached to survivors of rape crimes. Sanam Naraghi Anderlini recounts the question that Claudine, a Congolese peace activist, asked her in a workshop on transitional justice: 'What kind of peace do we have if the men who raped and killed women now sit in the government?' and for the Bosnian, Burundian, Colombian, Guatemalan, Kosovan, Palestinian and Rwandan women activists present, 'her words resonated deeply' (2005: 103). Anderlini summarizes their views that while political pragmatism often leads to amnesties to end war and it is better to tolerate impunity 'than to watch the violence go on', they all agreed that accountability for violence helped to end cycles of violence based on revenge and retribution. That is, 'true peace is possible and sustainable only if there is justice' (Anderlini 2005: 103).

Rwanda provides us with ample examples of injustice. Throughout the genocide, widespread sexual violence against predominantly Tutsi women occurred. Binaifer Nowrojee suggests that almost every defendant coming before the International Criminal Tribunal for Rwanda (ICTR) could be charged and convicted for perpetuating these acts or not preventing the acts of subordinates, yet on the tenth anniversary of the genocide, the court had handed down only 18 convictions and 90 per cent of these contained no rape convictions (2005: iv).[6] From 1996, Nowrojee talked to rape victims and in 2003 she interviewed them about their perceptions of the Tribunal. Nowrojee found that they repeatedly mentioned law, public acknowledgement and the process of justice. The women wanted information on whether to testify, what to expect, an enabling environment in the courtroom and following testimony, 'safety and protection from reprisal, exposure or stigma' (Nowrojee 2005: 4). They also wanted access to the AIDS medication provided to defendants in custody. 'Punishment and vengeance were astonishingly the least articulated reasons for why Rwandan women wanted and valued ICTR prosecutions of rape' (2005: 5). There was a straightforward explanation for breaking the silence. 'No punishment can ever adequately redress the injuries of, or restore to their previous state, the victims of genocide. Yet despite this, there remains something important to the victims about the act of acknowledgement' (Nowrojee 2005: 5). The importance of public truth and condemnation of atrocities is part of restoring the humanity of victims, which is essential to the realization of justice for women and men.

We have already noted that gender injustice perpetuates inequality and hinders women from realizing their capacities. What, then, constitutes gender justice in the context of armed conflict and its aftermath? How can women receive what is owed to them – their dignity? Clearly, gender justice must recognize the ways in which women distinctively experience harm and are denied dignity, but determining what constitutes justice is less straightforward. There is a human face to injustice, but there are many faces of justice. Different cultures, religions, eras and individuals have different ideas on what constitutes justice. How we define justice may depend on where we live. The definitions have profound implications on addressing justice and peace with compassion. The definitions also influence resource allocation. Should resources be pumped into something like the International Court of Justice in The Hague, with much money and few trials, or into developmental issues? How do we weigh legal versus distributive justice? There are always going to be limits to justice. Communitarians have argued strongly that liberal understandings of justice devalue 'benevolence, altruism, and communitarian sentiments' (Sandel 1982: 60), values which I argue are essential to feminist concepts of peacebuilding.[7] Precisely how we document truth about the past, how we restore dignity to victims, who is considered a victim and what constitutes meaningful reconciliation, are justice issues open to debate. Those who have suffered injustice have an emotive, intuitive sense of what would be meaningful justice for them. I endorse the principle of justice that Carol Gould proposes: it 'builds a recognition of difference and responsiveness to individuated needs, as well as the protection of the rights of difference into its basic conception' (1996: 180). Her point is that justice recognizes and considers relevant differences, 'it sees equal treatment as inherently responsive to and defined by difference' and requires 'empathy with the differentiated needs of others' as part of a feminist notion of care (1996: 180). To extend Gould's principle, gender justice responds to the specific injustices that women or girls face. A politics of compassion responds with empathetic understanding to particular narratives with differentiated needs and strives to address what is due.

Ensuring justice after conflict is a political and social imperative. Rama Mani suggests that typically there are three forms of distinct but 'mutually reinforcing' justice: rectificatory justice, which rectifies injustices that are direct consequences of conflicts; legal justice, to reinstate the rule of law where legal injustice is a typical symptom of conflict; and distributive justice, which stems from structural and systemic injustices that frequently trigger the causes of conflict (2005: 27). In addressing the reconstruction process Noeleen Heyzer, Director of UNIFEM, highlights key priorities for justice: security, governance, the rule of law, economic security and rights (in Danbolt *et al.* 2005: 45). In order to advocate on gender justice, and realize these priorities, security sector reform is needed to include women's rights, protect women from the link between HIV/AIDS violence and include women ex-combatants and the dependents of ex-fighters in DDR programmes. Women's participation in legal reform includes the drafting of the constitution as well as sharing information between rural and urban women's networks. Also, for there to be gender justice, 'the peace dividend' should bring economic security through 'inclusive economic policies and strategies' as well as land rights and access to basic services (Heyzer in Danbolt *et al.* 2005: 45). Women and girls spend so much time collecting firewood and water and caring for household members, so 'water, energy, feeder roads, health and education are fundamentally gender issues' that address justice (Heyzer in Danbolt *et al.* 2005: 46). Thus attending to injustices can include very practical things rather than necessarily legal solutions. Justice responds with compassion to the cry, 'that's not fair'. Justice responds differently to differing cries of what is owed.

Gender inequality and equality

Inequality is a form of injustice that fails to respect human diversity. Valuing diversity is fundamental for an inclusionary politics. Gender justice inevitably is tied to gender equality. Humans are born equal in fundamental dignity and it is in this sense that I use (in)equality. As argued previously, women's participation in conflict resolution and official negotiations is an essential dimension to equitable political representation.[8] Where there is insecurity, inequality prevails. Christine Chinkin offers a grim reminder: 'the reality is that there is no peace agreement that provides an overall model for appropriate provisions for ensuring that the needs of women within the conflict zone are served alongside those of the men' (2003: 2). She explains that 'typically peace agreements are framed in gender-neutral language', there is the assumption that the contents are 'equally applicable to, and equally appropriate for, the needs of both women and men' (2003: 2).[9]

As we have seen, this equal participation never occurs. Sumie Nakaya summarizes five key proposals that women's groups want to have incorporated into peace agreements, namely:

- 'statutory guarantee of women's rights and equal treatment';
- a minimum 30 per cent quota for women in decision-making processes;
- special measures that ensure the safe return and reintegration of displaced women;
- women's rights to property ownership and inheritance; and
- the end of impunity.

(2004: 144)

However, once there is some stability, gender equality is not straightforward. Nakaya suggests that it is contingent upon three extra factors: 'the institutional framework of post-conflict governance, including power-sharing arrangements'; social power relations of class and clan; and the degree of 'international support to gender mainstreaming in peacebuilding' (2004: 147). Structural reforms that attempt to promote intra- and inter-group equality can be problematic where antagonistic relations have not been fully broken down. For example, in post-genocide Rwanda, the recruitment of Tutsi women for high-level government positions may not be perceived as gender equality for Hutu women.

Chinkin stresses the importance of listening to the diverse experiences of local women who have lived through the conflict and have developed new skills and competencies as well as occupying positions previously filled by men who were absent in war. She gives examples of ways in which women prioritize issues within their own contexts that should be included in negotiating peace agreements in order to further gender equality. For example, it was important for women in Bougainville that communication and transport services were restored and that church groups should participate in the rehabilitation programme (Chinkin 2003: 14). In December 2001, the Afghan Women's Summit for Democracy ran as a parallel process to the summit where the Bonn Agreement was accepted. The women's summit 'urged provisions on education, media and culture; health; human rights and the constitution; refugees and internally displaced women' (Chinkin 2003: 14). For women in Burundi, equality issues were the protection of women and girls, the prosecution of crimes of sexual violence, access to education for girls and legislation of women's rights to inherit land. Without the active inclusion of women in peace negotiations, many of these issues which are specific to women and girls are not included in peace agreements and institutional reforms. Indeed, a 'stress on equality makes sense only as a way of attending to differences' (Volf 1996: 18). Global gender inequalities remain prevalent.

In Cambodia, East Timor and South Africa, women's groups organized to develop women's charters to ensure the centrality of equality to peacebuilding. The first stage in overcoming gender inequality is to enshrine the principle of equality in constitutional, electoral, legislative and judicial reforms. Yet anomalies exist. In Somalia, 100 women participated in peace negotiations and in August 2000 secured 25 seats from 245 in the Transitional National Assembly, but Somalian women continue to be marginalized and the implementation of peace agreements has stalled. 'In contrast, in Mozambique, women did not play a visible role during peace negotiations, nor were they granted statutory quotas. Yet, today Mozambique is one of the few countries in the world where women occupy more than 30 per cent of Parliament' (Nakaya 2004: 151). The gap between women's representation and gender equality is stark, as Mozambique ranks as one of the lowest on the UNDP's Human Development Index and its gender-related Development Index of life expectancy, literacy, income and economic participation (Nakaya 2004: 208). Whatever country we are discussing, 'the nexus between security and development is indisputable. Insecurity hampers development and the absence of inclusive development substantially exacerbates factors that lead to conflict' (Williams 2006: 31).

Denial or fulfilment of rights

Despite the fact that international humanitarian legislation governed by the Fourth Geneva Convention and Protocol 11 has occurred since 1949, few prosecutions of war crimes have occurred, with fewer still involving gender-based violence. Provisions prohibiting violence against women were inadequate. The atrocities in Bosnia and Rwanda put pressure on women's international organizations to take measures to enforce women's human rights. The UN Security Council set up the International Criminal Tribunal of Yugoslavia (ICTY) and the ICTR to prosecute war crimes. Anderlini explains that Bosnian and international women's human rights advocates 'demanded that sexual violence during the war be treated as a grave violation of international law, and not just a byproduct of war' (2005: 105). Human rights activists urged the inclusion of gender experts within the ICTY structures.

It would be possible to fill this book with cases of particular injustice, inequality and deprivation of rights, but I shall select only a few. In the case of Dusko Tadic in the ICTY (*Prosecutor* v. *Tadic*, Case No. IT-94-I-T), evidence of sexual violence was not treated as seriously as other crimes until the female member of the Trial Chamber, Judge Odio Benito, challenged the prosecutor after submissions from women's organizations. Tadic was not prosecuted for rape. In the *Kunarac* case (*Prosecutor* v. *Kunarac, Kovaca* and *Vukovic*, Case No. IT-96-23), rape was defined as a violation of sexual autonomy, an element of torture, 'as well as of enslavement as a crime against humanity. It was also the first indictment brought to an international tribunal exclusively on the basis of a crime of sexual violence against women' (UNRISD 2005: 246). With *Akayesu* in Rwanda (*Prosecutor* v. *Akayesu*, Case No. ICTR-96-4-T), initially, there were no charges of sexual violence. Again, a female, Judge Navanethem Pillay, drew out witnesses' testimonies and Akayesu was 'prosecuted and convicted for rape as a crime against humanity... For the first time rape was punished as an act of genocide aimed at destroying a group' (UNRISD 2005: 246). This 1998 decision by the ICTR is historically significant in setting an 'international precedent by defining rape as a crime against humanity and an instrument of genocide' (Anderlini 2005: 105). This is a huge step forward in acknowledging that sexual violence is a human rights abuse and that rape destroys human dignity. The importance of dignity is what makes a crime against humanity so abhorrent. Affirmation of dignity is fundamental to justice, equality and rights.

The Women's Caucus for Gender Justice was formed in 1997 and was a strong influence on the design and statues of the International Criminal Court (ICC). Judges at the ICC must have gender expertise. The ICC signals a new era of international justice and accountability for women. The Rome Statute of the ICC includes in the definition of crimes against humanity and war crimes, sexual violence, including rape, sexual slavery, forced prostitution, forced pregnancy and enforced sterilization. Trafficking of women and children is also listed as a crime against humanity. The commentary of the Statute explains further that rape and sexual violence can amount to genocide. Yet, in Rwanda, 'ten years after the genocide, there have only been two successful prosecutions for rape and one acquittal' (UNRISD 2005: 247). One important role of procedure is to guarantee witness protection for women who testify, thereby reducing the risk of retaliation against those women who have the courage to give evidence. Within the ICC, there is a Victim and Witnesses Unit to provide protection, trauma counselling and security.

SCR 1325 reaffirms 'the need to implement fully international and humanitarian and human rights law that protects the rights of women and girls during and after conflicts' (S/RES/1325 2000). With regard to issues of gender justice and equality, emphasis on human rights is absolutely crucial but not in itself sufficient. During all stages of armed conflict, violations occur that are rationalized as the consequences of war rather than human rights violations. For example, in addition to dubious claims about weapons of mass destruction, the plight of women in Afghanistan was invoked as a humanitarian calamity and partially used to justify the military intervention in Afghanistan post-9/11. Yet, 'the effort to redefine women's rights as human rights and not as "private" or "cultural" matters is an ongoing struggle', despite the Karzai government's claims to have overturned Taliban laws and to uphold international human rights laws (El Jack 2003: 22). Amani El Jack gives examples that women are still imprisoned for travelling without a male accompaniment, female teachers are threatened with death and despite the shortage of medical doctors, women medical science students face opposition from their husbands at Kabul University. The Emergency Loya Jirga, the grand council held in June 2002, was the first opportunity in a post-Taliban period to listen to a wide range of voices. There were more than 200 women from 1,501 delegates, but there were widespread reports of intimidation of women delegates who complained that when they went to speak, their microphones were cut off (Kandiyoti 2005: 18). During meetings of the constitutional future concerning post-war Iraq in April 2003, there were only six women from 250 delegates (El Jack 2003: 34).

Within the framework of universal human rights, the case must be made for gender-specific rights. The time of post-agreement reconstruction is a time when new norms, laws, institutions and leaders emerge. The right to participate meaningfully in these aspects of rebuilding the polity and redistributing resources include 'the right to build a gender-equitable society for lasting peace and prosperity' (Zuckerman and Greenberg 2005: 70). There are positive examples of women gaining political rights. The dominant parties in South Africa (ANC), Mozambique (Frelimo) and Namibia (Swapo) all established women's quotas on candidates' lists and Afghanistan, Rwanda and Timor Leste provide other examples. Many situations of conflict concern disputes over land or territory and hence property rights are crucial. Yet, 'in Namibia, Rwanda, and Uganda, customary law, which does not recognize women's rights to own property, prevails even after new civil laws which uphold gender equality are promulgated' (Zuckerman and Greenburg 2005: 72). Where women gain training in literacy skills they tend to have more understanding of their legal rights. The right to freedom from violence is a right for all people. Male soldiers, accustomed to a military subculture of force and weapons, are often 'unfamiliar with respectful, equitable gender relations' when they are demobilized (Zuckerman and Greenberg 2005: 72). Gender-equitable laws and policies are more likely to occur when there is a critical mass of capable women who defend women's rights to other women and convince men of the need for equal rights.

There were successful practices in East Timor. The first Congress of Women in East Timor was held in June 2000, bringing together 500 women. The East Timorese Women's Political Caucus was formed and a 'Platform for Action for the Advancement of the Women of Timor Loro Sae' was developed. The group working on women and the Constitution organized meetings with women's groups to hear the pertinent issues affecting women. This led to the 'Women's Charter of Rights in Timor-Leste', a historical milestone in women's commitment to peace, security and justice. UNIFEM, regional contributors, particularly Australians and UNTAET trained 150 women during a critical skills workshop aimed at increasing knowledge in informed democratic decision-making. The Women's Caucus went out to the districts to provide economic and moral support to women candidates and was indeed a best practice, applicable elsewhere. The election of 15 September 2001 saw women returned as 27 per cent of those elected to the Constituent Assembly. However, massive problems linger. While electoral representation is significant, widespread practical reforms are necessary to see the fruits of equality. Timor remains one of Asia's poorest countries and the 2006 resurgence of violence was a setback to women's rights.

Universal principles and particular adaptability

I have given examples of gender injustice, inequality and the denial of rights and made some suggestions as to how progress can be furthered. I now seek to develop the conceptual framework in which justice, equality and rights can be achieved for men and women. I explore the moral demands of justice, equality and human rights to achieve sustainable peace. My framework has three components, a defence of universality and particularity, our obligation to restore violated dignity and the need for security as fundamental to peace with justice.

As outlined in Chapter 2, this book seeks to transcend dualistic frameworks. In this section, I seek to put flesh on what it means 'to live caught in the permanent tug of war between the vision of the universal and the attachments of the particular' (Benhabib 2005: 16).[10] If I am stressing the importance of difference – in this case gender – why is it important to pay attention to the universal? In response to this question, Judith Butler argues that 'there are cultural conditions for its articulation that are not always the same, and that the term gains its meaning for us precisely through these decidedly less than universal conditions' (1996: 45–46). She points out that this is a paradox, which is different from a dualism. A paradox seems to be contradictory, such as the desire for justice and for peace, or that universals have cultural adaptations, but it is not necessarily antagonistically opposed. There are awkward tensions in dealing with paradoxes, part of the messiness of moral complexity. It is a paradox that in dealing with past atrocities, 'the need to remember is bound up with the competing, survival urge to forget' (Rooney 2000: 219). In many ways, a key advantage with the Beijing PFA is that it presents universal goals 'of what a gender-just world could be when women's status has achieved equality with men's' (McKay 2000: 561). The importance lies also in articulating what particular conditions are needed for women to achieve these universal goals.

Why is it important when addressing the universality of justice to pay attention to the particular? Traditional concepts of justice consider that difference (like gender), context or particularity blur impartiality. But in everyday life, questions of justice arise as a direct response to actual predicaments of humans caught in the swirl of injustices and complex contexts. Questions arise because people feel aggrieved and say, 'that's not fair' or, 'why am I not getting what's due?' in many different ways, for many different reasons. The principles of justice 'demand only the rejection of principles that cannot be shared by all members of a plurality' (O'Neill 1993: 321). What Onora O'Neill is arguing is that 'justice requires judgments about cases as well as abstract principles; care is principled as well as responsive to differences' (1993: 311). It is this responsiveness to difference that is so important in understanding the politics of tradition within women's lives and the extent to which they internalize community expectations with regard to common practices such as 'FGM, honour killings, bride burnings, acid attacks, sharia stoning to death for adultery', (Vlachová and Biason 2005: 25) where many women understand that in order to survive, they must continue engaging in practices with which they do not always agree.

The cases we are examining require us 'to give language to pain, to experience the pain of the Other inside you' (Baxi 1999: 126) as intrinsic to the politics of compassion. Upendra Baxi distinguishes between three Hegelian moments: abstract universality, abstract particularity and concrete universality. The abstract universality reflects the UN Declaration of Human Rights, that all human beings possess rights and dignity. The abstract particularity refers to the need to assert specific rights, such as women's rights as human rights, the rights of indigenous peoples or the rights of children and migrants in order to realize universal rights. These particularities 'differentiate the *abstract human* in the UNDHR' (Baxi 1999: 128; emphasis in original). They are abstract only until they attend to a specific subject. 'Concrete universality is where rights come home, as it were, in lived and embodied circumstances of being human in time and place marked by finite individual existence' (Baxi 1999: 128).

There are universal principles of equal rights embodied in the Universal Declaration of Human Rights that must realize particular adaptability. When the adaptability is subject to the whims of gendered cultural constraints, concrete universality breaks down. Deniz Kandiyoti writes critically about notions of modern citizenship that tie rights to social membership because 'the domestic domain and the control of women are among the most jealously guarded areas in the reproduction of sub-national identities' (2005: 12). Gould also offers insight into the intrinsic connection between rights and reciprocity, that is, 'in asserting one's own right, one acknowledges the validity of the other's claim as a right by virtue of reciprocally recognizing it as like one's own' (2004: 41). Gould suggests that while the concept of care has had an impact on political philosophy and in IR theory, 'this care discussion has as yet had almost no impact on conceptualizing human rights', given that rights are considered to be universal and care is thought to be particular (2004: 143). The connection between rights and care is deep. Underlying human rights is our fundamental equality as humans which has a 'justice-based judgment', but this equality 'grows out of a shared feeling of commonality with others, on the grounds of common needs, suffering, and aspirations – in short, as being like ourselves' (Gould 2004: 145). Justice, equality and rights are linked tightly. Without universal principles, there are no grounds for defending an assertion that all humans have the equal right to justice or to claim what is their due. Without particular adaptability, this assertion has little practical relevance.

Moral obligation to restore dignity

I tie the search for justice to the restoration of human dignity. When one has been seriously wronged within a violent society, a search for justice usually is about restoring one's sense of worth and seeing justice done, which can mean acknowledgement of perpetrator wrongdoing, punishment or accountability, or victim compensation. In this book, the underlying assumption behind peace-building is premised on the human dignity of all persons. As Martha Nussbaum expresses it, this idea of human dignity is based on a notion of '*equal* worth', namely that 'all are equally deserving of respect, just in virtue of being human ... But human dignity is frequently violated on grounds of sex or sexuality' (1999: 5; emphasis in original). Within deeply divided societies, the violation of dignity is profound, and even when the violence has ceased or slowed down, deeply held animosity remains and strengthens vicious forms of discrimination. 'Discrimination on the basis of race, religion, sex, national origin, cast, or ethnicity is ... a type of indignity or humiliation' (Nussbaum 2000: 86).

People experience indignity for different reasons and express humiliation in different ways. For example, many unionists in Northern Ireland were outraged at the early release of prisoners who had been convicted of Irish Republican Army (IRA) crimes, even if the release adhered to the 1998 Good Friday Agreement. Under the Agreement the old police force, which was almost completely Protestant and viewed with great suspicion by Catholics, was renamed and overhauled in order to make it more responsive and representative. Many from republican backgrounds refused to legitimize the Police Service of Northern Ireland until its 2007 acceptance by Sinn Féin. All people have the right to trust the police and use a court system to achieve justice. Under the Agreement, paramilitary groups decommissioned weapons, but widespread suspicion hovered as to the extent of decommissioning despite international weapons inspections. Similarly, struggles for justice occurred in South Africa, where many considered that giving amnesty to those guilty of murder and torture was unjustified, even if the acts were politically motivated. Biggar defends his thesis that peace and justice can be negotiated by arguing that 'justice is *primarily* not about the punishment of the perpetrator, but about the vindication of the victims' (2003: 7; emphasis in original). (I will discuss victims shortly.) I would add to this argument that peace and justice warrant the conditions that permit the flourishing of human dignity and that furthermore, these conditions may differ for women and men.

Nussbaum adopts a feminist internationalist perspective whereby 'individuals have moral obligations to promote justice for people outside their national boundaries and that their governments do also' (1999: 6). She suggests that it is 'in the contingency of birth location' affecting people's lives that requires us to conceive of the humanity, dignity and needs of distant human beings (Nussbaum 1999: 7). Nussbaum defends an approach that addresses the social minimum that meets basic human needs and rights through developing universal human capabilities. To the accusation that such universal obligations pose an assault on local traditions she is defiant, that such traditions women typically face, such as self-sacrifice, deference and unquestioning obedience, are unjust and that 'there are universal obligations to protect human functioning and its dignity', including the equal dignity of women (1999: 30). She argues that 'the capabilities can be the object of an *overlapping consensus* among people who otherwise have very different comprehensive conceptions of the good' (2000: 5; emphasis in original).[11] Aware that feminist theorists frequently are sceptical of universal norms in disregarding difference, Nussbaum defends the framework 'that is strongly universalist, committed to cross-cultural norms of justice, equality, and rights, and at the same time sensitive to local particularity, and the many ways in which circumstances shape not only options but also beliefs and preferences' (2000: 7). Her central question is: 'what activities characteristically performed by human beings are so central that they seem definitive of a life that is truly human' (1999: 39)? She is looking at the gaps between imagining humanity at its full potential and the real disparity of so many people's lives. Accordingly, Nussbaum develops ten central human functional capabilities.[12] Women have the potential to fulfil these capabilities and thus 'their unequal failure in capability is a problem of justice' (1999: 54). The struggle for justice and the realization of human rights is part of striving towards compassionate societies which respond to differentiated needs.

Compassion 'helps us recognize our justice obligations to those distant from us' (Clement 1996: 85). There is no false dichotomy between justice and compassion, rather considerations of justice emerge because of the care we have for fellow human beings, in the desire to see people get what they deserve and have lost dignity restored. I argue that the defence of the need for compassion is tied intimately to a defence for the rights of justice. Justice and compassion are compatible. I also argue that the defence of compassionate justice is important because of women's historical experience of injustice and traditional association with caring. It is not care alone that enables compassionate responsibility, but a merging of the compassionate drive with a search for justice, equality and rights that is more likely to address people's needs in a meaningful manner. Global boundaries have expanded and obligations of justice now extend globally. These cosmopolitan, moral obligations require us to respect universal human rights and respect each other as particular human beings. We deserve to be treated with dignity and this includes the appropriate treatment of perpetrators of violence and ex-combatants as well as the compassionate care of victims or survivors.

Security, peace and justice

SCR 1325 is unprecedented in acknowledging the importance of involving women in all peacebuilding measures. It requires action in increasing the participation of women in decision-making, peace processes and peacekeeping; protecting women; and integrating gender mainstreaming in implementation mechanisms.[13] It makes a gender perspective relevant to all aspects of peace processes. While progress has occurred in peacekeeping and humanitarian arenas in terms of new policies, gender expertise and training initiatives, 'in no area of peace and security work are gender perspectives systematically incorporated in planning, implementation, monitoring and reporting' (UN OSAGI 2004a: 2). I suggest that there are limiting views on peacebuilding that impact on the interpretation and efficacy of the resolution, and argue that peacebuilding processes flow through the pre-conflict, conflict and post-accord stages. I have noted already how women are marginalized in formal peace processes but are conspicuous in informal practical peace work.

It is unsurprising that women who face insecurity and injustice have expansive notions of peacebuilding linked to security and justice. Human security incorporates all dimensions of what is necessary to feel safe. As explained earlier, the cessation of explicit violence does not guarantee security because 'the violence of a regime begets a general culture of violence' (Turshen 1998: 8). In such contexts, gendered violence is 'legitimized by structural violence' (Caprioli 2004: 413). Thus, it is important to expand traditional definitions of national, territorial and military security to include all factors that are crucial to human security. Gender justice is part of this human security. 'Gender justice refers to the protection and promotion of civil, political, economic and social rights on the basis of gender equality' (Anderlini and Stanski 2004: 39; see Spees 2004: 9). For women in conflict zones, peace and security involve multi-faceted factors of what is needed to build sustainable peace, and this includes social justice, rights, coexistence, tolerance, participatory democracy, transparency, open dialogue and attention to differences. Peace has to be grounded in the immediacy of fulfilling ordinary daily needs. It is often apparently 'mundane aspects of peacebuilding' which have an impact on a community, such as immunization programmes or water projects (Knight 2004: 378). As prime carers, it is no surprise that women are active in 'mundane peacebuilding'. Peace and justice are connected. This is not a lightweight cliché. The conditions that enhance human security are those that free people from poverty, exclusion, injustice and oppression. These conditions broaden the parameters of peacebuilding to include all the concrete, local and practical processes needed to build peace with justice.

We noted in Chapter 1 how security means figuring out how to meet all the material, social, emotional and spiritual requirements of life that are necessary conditions for meaningful peace. We noted in Chapter 3 how, despite cultural differences, women's groups collaborate on practical issues of security and justice by concentrating not on antagonistic ethnic, racial and religious differences which have caused violent conflict, but on the urgency to find commonalities that permit coalitions to form and are respectful of differences. Human rights are a crucial component of human security. Human security provides a holistic framework for integrating aspects of peace, security, justice, equality, human rights and development. Anything that threatens security violates human rights, including 'gender-specific violations long considered to be normal, private or inevitable outcomes of war' (El Jack 2003: 22).

Gender analyses of security (Basch 2004; Blanchard 2003) listen to the voices of those women who experience daily insecurity. Charlotte Bunch (2004) and Linda Basch (2004) make the important point that the concept of human security emphasizes both the protection of victims and empowerment of agents. To be a victim is (as I will expand shortly) also to be a potential survivor. In breaking down polarizations, 'security is not only about the recognition of threats but also about building capacities to create secure spaces' (Hoogensen and Stuvøy 2006: 222). One cannot feel secure in a context of violence, poverty, injustice, inequality, suppression of rights and exclusion. Security is enhanced when there is fair access to resources and decision-making processes in a context of social justice and respect for human dignity.[14]

Victims: restoring dignity

Who is a victim?

The nature of victimhood created by violent conflict is various.[15] It includes those who are bereaved, maimed, scarred, injured, tortured, intimidated, humiliated, raped and those who suffer from the loss of home, land, dignity and loved ones. As we shall see in Chapter 6, 'victims are the heart of all dimensions of the reconciliation process in societies emerging from years of violent conflict' (Huyse 2003b: 54). Victims suffer trauma.[16] Hence, it is a curious feature of conflict societies that there may be disputes in deciding who is actually a victim. In places such as Northern Ireland, 'cultures of contemporary loyalism and republicanism are cultures of victimhood' (Smyth 2003: 126), where both sides have used their status as victims of terrorism or victims of British imperialism, and both are guilty of sectarianism to justify their recourse to armed conflict. 'The acquisition of the status of victim becomes an institutionalized way of escaping guilt, shame, or responsibility' (Smyth 2003: 127).[17] As Marie Smyth points out, victimhood is a contested issue, but over-inclusive definitions that simply equate victimhood with suffering are not helpful because further grievance is created by equating 'the enormous suffering of some with a lesser suffering of others' (2003: 128). A faultline developed in Northern Ireland, not along the usual politico-religious divide, 'but between those who supported and those who opposed the Good Friday Agreement of 1998' with the latter group using terms such as 'innocent' and 'real' in order 'to exclude others from the category of genuine victimhood' (Smyth 2003: 128). The exclusive approaches of victims' groups talked of themselves as representing 'victims of terrorism', 'innocent victims' or 'victims of nationalist terror', and opposed the prisoner releases that were part of the Good Friday Agreement.

In the South African Truth and Reconciliation Act of 1995, the definition of 'victim' included the relatives and dependents of victims. 'This is very important because it locates wives, mothers and children in center stage as having suffered "the gross violations of human rights"' (Goldblatt and Meintjes 1998: 34). This broad inclusive definition was very important in a context where being a widow could mean not only loss of status in the community, but being deprived of 'standing, almost illegitimate' (Goldblatt and Meintjes 1998: 35).

Again, it is important to draw attention to the fact that while violent conflict causes human suffering to many, it may have a different impact on women and men and thus the nature of victimization may have gender-specific connotations. As we shall see more fully in the next chapter, women generally are reluctant to testify to the abuses that they have suffered, particularly when it is of a sexual nature, because of shame, cultural conventions against speaking about sexual matters and the stigmatization that follows in admitting to being abused. Also, we should note that 'victimization may not cease with the establishment of a peace agreement. Cases from Cambodia and Sierra Leone demonstrate that sexual abuse unfortunately often continues with the appearance of peacekeepers and humanitarian workers' (Huyse 2003b: 56). Peacekeepers come into zones with money and peacekeeping missions create artificial economies which become ripe for the sexual exploitation of local women and girls, particularly in a crisis such as the Democratic Republic of Congo, where the age of consent is 14.[18]

Gender-specific violence in war includes rape, sexual assault and trafficking. Examples given by Human Rights Watch (2001) are numerous. The fragile July 1999 Lomé Peace Accord in Sierra Leone granted a blanket amnesty to the Revolutionary United Front rebels, led by Foday Sankoh, for their atrocities, which included sexual violence. The Accord collapsed in May 2000 but rapes, sexual assaults and mutilation continued with the police and UN Mission in Sierra Leone (UNAMSIL) doing little to protect women or punish men. Russian soldiers raped women with impunity in Chechnya during 2000. Impunity may lead to an immediate ceasefire but where there is a lack of accountability, violence frequently continues and there can be no lasting peace. In Algeria, armed Islamist groups treated women who lived in villages that opposed their rule as spoils of war, raping about 5,000 women between 1995 and 1998, abducting and killing some. In East Timor, pro-Indonesian militia and Indonesian soldiers raped many women in the lead-up to the 1999 referendum on East Timorese independence. Taliban members in Afghanistan abducted and raped Hazara and Tajik women with impunity. Sexual violence against women is a constant feature in the Democratic Republic of Congo. Even in post-conflict settings such crimes violate women's human rights, such as in Kosovo, where women suffered a rise in domestic violence, rape, trafficking and abductions following the war.

The Independent Experts' assessment on the impact of armed conflict on women writes that one of the most disturbing findings 'was the association, in the vast majority of peacekeeping environments, between the arrival of peacekeeping personnel and increased prostitution, sexual exploitation and HIV/AIDS infection' (Rehn and Johnson-Sirleaf 2002: 61). Accordingly, the UN has deployed gender specialists in the Democratic Republic of Congo (MONUC), East Timor (UNTAET), Kosovo (UNMIK) and Sierra Leone (UNAMSIL). On the first anniversary of the adoption of SCR 1325, the late Sergio Vieira de Mello, Special Representative of the Secretary-General in UNTAET, said, 'I was against the creation of a Gender Affairs Unit for the UNTAET. I did not think a Gender Unit would help rebuild institutions from the ashes of what the militia left. I was wrong' (de Mello in Spees 2004: 14). UNTAET established the first ever Gender Affairs Unit in a peacekeeping mission which was focused on raising awareness, promoting gender equality and stressing the differential impact of conflict and reconstruction for women and men. The unit worked in close collaboration with local women activists to mainstream gender and promote women's rights. The unit 'could serve as a model for other operations' (Mazurana 2002: 47).[19]

In her work with traumatized women in Bosnia-Herzegovina, Monika Kleck writes that 'traumatic experiences often cause the survivor to question their view of reality, robbing them of their sense of integrity and wholeness and leading to the loss of self-esteem' (2006: 345). She is right to suggest that the key criterion when planning appropriate measures to rebuild war-torn societies is 'not statistical benchmarks', but the rebuilding of human dignity (2006: 345). However, there are other considerations that affect all women as potential victims. For example, typically, no money is spent on women's health during war, and yet with the stresses of conflict, there may be a greater demand for health care. Mobile gynecological clinics can provide services for women who have no access or resources to such services.

A victim is robbed of self-dignity. It is a useful reminder that some people cringe at the notion of being a victim. For example, in South Africa, some 'consider ourselves to be either survivors of apartheid or more importantly, victors over apartheid' (Lapsley 1998: 744). It is important to qualify also that 'the distinction between "victims" and "perpetrators", as it is often used, is logically simplistic, ethically unfair, psychologically misleading, and prudentially undermining' (Govier and Verwoerd 2004: 371). In the aftermath of violent conflict, those individuals who have been labelled as 'offender', 'perpetrator', 'terrorist', 'murderer', 'combatant', 'paramilitary', 'ex-combatant' or 'ex-prisoner' often change in positive ways, some through education while imprisoned, some through the assistance of the international community and others through realizing that violence will not progress democratic change. Also 'some persons are both victims and perpetrators' (Govier and Verwoerd 2004: 372), and thus condescending talk of 'terrorists loose on the streets' (2004: 374) fails to understand the nuance of social identities and the importance of reintegrating ex-combatants into some semblance of normal life. While victims usually see themselves as innocents who have suffered and view ex-combatants as those willfully guilty of inflicting harm, there are alternative approaches.

A commitment to norms of human dignity and rights carries with it a commitment to the possibility of moral change in any human being. To regard ex-combatants as irredeemably evil is to disregard their humanity – and to ignore the reality that some have gone on to make profound contributions in their community and internationally.

(Govier and Verwoerd 2004: 376)

When asked where the quest for justice ends and the quest for revenge begins, Václav Havel[20] illuminates the balance between being humane and not escaping the past. He states that 'such a limit could be defined only by something intangible, certain human qualities like feelings, taste, understanding, wisdom, something that is not easily expressed in legal norms' (Michnik and Havel 1993: 24). The urge toward vengeance is more likely when there is a feeling that justice is being denied. Such a feeling may arise in places where amnesty occurs. How is one to discern 'whether executive endorsement of an amnesty law represents an unprincipled capitulation to the perpetrators of the past or an honest effort to move the country forward towards true reconciliation and healing' (Sarkin and Daly 2004: 689)? As we shall see more fully in Chapter 6, the relationship between reconciliation and justice is complex. For those who define the need for justice in punitive measures, redress or even vengeance, reconciliation's tendencies toward forgiveness, mercy and amnesty may seem purely pragmatic. The relationship between justice and reconciliation can be mutually reinforcing where justice vindicates victims and 'strong reconciliation' (Porter 2003) occurs. Where there is a vicious cycle of impunity, gross atrocities go unacknowledged, unpunished and without redress. Most legislations that address amnesty pardon those crimes that are explicitly political in nature.

In the South African TRC, there was no general amnesty. Individuals who had been involved in violence and human rights abuses made an application to appear before a panel, which decided whether the applicant satisfied stringent political conditions for considering amnesty. Tutu remarks that 'general amnesty was really amnesia. It was pointed out that we, none of us, have the power to say, "let bygones be bygones"' (1999: 31). However, the perpetrators were not required to demonstrate repentance, apologize or initiate reparation, but to make a public confession. This created a perception that victims' rights to seek legal redress were obliterated. 'The framing of amnesty by the need to "advance reconciliation", coupled with Tutu's zeal for forgiveness, was perceived as at least putting undue pressure on victims to forgive' (Verwoerd 2003: 264). However, Digeser argues that the amnesty required 'that a minimal level of justice be met and a public accounting of who did what to whom' resulted in a form of 'political forgiveness' (2001: 74). Tutu maintains that the process of granting amnesty to those who plead guilty and accept responsibility for their actions supports a culture of respect for human rights, acknowledgement of responsibility and accountability and is a form of justice 'for a limited and definite period and purpose' (1999: 51).

Restorative justice

Where there is no desire for violent reprisal or retaliation, is there a form of justice that takes a caring approach toward victims? Retributive justice might avoid unbridled revenge; protect against the return to power of perpetrators; fulfill an obligation to victims; individualize guilt; and break the cycle of impunity (Huyse 2003c: 98). Yet punishment and prosecution is not always appropriate in transitional times where delicate choices need to be made over pragmatic compromises that stall violence, even temporarily. Retributive justice risks destabilizing a fragile peace settlement, provokes hostile subcultures and networks, and causes crippling effects on governance (Huyse 2003c: 103). Thus, it is restorative justice to which many peacebuilders turn. Restorative justice draws strongly on indigenous mediation-based ideas and practices coming from Africa, Australia, Canada, New Zealand and the Pacific Islands and constitutes an important paradigm shift.[21] It moves the emphasis from blame, punishment and dealing with the past to hurt, restoration of relationships and moving on. In this concluding section, I examine what is involved in restorative justice, explore why it is worth advocating and offer some examples. I maintain that restorative justice is consistent with a politics of compassion that attends to the suffering of victims, listens to their needs and responds wisely with justice and compassion.

Restorative justice reconceptualizes crime, the victim, the role of the community and the purpose of justice itself. Crime violates victims and through an inclusive process between the victim, perpetrator and affected community members, the purpose of restorative justice is transformative, not adversarial. In a similiar fashion, it is consistent with the goals of reconciliation in being forward-looking, constructive, transformative and aimed at healing the victim.[22] Indeed, it achieves the balance between an ethics of justice and an ethics of care outlined in Chapter 2, what Marc Forget calls 'reconciliation between victim and offender' (2003: 111).

Restorative justice is a response to the shortcomings of criminal law that ignore the victim and social context. Restorative justice 'sees the offence as something that has happened to people and whose consequence is a rupture in relationships' (Tutu 1999: 52). It responds to the effects of violence on relation-ships that entail an obligation to set things right, by acknowledging victims' needs and requiring from the perpetrator of wrongdoing accountability, truth, apology, restitution and/or compensation. Those who advocate the benefits of restorative justice seek to restore losses to the victim and to the community that result from crime 'by reconciling the transgressor to the victim and the commu-nity, and by achieving these goals through the active participation of all the parties involved' (Digeser 2001: 41). The focus is on the victim who has been wronged. 'Far from being at odds with justice, forgiveness is understood as a necessary part of reparation and reconciliation' (Digeser 2001: 41). This undoubtedly requires a two-way process, whereby the offender expresses shame and remorse and the victim takes some initial step toward forgiveness. The point of this shame is not to stigmatize the wrongdoer but to express public disapproval of the wrongdoing. (In Chapter 6, I will argue that victims are not always morally obliged to forgive. Forgiveness is a gift.)

Why advocate restorative justice? It is understandable why those who are concerned with peacebuilding look to the concepts and practices of restorative justice as meaningful alternatives to revenge or retributive justice.[23] Restorative justice focuses on healing wounds, it is concerned with the humanity of both the victim and offender and seeks to restore their dignity. It recognizes the need for accountability for wrongdoing, but the target of justice lies in achieving the right relation between victim and perpetrator. 'Restorative justice seeks creative, positive nonviolent, and even noncoercive ways of putting things right (Acorn 2004: 21). As Annalise Acorn reminds us, what constitutes an 'appropriate means of righting the balance' is highly 'context-sensitive' (2004: 21). I have argued earlier that feelings of injustice are personal and what constitutes justice may differ for different individuals. Despite universal principles of justice, cultural interpretations result in different understandings of just responses. Acorn's argument is that the 'seductive vision' of restorative justice as a simplistic convergence between love, harmony and injustice is illusory (2004: 1–26). However, she suggests that there are three 'normative conditions for restorative compassion': a vivid awareness of complex concrete inner lives of others; mutuality and humility (2004: 138). She explains humility as 'humble recognition of one's own and others' implicatedness in the dual conditions of human existence: pain and the possibility of flourishing' (2004: 140). These conditions embody the three factors of compassion outlined earlier: feelings, empathy and co-suffering.

Hence, 'although restorative justice appeared to be a promising way to theorize political forgiveness, the central conflict between victims receiving what is their due (justice) and victims releasing what is their due (forgiveness) remains' (Digeser 2001: 43). Restorative justice will not be meaningful if it is (Elshtain (2003b: 59), 'cheap forgiveness' what Elshtain calls 'contrition chic' (2003b: 45). Elshtain was told repeatedly by several members of the Argentine Mothers of the Disappeared 'that they wanted justice and not vengeance and that they knew that not all of the guilty could be punished' (2003b: 60), and thus full reparation, compensation and just punishment are not possible when confronting the enormity of many political horrors.[24] As Elshtain explains, 'part of what is involved in restorative justice is a dramatic transformation in the horizon of expectations' (2003b: 61).

Jose Zalaquett, a member of Chile's National Commission on Truth and Reconciliation, interviewed thousands of relatives of people who were killed or disappeared under General Pinochet's regime, and reported the following:

> Certainly, many of them asked for justice. Hardly anyone, however, showed a desire for vengeance. Most of them stressed that in the end, what really mattered to them was to know the truth, that the memory of their loved ones would not be denigrated or forgotten, and that such terrible things would never happen again.

(in Walker 2006: 88)

Similarly, Pumla Gobodo-Madikezela, a psychologist on the staff of the South African TRC, explains 'the victim's resolve that "I cannot and will not return the evil you inflicted on me" not only as "the victim's triumph" but as "a kind of revenge"' (2003: 117). Mani proposes an alternative 'reparative justice' based on 'legal and psychological conceptions of reparation' (2005: 31). Reparative justice neither excludes punishment or prosecution but 'aims to be *sensitive* to the nature of offences and the impact on victims, offenders and societies, and *flexible* in devising a suitable combination of responses to them' (2005: 31; emphasis in original). In this sense her proposal is very similar to restorative justice, but she suggests that it is a more humble and realistic goal where repair may be more feasible than restoration.

Options to restore justice are necessarily open-ended. Traditional dispute resolution systems have differing ways of reconciling disputing parties and restoring harmonious relationships within communities. Sometimes this involves rituals such as sharing an animal, drinking certain drinks jointly and ceremonies for bringing people together. The Gujarat Harmony Project offers an example of restorative justice in the face of a failed retributive justice system. On 27 February 2002, a train was burned by a rioting mob, which catalyzed violence against Muslims. The project brings together 10 partnership organizations with CARE, a donor development agency. Underlying this project is the principle of restorative justice, which helps people to understand the reasons for a violent past, including the brutal loss of humanity, resulting in formulating new meanings for coping. The principle of forgiveness is important to this project. Theories of reciprocity and mutuality required by restorative justice come to the fore. 'While the person who forgives may annul the need for "punishment", the one who is forgiven has certain obligations to repair the past, and must acknowledge his or her personal accountability' (Ahmed 2005: 97). Further, as we shall see in the final chapter on forgiveness and reconciliation, reconciliation is based on transformative relations between perpetrators and victims. In a strong sense, restorative justice 'gives precedence to reconciliation and regards forgiveness as a legitimate ethic in public life' (Amstutz 2005: 92). It is an ongoing intellectual dilemma on ideas on transitional justice as to whether newly emerging democratic regimes should achieve justice and then pursue political reconciliation, or whether this is not possible because legal provisions of justice alone do not foster the right conditions for reconciled relations. 'Restorative justice emphasizes the transformation of subjective factors that impair community, such as anger, resentment, and desire for vengeance' (Amstutz 2005: 110). Attending to feelings of injury and dealing with past wrongdoing is part of a politics of compassion that also paves the way toward reconciliation. Restorative justice principles are based on an understanding of compassion, that everyone is equal in dignity and can contribute to the good society. Thus when a person becomes alienated or marginalized from society, it is the responsibility of communities to restore someone's undermined sense of self and relationship with the community. The response is restorative in the sense of repairing harm done by restoring dignity and a sense of well-being in the community.

In this chapter, I have argued that a politics of compassion feels pain, empathizes as a co-sufferer and responds wisely with judgement and, where appropriately, with mercy. Attentiveness and active listening are prerequisites to judicious, differentiated responses to victims' suffering. I also argued that compassion can be combined with justice and peace in demonstrating attentive care. There are too many examples of injustice, inequality and the denial of rights that abound in conflict zones and divided societies. Where there is an application of universal principles of justice, equality and rights to particular needs, violated dignity can be restored. Violence disrupts, demoralizes and destroys dignity. I concluded by advocating the principles of restorative justice as a way to repair relationships and restore dignity with compassion. There can be compassionate responses to the cry, 'that's not fair'. Due recognition underlies just compassion.

5 Memory and truth

> The moment we begin to fear the opinions of others and hesitate to tell the truth
> that is in us, and from motives of policy are silent when we should speak, the
> divine floods of light and life no longer flow into our souls.
>
> (Elizabeth Cady Stanton 1890)[1]

Dealing with the past

An important challenge of peacebuilding lies in a period of transitional justice
where nations are trying to respond to past evils. The objective of transitional
justice is to confront the legacies of human rights abuse and human suffering, to
ensure accountability for the past injustices while maintaining peace, the rule of
law, democratic processes and the need for reconciliation. This chapter examines the role of memory and truth in dealing with the past. Choices about what is
remembered and forgotten, and stories told truthfully and those covered over or
suppressed, have massive moral implications for individuals, groups, communities and politicians and influence the direction in which a country moves. While
we cannot change the past, we have choices in how to remember it, talk about it
and deal with it. 'History is not memory, but divergent re-rememberings, shaped
in culturally specific ways' (Cockburn 2004: 89). Collective memory of the past
is, in many ways, a social construction, handed down generationally or acquired
through marriage or political indoctrination. Different accounts of the same
historical narrative differ according to politics, religion, age, class, peer influence or personal bias. If we can choose what aspects of collective memory to
accept, question, contest or deny, we can also make choices about different
alternatives in how to deal with the past. Choice is the hallmark of moral
agency. A challenge for peacebuilders is to foster the healing process in victims
who become empowered as survivors, agents of choice. The past I am referring
to is one that has been ridden with conflict, tragedy and human pain. In particular, I refer to past evils.

In this chapter, I have four main aims. First, I explain some of the complexity in dealing with the past, particularly in confronting evil, acknowledging
wrongs and the turmoil of deciding what to remember and what to forget.
Second, acknowledgement is the first step for both victims and perpetrators in

facing the truth. I explain why women are silenced and why their choice of silence exhibits inner strength. Third, my aim is to highlight the impact of silencing and testimony in the special hearings in the South African TRC. I demonstrate the restorative potential in truth. Fourth, I examine the need for differentiated ways to compensate for the horrors of dealing with the past. Throughout each section, I argue that moral agency determines how we deal with the past. We can choose to face up to the truth of atrocities through forgetting, remembering, being silenced or choosing silence; confessing or denying atrocities committed; or attending to the needs of those who suffer because of potent truths.

Evil, retribution and moral choice

I begin with evil. In using the term 'evil' I make a deliberate moral judgement. Claudia Card offers an explicit definition of evils 'as reasonably foreseeable intolerable harms produced by culpable wrongdoing' (2004: 216). She describes 'atrocities' as 'particularly gross evils' (2004: 217). She defines 'intolerable harm' as 'deprivation of the basics ordinarily necessary to make a life tolerable and decent' (2004: 218).[2] The succinctness of these definitions is useful. Card suggests further that one of the biggest challenges is 'how to respond to evils without doing evil' (2004: 219). So often, revenge, retribution and self-righteousness go into overdrive, prompting responses that are as abhorrent as the original act of murder, terrorism, bombing or war. (I will return to retribution shortly.) Some evils are 'so severe that they are absolutely unforgivable' (Digeser 2001: 61). (I will examine forgiveness in the next chapter.) Some discussion is pertinent here because the notion of evil under discussion may be understood as 'the obliteration of personhood and hence the deprivation of all the personal and political rights of one, two, some, or many' (Kateb 1992: 201). The consequence of being subject to the enormity of evil, whereby one's personhood has been shattered, is a challenge for victims in ascertaining what justice might mean for them. How do victims respond to those who assigned and executed the orders to torture, maim, rape, murder and make people disappear? It is in this sense that Digeser argues that while victims of evil may not find 'recourse that could make them whole, ... evil can be defined as that action in which victims push for justice, not because it rectifies the wrong, but because it is, at least, a response' (Digeser 2001: 61). Such victims cannot just sit patiently waiting for justice, often they are driven with passion to do something to ease their pain. Hence Digeser intimates that 'perhaps evil is politically unforgivable' because those who have committed evil acts cannot expect victims to put the past behind them, forgive and get on with life (2001: 61). (As we will discover in the next chapter, this does not mean that individuals do not forgive those who have committed evil deeds, because many do.)

Digeser offers important qualifiers in distinguishing the actors from their actions, the sinner from the sin. His position is that 'while certain deeds may be unforgivable, all actors possess the capacity for moral change' (2001: 61). Not to hold this position is to 'fail to acknowledge the intellectual and moral capacities of persons' (Govier 1999: 70) to change, forgive and reconcile. All throughout this book I have emphasized the importance of respecting the moral worth of people, their intrinsic dignity, and it is only with this foundational premise that I can support Digeser's view that 'no perpetrator is absolutely unforgivable. Evil, therefore, should not be understood as beyond the reach of political forgiveness' (2001: 61).[3] Peacebuilders cling onto the possibility of moral and social change. (The idea of humanization of our enemies is exceptionally difficult and is the subject of the next chapter.)

Claiming responsibility for evil is part of the process of reconciliation. From a South-African perspective, Antjie Krog, poet and journalist, writes that 'reconciliation will only be possible if whites say: Apartheid was evil and we were responsible for it' (1998: 58). She writes further that reconciliation will only occur 'the day whites also feel offended by racism, instead of feeling sorry for blacks' (Krog 1998: 111). Certainly, in the TRC, Tutu kept the moral language of good and evil central, trying to ensure that injustice, oppression and lies did not prevail over justice, freedom and truth. As Tutu listened to the stories of perpetrators talking about their violations, he realized:

> How each of us has this capacity for the most awful evil – all of us. None of us could predict that if we had been subjected to the same influences, the same conditioning, we would not have turned out as these perpetrators. This is not to condone or excuse what they did. It is to be filled more and more with … compassion.
>
> (Tutu 1999: 76)

This position embodies the politics of compassion in imagining how different it might be if you or I were in different positions, whereby we had to defend the integrity of our family or community. It is a sober reminder against hasty judgement that within us we have the capacity for good and evil. Increasingly, in global politics and media reports, the evils of sexual slavery, trafficking, child pornography, war rape, torture, terrorism (ideological, religious, political and state) and genocide are named as evils. Such wrongs are never redeemable, but some perpetrators of even the vilest evils do change. The acknowledgement of wrong gives people the opportunity to change. As moral agents, both victims and perpetrators of human rights abuse and violence are capable of change, not regardless of, but in spite of the loss, suffering and undermining of self-respect or having committed gross violations. In order to deal with the past, victims must have their needs addressed, perpetrators and ex-combatants need to become responsible citizens, communities need to rebuild solidarity and nations require healing. Some victims choose to remain embittered. Many perpetrators of violence do not seek a changed life. Most ex-combatants retain militarist or violent tendencies. However, I am emphasizing positive lessons that we can learn from history. Before exploring these lessons, it is worth understanding a little more of what is involved in retribution.

I disregard all forms of revenge that result in 'tit-for-tat' murders, personal vendettas, revenge killings, tribal retaliations and a negative spiral of vengeance. Instead, I examine the concept of retribution, which 'reflects a belief that wrongdoers deserve blame and punishment in direct proportion to the harm inflicted' (Minow 1998: 12). The motivation for retribution is a sense of justice as fairness. Martha Minow talks about the need for limitations placed on retribution 'such as mercy and moral decency', otherwise it has the potential to threaten the 'bounds of proportionality and decency' (1998: 12). Similarly, Donald Shriver argues that 'the justice of truth-telling needs the justice of forbearance from revenge' (2003: 32), otherwise, bitterness can prompt a preoccupation with justice, which leads readily to revenge. While it is common to think that the desire for retribution only leads to further violence, the desire is more complex, it stems from self-respect. What often drives this desire is anger, particularly anger at injustice, at being ignored, and no one listening to the personal cry of 'that's not fair'. Anger also drives the realization that 'one's tendency to easily forgive can be seen as a symptom of one's lack of self-respect' (Babic 2000: 59). Forgiving readily might seem an easy option, but it does not address one's personal hurt. Anger is a basic emotion, a response to extreme offence, violation and injustice and motivates revenge, forgiveness or the accumulation of hurt as well as a passionate desire to see justice realized.

Thomas Brudholm (2006) writes against an overemphasis on negative emotions such as anger, hatred and resentment in the wake of genocide, and looks for a redemptive project of emotional transformation where victims can overcome anger and the desire for revenge. However, Brudholm argues that 'the disqualification of anger and resentment also insinuates and promulgates an uncritical conception of forgiving as always noble and praiseworthy' (2006: 10). He explores the values that are at stake when anger is morally disqualified and when advocates of forgiveness are impervious to the case presented by unforgiving victims. He accepts that the refusal to forgive can be pathological and unjustified, particularly when people wallow in a victim identity or are so consumed by anger that they dehumanize 'the enemy' and carry out atrocious acts of intense revenge. Rage against past abuse is legitimate, but often societies tire of the persistence of angry victims who cannot let go of the past. Yet, Brudholm maintains that 'after the atrocity, forgiveness can be refused and resentment can be retained on genuinely moral grounds' (2006: 22) in places such as Algeria, Armenia, Bosnia, Cambodia, Rwanda and South Africa. He explains that resentment, as he is using it, is not merely an emotion but a response to the injustice, injury or violation. The point of moral boundaries is to signal what is and is not morally acceptable. Thus Brudholm argues that in the face of evil, anger, outrage, resentment and a bitter struggle for accountability 'can be testimony of moral commitment to norms that have been breached' – that is, 'the reflex of a moral protest' (2006: 23). What we learn from these arguments is the incredible moral complexity of anger, atrocity and the choice to resist or forgive.

Minow (1998) talks about the delicate negotiations in walking the path 'between vengeance and forgiveness' and the variety of reasons or goals to walk this path. I relate comfortably to her argument – in walking the path, you choose which path or divergent track to take. Therapeutic goals promote healing for victims, witnesses and offenders. Political goals create a climate conducive to human rights and democratic processes that move governments away from mass violence. Goals of reconciliation across divisions restore dignity to victims and deal 'respectfully with those who assisted or were complicit with the violence' (1998: 23). Minow places high importance on the value of trials in transferring 'individuals' desires for revenge to the state or official bodies', thereby interrupting the vicious cycle of blame that often leads to sustained feuds (1998: 26). How, then, can societies respond to past evils and withhold the urge for revenge?

In responding to these challenges of past atrocities, David Crocker (2003) posits a normative outline of eight goals that societies can use as a framework to discuss morally appropriate, culturally sensitive responses. Debates about how to actualize these goals are always contentious. First, actualizing the goals involves investigating, establishing and publicly disseminating the truth. Second, victims and their families need a public 'platform to tell their stories and have their testimony publicly acknowledged' (Crocker 2003: 47). (Later, I will provide instances of women telling their stories and explain why personal narrative is a crucial part of the process of healing and reconciliation.) In giving one's account of one's suffering and being listened to, some lost dignity is restored, in contrast to being treated with contempt. Third, accountability for past crimes and corresponding appropriate sanctions or punishment are part of the ethically defensible treatment of past wrongs. Crocker suggests that a perpetrator's moral guilt is proportional to their knowledge, freedom or power to commit or prevent evil and the personal risks taken in performing a rights violation (2003: 48).[4] Fourth, due process, fairness, publicity and impartiality are part of the rule of law in dealing with the past. Fifth, compensation to victims should be paid when rights have been violated and compensation incorporates a wide variety of options. Sixth, in order for long-term development, institutional reform of basic social, political and economic institutions are needed. Reforms within the judiciary, police, military, land tenure system, tax system and the structure of economic opportunities are essential. Seven, the goal of reconciliation is important in dealing with the past because it aims to reconcile former enemies. Finally, public spaces, debate and deliberation are crucial to honest dealings with past atrocities. The eight goals are not a blueprint, but provide a culturally adaptable structure for dealing with evil.

It is important to say from the outset that opening up the past may not always be appropriate. While the goal may be to deal with the hurt of the past, reliving past traumas inevitably reawakens hurt. Those who relive past traumas 'are often people whose core identity is as a victim' (Rigby 2001: 1). When we analyse the examples in this chapter, we will discover that women frequently are victims, reluctant to tell their stories because their personal pain is experienced as a deep inner shame. Such women do not choose an identity as victim.

Acknowledgement

A first step in beginning the process of dealing with the past is acknowledgement that someone has been wronged (victim or communities of victims) and that someone (perpetrator) or something (state) has done wrong. Acknowledgement arises because there are abhorrent things to admit, it indicates some willingness to make amends and commit to positive change. The refusal to acknowledge wrong is harmful, the wound of denial festers and damages others' ability to heal because it treats people as if their stories do not count or are not worth hearing. It is a misrecognition of what is needed to affirm identity. In contrast, acknowledgement of past wrongs deals with people's real pain and suffering.[5] In an important sense, as Trudy Govier argues, to receive acknowledgement that certain things did happen, and that 'they were wrong and should not have happened, is to receive confirmation, validation, of one's dignity and status as a human being, and a moral being of equal worth' (2003: 85). In the context of profound wrongs, acknowledgement is important to victims because it provides moral recognition of one's humanity; it is this restoration of dignity that underlies the work of many of the authors I draw on and cements the arguments in this book. Govier situates the defence of her argument in the social nature of selfhood, the *ubuntu* of humanity. As I will elaborate more fully later, Commissioners in the South African TRC 'were exhorted by our enabling legislation to rehabilitate the human and civil dignity of victims' (Tutu 1999: 33). I argue that we have a moral obligation to acknowledge, recognize and affirm the dignity of victims.

In Northern Ireland, a 'Healing Through Remembering' project explores the primary question of how people should remember the effects of the violent conflict and, in doing so, contributes to the healing of social wounds.[6] The project accepted that the distribution of suffering is uneven, that some individuals, groups and communities have suffered more than others, but that no one's hurt 'is more important or less valid than another' (Healing Through Remembering 2002: 15). The project makes an important point that there is no inherent value in remembering for the sake of it; remembering only has significance when it leads to positive changes. Hence for many, the key goal of remembering is to help ease the suffering of victims. The 'acknowledgement that there is no single solution to dealing with the past' (Healing Through Remembering 2002: 38) is incredibly important, no matter how ambiguous the consequences of this acknowledgement. Further, it recommends that acknowledgement involves all the organizations and institutions that engaged in conflict, who 'should honestly and publicly acknowledge responsibility for past political violence due to their acts of omission and commission' (Healing Through Remembering 2002: 50). Such acknowledgement recognizes state complicity in suffering and is crucial in establishing the truth.

Remembering and forgetting

Before getting to the complex issue of truth, it is important to state the need for a 'balance between too much remembering and too much forgetting' (Sarkin and Daly 2004: 706). In many ways, as Tutu puts it, 'it is *important* to remember, so that we should not let such atrocities happen again' (1999: 219; emphasis in original). However, Eilish Rooney from Belfast writes poignantly that 'some things are actively forgotten – have to be forgotten, because to remember is too painful and dehumanizing. Some things are remembered involuntarily' (2000: 224). In terms of her own story, she writes that 'the time for telling is not yet. ... Not telling, and forgetting, are ways of coping' (2000: 226). Roberto Cabrera writes similarly of how, in Guatemala, repression took away people's right to speak, hence 'when considering the question *should we remember?*, it is very important to first ask, has any victim forgotten?' (1998: 27; emphasis in original). Cabrera writes that people 'remember because they have not forgotten' (1998: 28).

As mentioned in the previous chapter, retrieving victims' memories often reignites flames of pain unless there is a context, specifically, a search for justice and the chance to redeem dignity. 'You can have too much memory. Too great a concern with remembering the past can mean that the divisions and conflicts of old never die, the wounds are never healed' (Rigby 2001: 2). This is obvious in places where seemingly intractable long-term conflicts remain, always poised on the brink of eruption. As Andrew Rigby continues, 'the dilemma is how to preserve the memory without letting it poison the future' (2001: 76). On the other hand, we should not try 'to bury the past by deliberate forgetting' of trauma (Biggar 2003: 5). Nigel Biggar (2003) offers three reasons for this. First, while some can forget the past, victims cannot.[7] Second, if governments do not attend to the injuries of victims, they fail in their role of protection. Third, 'grievances without redress tend to fester' (Biggar 2003: 5). Particularly where the fate of a loved one is unknown, the truth can be liberating for relatives freed from unbearable uncertainty.

Examples of never forgetting abound. As the *Madres de Plaza de Mayo* in Argentina demonstrate, and Palestinian mothers who have lost children during the *intifada* know, and those whose loved ones were shot by the IRA and buried in unknown places understand, not to know is emotionally draining. It tears at one's soul. Most people want to know what happened to their loved ones, when they were killed or taken away, what was done to them in the process, how long they lived before they died and where the bodies remain. The truth of these facts is shocking, but most people crave this truth. The *Madres of the Plaza de Mayo* in Argentina are a strong reminder that, despite knowing that nothing can be done to replace their missing loved ones, the importance of demonstrating outrage and anger is part of the way in which these women choose to deal with the past. The ironies of this position are acute, given that the UN Declaration of Basic Principles of Justice for Victims of Crime and Abuse of Power requires 'access to justice' as part of the minimum standards of which victims must be assured. People deal with the past in different ways.

Truth and silence

Acknowledgement of evil wrongs and wrongdoings is an important first step in dealing with the past. In order to move positively into the future, truth, silence, historical commissions, commissions on the disappeared, truth commissions and commissions of inquiry are important.[8] As we already know, the nature of truth is complex, what constitutes hearsay, myth or half-truth is one thing, another is all the variance of stories within one truth narrative. Enormous harm is caused when individuals, groups, clans, tribes, states, nations, religious organizations or churches claim that they possess exclusive truth. What is the truth about ethnic cleansing, war rape, collateral damage and men dominating negotiation processes? Whose versions of truth are more reliable or trustworthy? How do we assess what is true when the range of stories about the same event are so varied? There are different types of truths. For example, in Northern Ireland, 'a broader truth-eliciting process might be tasked with establishing particular truths that cumulatively, contribute to truth (rather than establishing *the* truth)' (Bell *et al.* 2004: 316; emphasis in original). Hence it is useful to talk of truths, rather than a singular truth. In this sense, what is called 'forensic factual truths' are clearly verifiable and documentable, social truths emerge through communal experiences and are affirmed through discussions, and personal truth is the 'truth of wounded memories' (Judge Mahomed in Tutu 1999: 33), which is highly individualistic, subjective and not open to debate because of the differential way in which people absorb pain. In the main, I concentrate in this chapter on this latter type of truth, the subjective truth of rape, exclusion, marginalization, injustice and silencing experienced by women from conflict zones. Concepts of truth have cultural variations. Take, for example, the 1994 Akobo Peace Conference between the Nuer and Dinka communities. 'In this part of Sudan, women's authority as truth tellers cannot be challenged because women are perceived as "mothers of the nation" and as socializers of the young who must therefore act correctly' and so the women participants in the conference saw their role as truth-tellers (Tripp 2000a: 660).

Silencing

Silence, or the withholding of information, is a crucial dimension in understanding the complexity of truth. We probably all have aspects of our lives that we would rather others did not know about, for reasons we choose to keep to ourselves or to our closest friends. In the case of conflict, war and violence, the politics of silencing is profound. In Kosovo in 1999, thousands of displaced women, men and children gathered in a stadium. An official made a broadcast requesting all women who had been raped to report to a particular area, and not one woman did, unprepared for the inevitable stigma or political repercussion of such a public identification. Certainly, the approach was hardly ideal, but the silencing was understandable and the consequences acute; it meant there could be no support given or the chance to hold the aggressors accountable. Silencing also occurred for women at the South African TRC (which I examine in more detail later). At this stage, I simply elaborate on the significance of silence and silencing in women's lives. Regarding the special women's hearings at the TRC:

> In more ways than one, it was easier to keep silent. Female Premiers, Ministers, businesswomen – kept silent. Some of them had been tortured, some of them raped. One of them gave birth in jail in front of a horde of laughing, jeering wardens. All of them are formidable women. Yet they did not come forward. They did not speak.
>
> (Krog 2001: 205)

None of these women wanted to lose the social standing they had achieved in the community or to be reminded of the shame of the past. The past and the future slide uneasily together and the need to move on takes precedence. These are examples of deliberately keeping silent for reasons unique to each person. Krog reminds us that these are remarkable women, yet they kept silent.

Then there is the choice to keep silent about the issues that one ought to admit to, but again, this is rarely straightforward. While it is true that 'silence makes us complicit bystanders to the perpetrators of yesterday' (Zorbas 2004: 30), many who feel powerless, shamed or without voice do not have the opportunity to break the silence. However, 'silence and amnesia are the enemies of justice...But "truth" in itself will not bring reconciliation' (Huyse 2003a; 23,24).[9] The army, the state, paramilitary groups and warlords all rely on creating a climate of fear to silence dissent. Silencing is a form of control and internalized repression often manifests itself through further violence. Elena, a leader of a Mayan women's cultural organization, explains the dangers in talking, of being taken as a guerrilla and the fear of being killed:

> In this situation one had to remain quiet, one could not say what one felt, what one thought, like one was sleeping. One's conscience was sleeping.... It was dangerous to speak for the security of one's own life.
>
> (in Stern 2005: 92)

Stories of such silencing abound in the search for truth. Bina D'Costa writes of survivors of gender-based violence during and after the Independence War of Bangladesh. She suggests that 'pathologizing the helplessness, frustration, and anger of rape survivors diverted attention' from the daily subjection that they faced and from demanding justice (2006: 132). However, during her fieldwork in 1999–2001, she found it difficult to find survivors who were willing to speak because the stigma, shame and humiliation remained: to speak meant possible ostracization from their communities. She 'learned that the enduring reality of war and survival after the war was articulated not only in women's uttered words, but also in those pregnant pauses during the conversations' (D'Costa 2006: 148). The issue of choice and silencing is complex. For Muslim women, sometimes the veil or *burqa* is worn willingly, there is no feeling of being silenced and it is a mistake to think that women who wear a veil do not have a voice. For other women, when it is a cultural constraint, there is no element of choice and so it may be a form of silencing. Silence is on the far end of the spectrum from truth.

Truth commissions

In this chapter, I do not examine the full implications of truth commissions for peacebuilding. I situate my discussion of commissions in the light of their effects on women. Truth commissions create opportunities for the public recording of violations and people's suffering. Since 1974, there have been truth commissions in Argentina, Bolivia, Chad, Chile, East Timor, Ecuador, El Salvador, Germany, Ghana, Guatemala, Haiti, Nepal, Nigeria, Panama, Peru, Philippines, Serbia and Montenegro (former Federation Republic of Yugoslavia), Sierra Leone, South Africa, South Korea, Sri Lanka, Uganda, Uruguay and Zimbabwe.[10] Their main purpose varies, from seeking information about the disappeared in Argentina, Sri Lanka, Uganda and Uruguay,[11] to working toward truth and justice in Ecuador and Haiti, or seeking truth and reconciliation in Chile, East Timor, the Federal Republic of Yugoslavia, Peru and South Africa (UNRISD 2005: 248). Some commissions have provided full amnesty for perpetrators who agree to participate in them.[12] The danger is that amnesty and pardon 'institutionalizes forgetfulness, and sacrifices justice' (Minow 1998: 15). In the case of Guatemala, Sierra Leone and Uganda, some claim that while the perpetrators of violence can act with impunity, the victims of violence are denied justice. The relationship between truth-telling and amnesty is controversial (as mentioned briefly in Chapter 4) – where amnesty is assured in return for the truth, victims may feel deprived of justice.

Generally, truth commissions are temporary bodies of usually between one to two years, officially sanctioned by the state as well as the peace accord, non-judicial bodies and created at a point of political transition. They focus on the past, investigate patterns of views on violations over a period of time, focus on violations of human rights and humanitarian norms and complete their work with a final report containing recommendations. The potential benefits for establishing a truth commission include:

- having to establish the truth about the past;
- promoting the accountability of perpetrators of human rights violations;
- providing a public platform for victims;
- informing public debate;
- recommending victim reparation;
- recommending legal and institutional reforms;
- promoting social reconciliation; and
- consolidating a democratic transition.

(Freeman and Hayner 2003: 125)

Most truth commissions focus on the victims rather than the perpetrators of violence in order to uncover those truths which have been deliberately suppressed by the state, paramilitary groups, terrorist organizations and separatist movements with warring rebels. There are different types of truth. Alex Bouraine (2005) posits four aspects of truth evident in the South African TRC. First, there is objective, factual or forensic truth, as evidenced by the apartheid state with its torture by state security forces. Second, there are personal narrative dimensions of truth told in the stories by victims and perpetrators. Third, there is a dialogical truth that can emerge through interaction, transparency and mutual respect. Fourth, there is a healing that comes with restorative truth, that 'knowledge in itself is not enough. Knowledge must be accompanied by acknowledgement and acceptance of accountability' (Bouraine 2005: 329). There are useful distinctions in recognizing the multiple understandings of truths. Juan Méndez, a survivor of torture by the Argentinian military dictatorship, suggests that truth commissions may be useful when large numbers of 'human rights violations have been characterized by denial, deception, or imposed silence' (2001: 29) and a well-organized effort is needed to uncover and disclose the truth. Furthermore, he clarifies that truth commissions 'work best when conceived as a key component in a holistic process of truth-telling, justice, reparations, and eventual reconciliation' (2001: 29). This process is integral in demonstrating a commitment to accountability. (As argued in the concluding chapter, reconciliation comes after truth is exposed and justice realized.)

Truth commissions are not always used for the following considerations:

- fear of ongoing or renewed violence;
- ongoing conflict;
- lack of political interest;
- insufficient capacity or resources;
- alternative preferences; or
- other urgent priorities.

(Freeman and Hayner 2003: 127)

Sometimes, as I will expand later, there are real shortcomings in truth commissions. For example, Tutu suggests that one great weakness of the South African TRC was the failure 'to attract the bulk of the white community to participate enthusiastically' (1999: 184). He suggests that part of the reason for this was resentment at having lost some political power.[13] Truth commissions are effective when affected individuals and communities feel a degree of ownership in the process. As we shall see, those truth commissions that incorporate gender-sensitive mandates and procedures legitimize women's experiences and make them part of the official public record.

War rape

When I began this book, I intended to avoid the issue of rape in order to concentrate on the positive aspects of peacebuilding. It has proved impossible to avoid as its horrors are stark. One of the clearest needs for gender-specific sensitivities in truth commissions is accountability for war rape. Throughout history, there has been a failure to deal with crimes committed against women. In 1977, the Protocols to the Geneva Conventions mentioned 'rape, forced prostitution and any other forms of indecent assault', but only as 'humiliating and degrading treatment' which, as Rhonda Copelon points out, reinforces 'the secondary importance as well as shame and stigma of the victimized women' (2000: 221). While women were the object of shameful attack, and thus needed protection, there was little talk of women as subjects of rights. Before the 1990s, the truth of sexual violence in wars was trivialized or considered a private matter, and rape was justified tacitly as a reasonable trophy for soldiers or totally ignored. An international court has not tried the sexual enslavement of about 200,000 women and girls taken by the Japanese Army during the Second World War as 'comfort women'. This glaring injustice and misrecognition led a coalition of grass roots NGOs to convene a people's tribunal in December 2000. 'Seventy-five survivors came to testify before the Women's International War Crimes Tribunal on Japan's Military Sexual Slavery. What drove the women to appear before the Tribunal was the wish to tell the story before it was lost history' (Rehn and Johnson-Sirleaf 2000: 90). Truth and justice are closely linked. The point of such a tribunal is to give the victims of atrocities the opportunity to know that their grievances have been heard and documented, in the hope that future similar crimes can be prevented.

Shame presses in on women. A woman in the Democratic Republic of Congo confided:

> In my culture, it is not common to talk about sex with men, let alone strange men. Many of the women who were raped like I was can identify their attackers, but find it difficult to report them to the police. We can talk to you because you are women like us. But we can't talk about these things with men.
>
> (in Rehn and Johnson-Sirleaf 2002: 69)

This woman suggested the importance of having women police as part of the peacekeeping force to whom women can go to report attacks. In 2007, Indian policewomen went to Liberia as part of the peacekeeping mission. In East Timor, the local women's movement and the UN Gender Unit launched an awareness campaign on domestic violence and established a special civilian police unit staffed by women to handle rape, domestic violence and gender-related crimes, thereby creating an environment where women felt safe to report cases. Similarly, in Cambodia and Bosnia-Herzegovina, women's groups supported by UNIFEM sensitized police forces and community leaders to violence against women.

Frequently, meaningful initiatives only occur after horrible acts have been committed. The atrocities in Rwanda occurred after the world had become aware of widespread rape and sexual violence in the former Yugoslavia and after rape was listed as a crime against humanity in the Statute of the ICTY. Yet observers of genocide in Rwanda failed to report the massive occurrence of rape during the genocide. In Rwanda, rape was rendered invisible as if it was not happening, or worse, as if it did not matter that it was happening. Genocide has an intense impact on memory, indelibly etched like an ongoing nightmare. 'A most appalling goal of the genocides, the massacres, systematic rapes, and tortures has been the destruction of the remembrance of individuals as well as of their lives and dignity' (Minow 1998: 1). Since 1955, there have been 29 countries that have experienced episodes of genocide[14] or politicide, attempts to remove politicized ethnic groups with drastic statistics in Afghanistan during 1978–1992, Cambodia during 1975–1979, Indonesia during 1965–1966, Pakistan in 1971 and Rwanda in 1994 (Marshall and Gurr 2005: 58). As noted in the previous chapter, rape was included as a crime against humanity in the Statute of the ICTR and it was mentioned as an example of the war crime of humiliating and degrading treatment, yet 'rape formed no part of the first series of ICTR indictments' (Copelon 2000: 224). It was true that women did not talk about rape. However, as previously mentioned, this changed when Judge Navanethem Pillay, the only woman judge on the ICTR Trial Chamber, was hearing a case and pursued her inquiry with two women who were called to testify to other crimes. A witness's testimony linked Akayesu to rapes.

> *Akayesu* was a landmark: the first international conviction for genocide, the first judgment to recognize rape and sexual violence as constitutive acts of genocide, and the first to advance a broad definition of rape as a physical invasion of a sexual nature.
>
> (Copelon 2000: 227)

The further significance of this landmark case was that the judgment empha-sized the ethnic targeting of Tutsi women as part of the genocide. The inter-national women's human rights movement mobilized to support the election of women judges, and prevent harassment of and discrimination against victims of witnesses.

In 2001, the ICTY found three Bosnian Serb military and paramilitary men guilty for the multiple rape, torture and enslavement of Bosnian Muslim women. Although rape had been successfully charged at the ICTY, the so-called *Foča* trial (*Prosecutor* v. *Krnojelac*, Case No. IT-97-25) was significant for a range of reasons.[15] After the *Akayesu* judgment referred to previously, the *Foča* judgment sets the second precedent in international criminal law in prosecuting rape as a crime against humanity. The trial shed light on the large-scale systematic sexual-ized assault on Muslim women and on the role that this violence played in the war in Bosnia-Herzegovina. It also was the first trial to successfully prosecute enslavement, in this case sexual enslavement as a crime against humanity. There were no rape charges at the Nuremberg trials of prominent Nazis after the Second World War. The Tokyo trials did not deal with the enslavement of Korean women who were forced to serve as prostitutes for Japanese soldiers. Truth matters. The silence about rape in war can no longer continue. If the stories of these rapes are so disturbing, the realities of the trauma are horrifying.

Slavenka Drakulic, reporting on the ICTY,[16] discusses the case of Radomir Kovac. During the war, he took a girl of 12, enslaved her with other girls, sold her to a Montenegrin soldier and she was never heard of again. This girl's mother came to the Tribunal to testify against him. She had not seen her daughter since she boarded a bus that was transporting people out of *Foča*. When the prosecutor showed her a photo of her daughter and asked how old she was at the time, this mother cried, sobbing, so deeply wounded that she could only howl. Zoran Vukovic confessed to the Tribunal that he told one 15-year-old girl that he could have been more brutal, except for the fact that he had a daughter of the same age. This is shocking of course, but it is morally troubling because it suggests some distinguishing between degrees of brutality. However in this instance, there is no acceptable level of violence, there is only evil. Uncertainties still linger as to how it is possible that ordinary men who had been neighbours, relatives, teachers, local shopkeepers, waiters or policeman could turn into torturers. It is apt to recall Tutu's quotation earlier in this chapter, that 'each of us has this capacity for the most awful evil' (1999: 76). Each of us also has the capacity for profound good.

It is important to note that the most powerful female member of the pre-genocide Rwandan government, Pauline Nyiramasuhuko, the National Minister of Family and Women's Affairs in 1994, donned fatigues, picked up a gun and ordered the *Interahamwe* (the civilian death squads) to rape Tutsi women. Nyiramasuhuko faces 11 charges in the ICTR, including genocide, crimes against humanity and war crimes. She is the first woman to be charged with these crimes in an international court. She is also the first woman ever to be charged with rape as a crime against humanity.[17]

Truth is an essential aspect to peacebuilding, but in the case of rape, the truth of the assault is not just physical, it is deeply psychological and cannot always be articulated explicitly. Feminists across the globe recognize the potential within the ICC to integrate gender into international criminal law. The ICC Women's Caucus draws on regional diversity and a wide range of experience in advocacy, legislation, monitoring ad hoc tribunals and working with survivors of sexual violence. Accordingly, the Statute of the International Criminal Court represents another landmark. It has codified crimes of sexual and gender violence as part of the jurisdiction of the Court, and 'a range of structures and procedures necessary to ensure that these crimes and those victimized by them will remain on the agenda and properly treated in the process of justice' (Copelon 2000: 233). This means that sexual violence cannot be seen just as part of other forms of violence that accompany war, enslavement, torture, genocide and inhumane treatment. Wherever human dignity is destroyed, there is a need for peacebuilders to repair fragile souls.

Gender-specific concerns with truth commissions

Truth recovery processes require safe spaces in which stories can be told, and where there is public acknowledgment that there are different understandings of truths experienced by different people about the same event. 'Equitable access to truth commissions or other legal proceedings may be particularly problematic for women and adolescent girls who wish to testify but fear reprisals from their unpunished torturers and rapists who often continue living alongside them' (UN Secretary-General 2002: 113), as was particularly the case in the former Yugoslavia. Indeed, 'the most common abuses under-reported to Truth Commissions are those suffered by women, as indeed are those least prosecuted. Women may find it impossible to speak out' (UNRISD 2005: 248). Some of the reasons why women keep silent have been discussed previously. Fear, shame, silencing and being silenced freeze the emotions. Nomfundo Walaza, a clinical psychologist, discusses the difference between guilt and shame as expressed in the South African TRC. She suggests that:

> Guilt is such a useless thing. Guilt immobilizes you... Feelings of guilt are also open to abuse by those who suffered ... I prefer shame. Because when you feel shame about something you really want to change it, because it's not comfortable to sit with shame.
>
> (Walaza in Krog 1998: 161)

Shame can immobilize too when it is kept inside. The importance of truth-telling and exposing the horrors of abuse and violence is to release the debilitating potential of shame. Brandon Hamber, talking about the potential for truth commissions, writes that 'psychological restoration and healing can only occur through providing space for survivors of violence to be heard, and for every detail of the traumatic event to be re-experienced in a safe environment' (2003b: 158). This is not always the case with women who have been raped, who do not want to relive every horrible detail of the past. Yet some raped women are not given the opportunity to testify or choose what details to relive. The 'Salvadoran Commission on Truth in 1993 did not include reports of rape at all in its final report because they were seen as outside of its mandate to report on "politically-motivated acts"' (International Alert and Women Waging Peace 2004, part 4: 5).

In order to demonstrate how a politics of compassion might be useful in truth commissions in attending to specific needs, listening to troubled narratives and responding with wise judgements, I draw on Fiona Ross's response to the need for gender-specific attention to truth commissions. She presents a moving account of what it means to bear witness to the truth. She questions conventional ways of attending to suffering and recovery. In particular, Ross's response is a reaction to those testimonies in the South African TRC which, when narrated, were simply distilled and recorded as data rather than 'narratives of pain' (2003: 14). Ross pays attention to the testimonies and experiences of women who were activists in the struggle against apartheid and she develops a 'politics of intimacy' (2003: 2) which overlaps with my politics of compassion. Ross attempts to address the absence of an empathetic listener who can hear the anguish within a story. Her emphasis on witnessing is on 'recognizing and acknowledging suffering' (2003: 3). Her political point is that 'witnessing calls for action – a "not-turning away" from seeing and hearing' (2003: 5). Ross draws on the ideas of Veena Das, who argues that:

> Denial of the other's pain is not about the failings of the intellect but the failings of the spirit. In the register of the imaginary, the pain of the other not only asks for a home in language but also seeks a home in the body.
>
> (Das 1996: 88)

To bear witness to the truth is to absorb multiple layers of intricate parts that contribute to the agony within a personal narrative. 'Witnessing is an integral part of the dialogical process of establishing social recognition and meaning' (Humphrey 2002: 114). Earlier chapters have stressed the importance of dialogue and recognition. Pain must be acknowledged in order to be recognized. In acknowledging the pain and recognizing the depths of anguish, we begin the process of restoration of dignity that is fundamental to peacebuilding. Ross argues that 'the communication of pain rests on words, gestures and silences. Pain's recognition requires imaginative engagement' (2003: 49). This is part of the empathy within a politics of compassion. While the TRC relied on giving expression to truth, as already argued, silence can be recognized as a meaningful aspect to truth. Ross warns that this can only be discerned through probing 'the gaps between fragile words, in order to hear what it is that women say' (2003: 50). Attentive listening is necessary. Ross's conclusion is profound. She argues that prevailing conceptions of voice, 'particularly the equation of speaking subject with healed subject ... do not do justice to the range of women's experiences of harm and the diversity of efforts to cope' (2003: 165). A politics of intimacy cannot emerge without careful, discerning listening to the words, the lack of words, the gestures, the frozen body stares, the cries and the suppressed wails. That is, there can be integrity in wilful silence; it is part of the unfinished, fragmented nature of social and spiritual recovery.

In recognition that an incorporation of a gender approach to truth commissions is relatively new, a World Bank study reviewed gender-related aspects of truth commissions in Peru, Sierra Leone and South Africa (Mantilla 2006). The findings are interesting. For example (as argued in the previous chapter), notions of justice differ among different groups of women. Women affected by violence do not always seek prosecution as the form of justice most required:

> In many cases, women link 'justice' with adequate education, health services, and housing for their children. Many women who became pregnant after rape would rather have the perpetrator bear the costs of raising the child than go to jail.
>
> (Mantilla 2006: 28)

The question of customary law is always controversial because in the desire to respect indigenous ways, caution is needed around criticizing local traditions. However, customary law dictates the codes of justice in many societies, usually to the disadvantage of women's rights, and hence there needs to be the codification of customary law with international human rights law so that the opportunity for culturally sensitive justice may occur.

Peru's TRC considered the victims as 'the disappeared'. The crimes implicated in these disappearances were kidnapping, torture and murder. When a gender perspective is added, it renders a more complex understanding of who is a victim. It also discredits any gender-blind notion that violations of human rights affect men and women in similar ways, with similar consequences. In the public hearings in Peru, a similar pattern happened that has been well-documented in the South African TRC, namely that while men recounted their own stories, women recalled their husbands', brothers' and children's stories with greater clarity than their own. To understand why this occurs, it is important to note that women in most cultures are taught from an early age to prioritize the care of others, in particular their family members, over their own needs. In Peru, the need to document women's experience and adopt a gendered approach became clear. Sanam Naraghi Anderlini explains that some of the victims were women who were raped prior to disappearing, sometimes the female relatives of the disappeared went to look for them and were subject to violent crime. Such an exposure has 'an impact on the resources needed by the commission, the type of experts and expertise required, the (differential) approaches appropriate for taking testimony, the array of services for victims, and so forth' (in Mantilla 2006: 2).

Yasmin Sooka was a Commissioner on TRCs for South Africa and Sierra Leone. Her experience from South Africa was crucial in the training of commissioners in Sierra Leone, organizing hearings and drafting the final report. Sooka (2006) suggests that there are a number of key issues which a truth commission can address in the area of gender and women's empowerment, such as: disaggregating data relating to gender components; drawing attention to crimes against women, such as rape and sexual enslavement; and assisting in restoring the status and reintegration, and providing material support, of victims who suffer ostracism and the stigma of having been associated with perpetrator groupings, especially if they have had children as a result of their experiences. Also, truth commissions can empower women survivors through an affirmative participatory process: adding gender components to dispute resolution, peace negotiations, reconciliation and democracy-building; dealing with gender-based violence through law reform in the building of human rights culture; improving DDR programmes; ensuring a gender-specific component to a reparation and rehabilitation programme; and addressing the role of peacekeepers. As someone with considerable experience, she advises transitional justice practitioners and others in the international community to consider how to deal with 'the deficit between norms, principles, and the reality on the ground' (Sooka 2006: 180). Sooka's advice is incredibly practical and broadly applicable in culturally sensitive ways. In addition to truth commissions, the ICTY, ICTR and ICC reflect the resolve of human rights NGOs and activists that impunity should not be exchanged for peace at the negotiating table. The significance of these legal structures for our purposes is that they give distinct attention to gender-based crimes.

Truthful stories

In the previous section, I addressed the importance of understanding truth and silence. It is important now to explore some instances of memory and truth. We all know how selective our memories can be. We often deliberately choose to block out aspects of our life that we would rather not remember, including trivial examples in comparison to the sorts of recollections of past evils under discussion here. For example, the memories of Albanians and Serbs in Kosovo or Muslims and Serbs in Bosnia can vary extraordinarily. Memories haunt. Some people can be so caught in the past that their wounds never heal and thus they remain dominated by the bitterness of their scars. Wherever there are ethnic divisions, there are individuals, groups and leaders of political parties who deliberately keep alive those memories which have the potential to fuel the fires of hatred. As noted previously, there are multiple versions of truth and so too there are competing memories of the past. 'Given the dangers of too much memory, a society must try to attain the right delicate mixture of remembering and forgetting' (Huyse 2003a: 30). Memory has different connotations for different people. For victims, memory sustains the quest for justice; for perpetrators, historical memory may justify further acts of violence. Stories that have been remembered and are relayed to others rely on memory, and placing this memory into a meaningful context that makes sense to the listener as well as to the narrator. 'Hence memory (and thus remembered stories) are as much a part of the present as they are a part of the past. They are also shaped by expectations for the future' (Stern 2005: 62). Memory can be distorted, manipulated or incredibly accurate.

Special hearings of the South African TRC

The South African TRC was developed on principles established in the final days of the 1993 negotiations with an interim Constitution. The principles asserted 'a need for understanding but not for vengeance, a need for reparation but not for retaliation, and a need for *ubuntu* but not for victimization' (Burton 1998: 15). *Ubuntu* is an ancient African word meaning 'humanity to others'. It means 'I am what I am because of who we all are'. It is an understanding of ontology as self-in-relations, and an understanding of the meaning of life as fulfilment of the human dignity of all. The TRC explicitly connected truth and reconciliation. Mary Burton, a TRC Commissioner and a founding member and activist in the Black Sash, a woman's anti-apartheid movement, points to the problems of reopening old wounds without providing adequate mechanisms for dealing with trauma for both victims and perpetrators. She points to the 'generosity of forgiveness', which acts as a 'catharsis' for submerged anger when accompanied by 'the right to be heard and acknowledged with respect and empathy' (Burton 1998: 20). The language of the TRC is rich in moral overtones. Wilhelm Verwoerd[18] maintains that people's everyday concept of justice is 'a (passionate) protest against wrongdoing as well as a demand for rectification' (2003: 253). He suggests that while there clearly were limitations in what the Commission could achieve, the main story of the TRC is a '"morality of the depths" of moral *evils*, past *injustices*, *gross* human rights *violations*' (2003: 268; emphasis in original). My focus in examining the TRC targets women's versions of truth on such evils, injustice and rights violation as well as their silence, confession and witnessing.

Within South Africa, women play an important role in shaping the post-apartheid transitional justice process. A project initiated by the Women Waging Peace Policy Commission found a number of key findings about the TRC (Gobodo-Madikizela 2005). Women were influential in ensuring inclusivity and consultation with regard to who was chosen as Commissioners. The Commission often relied on women in NGOs and community-based organizations to identify potential witnesses. Women Commissioners focused on establishing a 'victim-friendly' process to ease the trauma of testifying. Separate structures for women, such as the Johannesburg Women's Hearings, gave them the safe space to testify about crimes such as sexual violence. Interviews with members of the Commissioners suggest that many men focused on a strict interpretation of law, whereas women Commissioners and staff focused on the human element of nurturing the participation of witnesses and facilitating the collection of testimonies. Commissioners attempted to engage with witnesses by letting them know how their testimonies touched them.

It is important to understand the contextual background as to why special hearings for women became necessary. While men testified about what had happened to themselves, 'more than half of the statements received by the Commission were made by women, with black African women accounting for approximately 60 per cent of these statements' (Gobodo-Madikizela 2005: vii). As we saw in the previous chapter with regard to the political significance of silence, the victims of crimes who testified in the special hearings in the South African TRC did not always want to speak of the crimes involving rape or sexualized brutality. These particular atrocities 'escaped the bounds of language – of the talking cure, of the healing truth – and fell outside the remit of apology' (Warner 2002: 14). This is what is meant by 'unspeakable truths'. The absences, silences and gaps were stark. 'The Commission established statistically that when women came to testify to the Commission they almost always told the story of what had happened to somebody else' (Tutu 1999: 182). In the main, women addressed the suffering of sons and husbands and were circumspect about their own experience of human rights abuse. Yet the motivation for this was complex. Pumla Gobodo-Madikizela, a member of the Human Rights Violation Committee, writes that, 'women witnesses often addressed the suffering of others, usually sons and husbands, in testimonies as a conscious means of generating empathy and taking on a broader responsibility for the collective sense of national healing' (2005: v). Special hearings on women with all-women panels were instituted because women were not coming forward to testify about themselves.[19]

In writing so poignantly of the voices of the victims who gave their accounts in the South African TRC, Krog writes powerfully:

She is sitting behind a microphone, dressed in beret or *kopdoek* and her Sunday best. Everyone recognizes her. Truth has become Woman. Her voice, distorted behind a rough hand, has undermined Man as the source of truth. And yet. Nobody knows her. The truth and the illusion of truth as we have never known them.

(Krog 1998: 56)

For six months the voices of the victims were given space. Krog describes the second narrative as 'the Other. The Counter. The perpetrator. ... There can be no story without the balance of the antagonist. ... But it is there. And it is white. And male' (1998: 56). When Krog asks, 'Does truth have a gender?' (1998: 178), her accounts are disturbing in response, referring to the dehumanization that occurs during rape and of those imprisoned, being unable to wash when menstruating. During the special women's hearing in Johannesburg, Debra Matshoba said, 'when I look around, I marvel at how we battle to be normal – and no one knows how shattered we are inside' (in Krog 2001: 206). In the opening speech of the special women's hearings Thenjiwe Mthintso, Chairperson of the Gender Commission, said:

As women speak, they speak for us who are too cowardly to speak. They speak for us who are too owned by pain to speak. Because always, always in anger and frustration men use women's bodies as a terrain of struggle – as a battleground.... Your sexuality was used to strip away your dignity, to undermine your sense of self ... While writing this speech I realized how unready I am to talk about my experience in South African jails and ANC camps abroad. Even now, despite the general terms in which I have chosen to speak, I feel exposed and distraught.

(in Krog 1998: 178–179)

This is a powerful statement. Gobodo-Madikizela suggests that rather than undermining their own experiences, women were purposefully incorporating 'the relational element of public testimony' whereby 'women take on the onus of speaking out in order to engage others and *on behalf of* others' (2005: viii; emphasis in original). This is consistent with the *ubuntu* indigenous philosophy of seeking to restore a common sense of humanity. The relational aspect is also intrinsic to feminist ethics.

Marcella Naidoo, regional director of the TRC in Cape Town, talks of the 'gentleness in the way that we work together and with the members of the public', including trying to break down some of the anxiety in the whites who were in the employment of the apartheid government (in Gobodo-Madikizela 2005: 11). She is explicit about this approach:

It's just part of caring. Yes, that's it. It's women's *ethos* of care. It's that quality of being a woman that allows women to reach out to others without feeling that they'll be losing anything or compromising themselves in any way. Men, I think, are always afraid of losing something – their dignity, their power, and stuff like that. For me I know it was about how to make relationships in my team work.

(Naidoo in Gobodo-Madikizela 2005: 11)

It is important to recall that empathy and compassion often are seen as weak qualities and good reasons to exclude women from the hard world of politics and peace negotiations. So it is incredibly important for us to listen to the defence of empathy from women who have extensive experience in the hard world of fighting against apartheid, fighting in armed conflict. It is also significant as an example of the potential for change (as outlined in the start of this chapter). Burton also talked about 'a particular way – women do things with compassionate dedication' and talks of the essential need for empathy, of identifying with pain of the mothers' suffering (in Gobodo-Madikizela 2005: 1–12).

Gobodo-Madikizela also talks of a conscious decision made by some of the women Commissioners 'to lead the way with demonstrating how critical empathic connection with different participants on the TRC was, connecting with people who carried different identities to the TRC' (2005: 12). This is another example of women being willing to reach out across barriers. Further, Gobodo-Madikizela talks about the dilemma she was feeling, in that white people would not be visible at the public hearings. The Commission needed to figure out how to engage whites in the process and find something with which they could identify. The Commission came up with a curious way to draw white families in: army conscription implicated white families in apartheid's history, so they approached a woman whose son had been killed and asked her to tell her story. Many within the TRC were outraged by the suggestion, but this decision was a turning point in the way that white South Africans responded. While it is easy to understand empathy toward victims of conflict and violence, the example of listening to the white mother's story is a profound deviation from the norm within typical conflict resolution strategies. Gobodo-Madikizela's point is that it is important to be emotionally present in order to try to understand a perpetrator's reasons for systematic abuse 'without relinquishing one's moral stance' (2005: 13). This requires a conscious attempt to create the sort of space in which perpetrators can acknowledge wrongdoing without being judged too quickly or ostracized. Again, the imagery of a creative space for change is compelling. However, this example in no way justifies the abuse or excuses the abuser.

> That acknowledgement is what invites the victim to engage and to reach out with forgiveness, if not forgiveness with acceptance. Some measure of compassion is critical for this to happen, and this is why so many disclosures by perpetrators were accompanied by remorseful apologies.

(Gobodo-Madikizela 2005: 13)

Acknowledgement of wrongdoing, of committing evil against another, as well as acknowledgement of the wrong itself, is a way of recognizing the humanity of victims, survivors and perpetrators. This is why I began this chapter with the difficult discussion on evil and of the potential for moral change. Gobodo-Madikizela is quick to qualify that the men on the TRC were not low on emphatic skills but that women are 'more ready to show their compassion than men' (2005: 13). She suggests that 'without empathy, I don't think the notions of shared ideas about future and reconciliation – let alone forgiveness – would have been realized as the symbols of hope that they've represented in the collective minds of South Africans' (Gobodo-Madikizela 2005: 13).[20] An old township woman attending a truth and reconciliation public meeting in the Grahamstown Town Hall on 17 February 1997 spoke pointedly:

> Your lives have changed. It is all right for you to forgive and embrace the perpetrators of heinous crimes for the sake of reconciliation. Indeed it's all right for Nelson Mandela to forgive since his life has also changed. But our lives have not changed. We still live in the same shacks or matchbox houses. ... How can we forgive if our lives have not changed?
>
> (in Verwoerd 2003: 252–253)

The crucial aspect to truth-telling is to provoke an impetus to change. There is a restorative power of truth-telling, that 'when the work of knowing and telling the story has come to an end, the trauma then belongs to the past, the survivor can face the work of building a future' (Minow 1998: 67). Michael Lapsley's story bears witness to this restorative power.[21] He worked with a group of mothers whose sons had been taken in 1985 from a township outside Pretoria and shot but did not hear until 1995 what happened to them. In his 'Healing of Memories' workshops he was able to take the women to where their children were buried. 'The moral order can begin to be restored because these children can be buried with dignity. Their spirits can rest. Their mothers now know the truth in all its horror' (Lapsley 1998: 748). The *ubuntu* approach to truth and reconciliation, predicated on the belief that 'I am because we are', recognizes the value of truthful narrative and confession of wrong as part of transitional justice efforts. This approach was evident in many testimonies. Where it occurred, the ability to forgive perpetrators was more likely because of their respect for the humanity of the perpetrators.

Redress

How is it possible to restore that which is so deeply lost in a spiritual sense? What role is there for redress? What sort of redress is most likely to lead to sustainable peace? Is the symbolic significance of compensation important in acknowledging grave loss and the need to recompense? Can financial compensation ever suffice? Isha Dyfan is a survivor of Sierra Leone's civil war, where diamond-hungry rebels destroy homes as well as lives and abduct children for indoctrination as child rebel soldiers and diamond miners. She said, 'No one can put a price on what we've lost.... We cannot be compensated' (in Rehn and

Johnson-Sirleaf 2002: 88). However, she goes on to say that truth and reconciliation are necessary to rebuild the country, for justice is intangible, it is concrete
and mundane, and 'we need to hear that these atrocities are condemned to at
least relieve some of the shame and the grief. It is not just a legal issue. It is
about people's lives' (in Rehn and Johnson-Sirleaf 2002: 88). A special court
dealt with the planners of the war, and a TRC was to provide a safe place where
truth could be spoken without fear.

Truth is an integral part of justice. When a story remains deeply hidden or is
repressed because of inhibition, social taboos, fear of the consequences or most
typically because of the deep sense of shame, it remains private and silenced.
When a story is expressed through testimony, 'new meaning can be given to
private shame as it is transformed into political dignity' (McKay 2000: 564).
Yet, in listening to personal narratives we become implicated and thus in
bearing 'witness to the testimony, the responsibility for finding justice is shared'
(McKay 2000: 564). This is part of the moral obligation for others which I have
argued is part of a politics of compassion. The responsibility also requires
attending to redress. Redress differs according to different individuals, groups,
communities or even nations. Financial compensation is but one form of compensation. Digeser posits an interesting view that despite the extraordinary value
attributed to having transgressors punished and debts repaid, 'other goods may
be lost in a relentless pursuit of justice. The demand to be paid to the penny
forecloses opportunities for generosity or magnanimity' (2001: 53). Other
goods include restoring dignity or right relationships, or equalizing access to
scarce resources or economic and educational opportunities. Redress takes many
different forms.

The International Centre for Transitional Justice (ICTJ) conducted a large-
scale research project on reparations for victims of human rights abuse. This
study highlighted the absence of information and understanding of the gender
perspective. Reparation programmes aim to provide some justice to victims.
Hence the ICTJ undertook a research project on gender and reparations (Rubio-
Marín 2006).[22] For example, in 2000, the Gender Affairs Unit in East Timor
convened a group of 500 women to recommend gender-sensitive reparations
which have an impact on women's lives. The results of this are fascinating.
These women recommended reparations for the impact of the loss of a male
breadwinner, the cost of unpaid home labour, contributions for transporting children to school, vocational training and psychosocial counsel (International Alert
and Women Waging Peace 2004, part 4: 6). Again, these examples of redress
come from women's prime duty to attend to everyday material concerns of
nurture and cater for primary basic needs. As noted, the Commission for Reception, Truth and Reconciliation of Timor-Leste had a mandate that a gender
perspective should be integrated into all aspects of its work, including reparations. Women were Commissioners and staff in healing workshops. The ICTJ
found that women's leadership has been more obvious in community-based,
self-help widows' groups centred on issues of economic survival, demands for
practical manifestations of justice and disclosure of the position of the

disappeared, rather than reparations. Proposed reparations programmes likely to help women include training, micro-credit and services rather than simple economic compensation, as well as public education programmes that minimize the stigmatization of victims, particularly those subject to sexual violence.

In Guatemala, the Commission of Historical Clarification recommended the creation of the National Reparations Programme in 1999. Feminist organizations focused on current violence and victims' organizations on the search for justice related to the dead or disappeared relatives. In 2005, there were modifications to the programme when it became clear that there were still issues relating to sexual violence and rape as crimes that needed to be repaired. Other significant reparations include protecting women's right to property when their husbands have died during armed conflict. Programmes aim to cover economic and psychosocial reparations. In Peru, a comprehensive reparations plan emerged from the TRC, and the inclusion of rape among the crimes to be repaired and 'potentially covered by economic reparations, represents a major step forward, considering the prevailing belief in Peruvian society that rape is a collateral damage of war' (Guillerot in Rubio-Marín 2006: 170). In Sierra Leone, the National Commission for Social Action was the government agency recommended by the TRC to implement reparations programmes and it added war widows and immediate family members as a privileged category for reparations which included adequate medical and psychological treatment. Yet, while war widows are the beneficiaries of skills training, they will not receive pensions.

Where victims and their families have been denied justice, where perpetrators have not been punished, reparation is sensitive. 'For some it is unthinkable to accept money for the death of their loved ones' (Rigby 2001: 75). Rigby suggests that one of the most important forms of redress is 'the public naming and shaming of those directly responsible for their injuries, pain, and loss' (2001: 89). In this process, some dignity is restored to survivors. There is some of the acknowledgement of the violation of dignity, and this in itself can be transformative for survivors searching for the meaning, or even closure, of the suffering of the past. (I have already mentioned the historical significance of the Japanese government's admittance in 1993 of enslaving Korean, Chinese and Filipina women as prostitutes, so-called 'comfort-women' in the Second World War.)

Wole Soyinka, Nigerian poet, novelist and activist, talks of reparation as 'a process of recompense for loss, for denial and violation' (2000: 21). He qualifies this by saying that we can argue over the specific support that this really means, 'but what refuses to go away is the underlying principle of reparations, restitution, social or racial justice or whatever presents itself as a prerequisite of healing and reconciliation' (2000: 22). Soyinka reflects on the Atlantic slave trade and suggests that, while we 'must exorcize the burden of memory', it can only be done 'by such strategies that do not sanitize the residuum of an unexpiated past' (2000: 37). Insert a context and the call for reparations is a potent instrument. This remains a strong case for indigenous Australians, who still await an official apology from the Australian government for the appropriation of land and the pain incurred by the stolen generation, taken away as children, placed in white families and lost to their families, communities, language and culture.

This chapter has examined the evils of the past. I have supported the claim that no perpetrator of evil is potentially unforgivable, and this sets the basis for an extended discussion of forgiveness in the next chapter. The crux of this moral problem is human agency, that as we can choose evil, so too we can acknowledge that we have wronged someone, demonstrate remorse and change. I have argued that to deal with the past, there needs to be both an acknowledgement of wrongdoing by perpetrators and acknowledgement of the effects of the wrong on victims. The truth of atrocities is horrific, and memories influence what is subjectively remembered. There can be many versions of truths about the same interpretation of history and victimization. Listening to all stories is part of a serious consideration for peacebuilders. Truth matters and in the pauses of silence, profound statements are made, if we listen carefully.

6   Reconciliation and difference

There is no handy roadmap for reconciliation. There is no shortcut or simple pre-
scription for healing the wounds and divisions of a society in the aftermath of
sustained violence. Creating trust and understanding between former enemies is a
supremely difficult challenge. It is, however, an essential one to address in the
process of building a lasting peace.

(Tutu in Bloomfield *et al.* 2003: 3)

Understanding reconciliation

In many ways, the ideal of reconciliation brings together themes from the previous chapters: the importance of inclusivity and open dialogue, the need for fair
and just relationships and the importance of the recognition of differences. The
ideal also includes apology and forgiveness. Whereas forgiveness refers to the
past, reconciliation looks to the future. Whenever fear, anger, bitterness and
hatred has so accumulated that relationships are impaired, reconciliation is
required. Yet despite the term reconciliation being used widely, often it is not
clearly defined or understood. Reconciliation is needed to break down antagonistic relationships that exist because of polarized views. In many societies
recovering from conflict, different tensions, beliefs, interpretations of events and
incommensurate values remain about how to respond to these different tensions.
As we will see, reconciliation is a goal, ideal, principle and process that aims to
lessen tensions and rebuild relationships. While there are substantial differences
between Baghdad, Belfast, Belgrade, Cape Town, Colombo, Kabul, Kigali,
Mogadishu, Ramallah or Santo Domingo, there are some similarities in terms of
the long-term process of reconciliation, even though the path to reconciliation
differs for each society. Wilhelm Verwoerd is right when he says 'expect messiness' (2003: 264). Reconciliation is demanding, and the messiness comes from
dealing with fraught tensions, stressful relationships and aspirations to put aside
the factional disputes that have long divided a nation.

This chapter has four main aims. First, I begin by explaining a range of
different understandings of the concept and practice of reconciliation. Second,
I examine the central role that apology and forgiveness play in furthering
reconciliation. Third, I give examples of some significant practices of

reconciliation, with a particular focus on Rwanda. Fourth, I examine what it means to embrace difference, even to embrace our former enemy. Throughout these aims, I argue that, although it is immensely difficult, reconciliation is worth pursuing.

Diverse meanings of reconciliation

In this section, I aim to achieve three things. First, I outline some diverse meanings of reconciliation. Second, I stress the essentially idealistic nature of reconciliation. Third, I argue that reconciliation is an ongoing process. First, why is there such a diverse range of meanings of reconciliation? Particularly since the mid-1990s, there has been a striking increase in the use of the term reconciliation by governments throughout Africa, Asia, the Australia-Pacific region, Eastern Europe and Latin America, with some countries enacting legislation aimed at promoting reconciliation, others inaugurating TRCs and others establishing government ministries to promote reconciliation.[1] Jeremy Sarkin and Erin Daly write persuasively that reconciliation as an ideal 'is so easily invoked, so commonly promoted, and so immediately appealing' that few pay attention to what it means and how to achieve or promote it (2004: 664). The need for reconciliation arises after gross human rights violations, war rape, genocide, disappearings, torture, bombings and deaths have left relationships so twisted that people cannot find ways to work meaningfully together.

As we are saw in earlier chapters, there is a clear link between the need for reconciliation and a period of transitional justice that follows the disintegration of colonialism in some African, Asian, Caribbean and Pacific nations, or the replacing of military dictatorships in Latin American countries, such as in Argentina and Guatemala, the break-up of the Soviet Union, a move to self-determination in East Timor or the move from oppressive violent regimes moving toward embryonic democracies in Burundi, Democratic Republic of Congo and Sierra Leone. In all these places there is an urgent need to address the pain of the past and establish reconciled relationships. There is an extremely wide range of understandings of what reconciliation means and how it links to the other themes discussed in this book, such as truth, memory, justice and forgiveness. It is useful to say at the outset that there are limitations with reconciliation and times when it is not likely to happen. Whenever the past is based on several narratives of the meaning of conflict, 'where fundamentally different versions or continued denials about such important and painful events still exist, reconciliation may be only superficial' (Hayner 1999: 373). As we saw in Chapter 3, the more modest goal of coexistence can be achieved in places where reconciliation remains elusive.

John Paul Lederach articulates three working assumptions that undergird reconciliation. First, there is the 'notion that *relationship* is the basis of both the conflict and its long-term solution' (2004: 26; emphasis in original). Second, in order to address the past without getting stuck in a vicious cycle, 'engagement of the conflicting groups assumes an *encounter*' (2004: 26) which acknowledges the trauma of loss, grief and anger that accompanies pain, memory of injustices, experiences and validation of each others' stories. His idea of an encounter encapsulates the notion of a space where 'both the past and the future can meet' (2004: 27). This idea of a space that is fluid and contextual is useful. It signals movement, flexibility, cultural adaptability and a place where people come together. Third, Lederach writes as a self-confessed intuitive practitioner 'that reconciliation requires that we look outside the mainstream of international political traditions, discourse, and operational modalities if we are to find innovation' (2004: 27). Lederach's point, that the critical paradigm of reconciliation 'embraces paradox' (2004: 31), is of incredible importance to the argument of this book. Lederach suggests there are three specific paradoxes that reconciliation deals with. First, reconciliation is building in the space between the painful past and the search for a peaceful, hopeful future. Within the space, it is a refusal to let the past strangle the possibilities of hope. Second, he suggests that 'reconciliation provides a place for truth and mercy to meet' (2004: 31). In this place, people can tell their stories of what has happened to them and recount the pain, trauma and grief that they have suffered, but within the space there is also the opportunity to let go of bitterness, hatred and animosity toward the other in developing new attentive relationships. Third, 'reconciliation recognizes the need to give time and place to both justice and peace, where redressing the wrong is held together with the envisioning of a common, connected future' (Lederach 2004: 31).[2] It is interesting to note that, because Lederach understands reconciliation 'as a process of relationship building', he does not believe it is 'limited to the period of postsettlement restoration' but is relevant to every stage of peacebuilding (2004: 151). This understanding is important in affirming my argument.

There are cultural differences in the meanings and practices of reconciliation. In many cultures, traditional conflict resolution mechanisms are used, such as cleansing rituals, customary trauma-healing, religious services and dramatization. In Bougainville, armed militants of the Bougainville Revolutionary Army and the pro-Papua New Guinea Resistance forces joined together for an exchange of pigs and shells and the symbolic breaking of bows and arrows (Maclellan 2004: 535). In some of the major peace agreements in Somaliland, the reconciling parties agreed to exchange 50 wives. The practice is symbolic. 'You give a daughter to someone you trust, honour and wish to maintain an interaction with' (Farah and Lewis 1995: 55). Particularly when there has been loss of life, the offer of a marriageable partner is a customary atonement. The point at this stage is not to question these customs. Ed Garcia (2005) points to significant cultural dimensions to reconciliation – in South Africa the notion of *ubuntu* signifies that 'humanity is intertwined' and thus reconciliation is 'part of restoring *ubuntu*' (2005: 37). In Rwanda, *gacaca* is the traditional participatory court system predicated on justice and national reconciliation. In East Timor, *lia nain* involves traditional leaders who are crucial in providing credibility in the Commission for Reception, Truth and Reconciliation. In Guatemala, many church institutions supported victimized indigenous women so that the atrocities of sexual violence were recognized in the interests of furthering reconciliation. Whatever the cultural form, 'reconciliation is about building a just peace and constructing a society where people are able to work effectively side-by-side in a common quest' (Garcia 2005: 37).

The connotations surrounding reconciliation are not always viewed positively. Where relationships remain antagonistic, Jean Bethke Elshtain's idea of being 'enclosed within a single sociopolitical frame and enfolded within a common political–ethical horizon' seems impossible to imagine, and people continue thinking that the majority 'of one's fellow countrymen and women are outsiders and enemies' (2003b: 59). Creation of a shared vision for the future is hampered where there is a minimal accepted common base for notions of history, definitions of justice or degrees of responsibility for wrong in places such as Israel and Palestine, Northern Ireland and Sri Lanka. Other issues confuse the pursuit of reconciliation. For example, in the Israeli–Palestinian peace movement, the strong involvement of women often is perceived as an impediment in 'projecting a "soft" image' (Hermann 2004: 52). Peace activists, particularly women, are 'blamed for being unpatriotic ("Arab lovers"), for neglecting Israel's national security, and for over-identifying with the enemy by accepting its historical narrative as legitimate' (Hermann 2004: 53). In such a context, dialogue is 'viewed as fraternizing with the enemy' (Hermann 2004: 53) when the whole point of the dialogue is to bring down dualistic notions of friends/enemies, them/us.

In Australia, Mick Dodson, a prominent advocate on issues affecting Australian Aborigines and Torres Strait Islanders, criticizes the idea of 'practical reconciliation' as trying to ensure the good health, adequate housing and appropriate education of indigenous Australians. Dodson suggests that these do not lie at the 'soul of reconciliation. But they are, quite simply, the entitlements every Australian should enjoy' (in Gordon 2001: 106). Instead, Dodson suggests that reconciliation goes deeper, right into the 'nation, soul and spirit. Reconciliation is about the blood and flesh of the lives we must live together' (in Gordon 2001: 106). Part of the encounter with the 'blood and flesh' of Australia's past is grasping that (as I will develop more fully later), forgiveness clears the way for healing to begin. The words of an Aboriginal mother who was part of the stolen generation,[3] taken away from their communities, are written on a sculpture in Adelaide, my hometown. They read:

> And every morning as the sun came up the whole family would wail. They did that for 32 years until they saw me again. Who can imagine what a mother went through? But you have to learn to forgive.
>
> (in Habel 1999: 41)

In exploring past losses and injustices, there is inevitable suffering as past pain is uncovered, and this is part of the complexity of reconciliation. This woman's urge to forgive never ceases to move me as I stand and read her words. Donald Shriver talks about the relationship between practising 'a just forgiveness and a

forgiving justice' (2003: 28). This understanding breaks down dualistic limitations of either justice or forgiveness. As Miroslav Volf expresses it, 'forgiveness
is not a substitute for justice ... Forgiveness provides a framework in which the
quest for properly understood justice can be fruitfully pursued' (1996: 123).
When justice is not linked with forgiveness it might remove collective resentments and condemnations, but fail to establish fair inter-group relationships, so
the potential for further conflicts hovers.

   I turn now to the second part of clarifying the meaning of reconciliation, and
explain its idealistic nature. Reconciliation is normative, it expresses an ideal of
how relationships should be. Luc Huyse distinguishes between the ideal of
reconciliation in terms of personal healing, reparation of past injustices, rebuilding non-violent relationships and developing a common vision, and the fact that
'in practice such all-encompassing reconciliation is not easy to realize' (2003a:
19). Andrew Rigby also talks of 'a culture of reconciliation', which is more than
simply a symbolic nod to the values of peace, truth, justice and forgiveness and
actually means something in the everyday lives of people – that is, the values are
actually 'embodied and lived out in new relationships between people at all
levels of society' (2001: 189). The space of encounter is meaningful. Alex
Bouraine stresses that if reconciliation is to be successful, it 'must affect the life
chances of ordinary people' (2005: 330) and what often hinders this is 'the
silence or the denial of political leaders concerning their own responsibility and
the failure of the state' (2005: 331). For many, the ideal is too hard, unrealistic
or the excuse is given that the people are not ready for it.

   Norman Porter defends a 'version of strong reconciliation' (2003: 12), which
admits to the difficulty of achieving it; indeed, writing specifically in a Northern
Irish context, he calls reconciliation 'the elusive quest'. Porter argues that as a
moral and political ideal, 'it makes demands on how we live and think as social,
political and cultural beings' (2003: 12). He explains the features that 'are constitutive of reconciliation: the activities of engagement and embrace, a spirit of openness, and the goals of healing division, defining common purposes and expanding
horizons' (2003: 70). He argues that reconciliation requires three main things:

> (1) it requires *fair interactions* between members of opposing groups; (2) it
> requires that we overcome our antagonistic divisions by occupying *common
> ground*; and (3) it requires the presence of society in which all citizens have
> a sense of *belonging*.
>
> (Porter 2003: 94–95)

His use of the terms 'embrace' and 'engagement' imply non-instrumental fair
interactions which do not take any short cuts to achieve the goals of reconciliation. They imply 'that reconciliation is a morally taxing ideal' which is distorted by relationships that are utilitarian, calculative, masquerade the true
intent, dupe opponents or do not demonstrate 'parity of esteem' (2003: 103). He
argues that the ideal of 'strong reconciliation' is difficult but worth pursuing. In
this chapter, I defend this ideal.

Part of the compelling nature of reconciliation is that 'it not only implicates the worst that human beings are capable of, but the best as well' (Sarkin and Daly 2004: 664). As argued in the previous chapter, human nature is capable of evil but also of change and generosity of spirit. Thus reconciliation has the potential to transform hatred into forgiveness, trauma into survival and conflict into peace. Within all of us there is the possible 'spewing forth of harm, on the one hand, and the capacity to contain, or redress it, on the other (Prager 2003: 21).[4] Reconciliation has diverse understandings. Reconciliation is a demanding but valuable ideal. I proceed now to the third clarification, reconciliation is an ongoing process.

Reconciliation as a process

Reconciliation is a process and different writers and practitioners stress different aspects to this process – governing principles, goals, stages, strands and the psychological changes needed to move into what I call 'reconciliatory spaces'. Norman Habel (1999: 24) talks about three governing principles of the reconciliation process: truth, justice and identity principles, the forgiveness factor and the suffering dimensions. The truth principle (as explained in the previous chapter) involves the aggrieved telling their story and those responsible for harm conceding their part in the story. This principle accepts that there can be no reconciliation while stories are suppressed. The justice principle (as explained in Chapter 4) 'requires that past injustices, losses and evils inflicted on the weaker party are addressed by a mutually agreed procedure' (Habel 1999: 37). The identity principle (as explicated in Chapter 3) 'asserts that the cultural identity of both parties in a conflict, especially that of the oppressed party, is to be valued equally and not negated as alien or "other"' (Habel 1999: 39). Similarly, David Bloomfield suggests that reconciliation is both 'a *goal*' and 'a *process*' needed to achieve the goal (2003: 12). He goes on to define it as a process which includes the pursuit of truth, justice, forgiveness and healing in order 'to live alongside former enemies' and 'develop the degree of cooperation necessary to share our society with them' (Bloomfield 2003: 12).

The process of reconciliation is not linear and its starting point varies. It might be at the negotiating table, or when perpetrators are indicted and prosecuted, or when there is the release of political prisoners, or the acceptance of a new constitution or free and open elections for all (Bouraine 2005: 330). Huyse suggests three main stages are necessary for lasting reconciliation. First, fear must be replaced by 'non-violent coexistence between the antagonist individuals and groups' (Huyse 2003a: 20). In different places, this means different things. It may mean looking for alternatives to revenge, or when both victims and perpetrators free themselves from the potential for self-pity. Second, when fear no longer rules, 'coexistence evolves towards a relation of trust' (Huyse 2003a: 20) whereby victim and offender can grow gradually confident in dealing with each other. Institutions and structures such as an impartial judiciary, a well-functioning legislative structure and active civil society are necessary to the transition from violent conflict to sustainable peace. Much of the trust-building happens through informal contexts. Third, (as already alluded to in earlier chapters) reconciliation must be supported by democratic values that ensure human rights, economic justice and the honouring of political commitments.

Brandan Hamber and Gráinne Kelly suggest that the reconciliation process generally involves five interwoven strands:

* developing a shared vision of an interdependent and fair society;
* acknowledging and dealing with the past;
* building positive relationships;
* significant cultural and attitudinal change; and
* substantial social, economic and political change.

(2005a: 28; 2005b: 190)

They acknowledge the process to be long-term, unpredictable and containing paradoxes and contradictions that are integral to the building of democratic processes. The contradiction between rival notions of justice and how to assess the impact of reconciliation is one example of complexity. Immediately after a conflict it is important to establish personal security and the rule of law. When those enforcing security are not trusted, community leaders often 'present initiatives as "community justice" such as clan leaders in Somalia, the Local Peace Committees in South Africa and paramilitaries in Northern Ireland' (Pankhurst 1999b: 250). Donna Pankhurst points out that when this occurs, existing power structures are strengthened through violence capitulating to the issues that were part of the conflict, and 'this commonly perpetuates a high tolerance of violence against women' (1999b: 250).

The process toward reconciliation goes through emotive stages. Carlos Sluzki (2003: 23) suggests that in conflict there is hostility, contempt and elation; with coexistence there is resentment, anger and mistrust; with collaboration, ambivalence; when there is cooperation, there is cautious empathy; in an interdependence stage there is acceptance of the past and cautious trust; and in an integration stage, there is solidarity and friendly trust. The whole process of reconciliation thus entails a progressive psychological shift of dominant narratives from victimization to empowerment. Bringing together former enemies and defusing enemy imaging involves delving deeply into emotional baggage. Daniel Bar-Tal and Gemma Bennink maintain that psychological changes need to take place for reconciliatory processes to begin. These changes are not linear in having a beginning or ending and effective processes proceed from both the top and bottom simultaneously. Bar-Tal and Bennink (2004: 28) include a wide range of activities that contribute to reconciliation processes, such as apology (acknowledgement, addressing past injustices/grievances), TRCs, public trials, reparation payments, writing a common history, education, media, publicized meetings between various groups, the work of NGOs, joint projects and cultural exchanges. They suggest there are six significant factors that affect the reconciliation process:

* the peaceful resolution of conflict;
* conciliatory acts of goodwill;

- the determination of the leaders involved in peacemaking and the trustful relations that they build;
- the activism and strength of those who support the process;
- mobilizing society's institutions of politics, the military, society, culture, and education; and
- the contribution of the international community[5].

(Bar-Tal and Bennink 2004: 35–36)

As we saw in earlier chapters, differences of belief, opinion, ideology, religion and ethnicity often cause or trigger violence. As noted, many view the process of reconciliation as part of democratic processes. Democracy, with its principles of equality, representation, participation and accountability, is a form of governance that enables differences to be expressed through debate, disagreement, argument, compromise and cooperation without recourse to violence. After negotiated settlements, former enemies with long histories of 'antagonism, distrust, disrespect and, quite possibly, hurt and hatred' (Bloomfield 2003: 11) face the challenge of implementing newly negotiated structures together. This is not easy. The challenges are great. The pressing need is to address the tensions that act as barriers blocking reconciliation in order to prise open reluctant reconciliatory spaces. I agree with Bloomfield, who suggests that there is both a moral case 'that reconciliation is the right thing to do' and 'also a powerful pragmatic argument to be made' (2003: 11) because positive relationships will enable governments to thrive. I have outlined some diverse understandings of reconciliation, explained its idealistic nature and outlined different views on processes of reconciliation. I have maintained that despite its challenges, the benefits in opening what I am calling 'reconciliatory spaces' are immense in a personal, national and political sense.

Amnesty

In exploring whether amnesty contributes to reconciliation, I return necessarily to some issues already introduced in Chapter 4. Despite admirable ideals in reconciliation, this is not always what the people want, particularly if they perceive that the price of reconciliation is amnesty and justice is not being done. Now it is possible to argue that if reconciliation is such a positive ideal, ultimately such fears are misguided. However, this would be to dismiss people's fears in a way that does not take their emotions and desires seriously. Fiji is a good example. The Fijian Reconciliation, Tolerance and Unity Bill 2005 provides for the establishment of a Reconciliation and Unity Commission and a Promotion of Reconciliation, Tolerance and Unity Council.[6] The Bill is based on the principle of restorative justice in order to grant reparation to the victims of gross violations of human rights and civil dignity. The reparation aims to avoid vengeance, retaliation and victimization between victims and offenders and their families and thereby restore human dignity within the community through understanding, reparation and forgiveness. On all appearances, these seem to be

eminently worthwhile aspects of a bill. However, during 2005 there were many
objections to the Reconciliation Bill, including from women's groups who
feared that it appeared to grant amnesty to the perpetrators of the 2000 coup, and
thus support for the Bill seemed to threaten the future stability of the country.
The concept of restorative justice is not new within indigenous cultures including in Fijian culture. Within traditional Fijian culture, there must be prior agreement between the perpetrators and the victims in order to avoid a unilateral
approach by the perpetrator that could lead to rejection, shame or simply deep-
ening of the injury to the victim. There must be an acceptance by the perpetrator
that a serious wrong has been committed which has damaged relations between
individuals, families and their communities. Such an admittance occurs at a
reconciliation ceremony, where forgiveness is requested from the victims and
reparations offered. The consultation in agreement with the victims is vital.
Many community groups and women's groups maintain that the Reconciliation
Bill makes the mistake of avoiding this crucial dimension to traditional Fijian
practices on restorative justice. The voice of victims must be accorded central
place in processes of restorative justice for there to be healing and reconciliation. The military opposed the Bill. In 2007, reconstruction work is needed
after the 2006 military coup.

In Rwanda, a general amnesty was out of the question for the Government of
National Unity, given the extent of the horrors of genocide and the strong
feeling that those responsible should be held accountable for their acts in order
to eradicate the culture of impunity, uphold principles of punishment for crimes
and reinforce a respect for law. In the East Timor Commission for Reception,
Truth and Reconciliation, exploring human rights violations committed on all
sides between 1974 and 1999, there was no amnesty. Its goals are truth-seeking,
community reconciliation and recommendations to government for further
actions needed to promote human rights and reconciliation. The Lomé Peace
Agreement, signed between the Government of Sierra Leone and the Revolutionary United Front, provided for a TRC enacted in law in 2000. An amnesty
offered in the Agreement means that some of the perpetrators of gruesome
crimes are free and victims will not be compensated. Justice is a precondition for
reconciliation. Where victims are denied justice, some seek retribution. The
TRC is not a court, it is a place where people say what they know, experienced,
did and saw. Truth processes are aimed at restoring the human dignity of victims
in promoting reconciliation.

The Commission on the Truth for El Salvador had a broad mandate to investigate serious acts of violence committed since 1980, and issued its report on the
12-year civil war in the country in 1993. Five days after the report was issued,
the government passed legislation granting amnesty to those named in the
report. In such an instance, amnesties discredit attempts at uncovering the truth
and do little to further reconciliation. The Law on the Establishment of the
Extraordinary Chambers in the courts of Cambodia (2001, amended 2004) limits
prosecutions to the senior leaders of the Khmer Rouge who were most responsible for committing serious crimes. This means that only a small number of

people fell within this remit to be tried and the justification for this is that it would facilitate justice, truth and national reconciliation. To many, this is a limited notion of reconciliation.

The situation in Algeria is a concern. During the 1990s there were more than 200,000 deaths and 8,000 disappearances and 'for most Algerians, including moderate Islamists, the conflict was not a civil war, which is an idea too painful to articulate, but *le terrisme*: armed insurgents against the state and those that the state had armed for self-defence' (Kristianasen 2006). In 1999, a civil harmony law offered reduced sentences or immunity to the members of armed groups who surrendered their arms and disclosed their activities. In 2005, there was a referendum based on a simple proposition: were people for or against peace? There was an overwhelming 98 per cent approval. Yet, despite this, there is fierce opposition to the new Charter for Peace and National Reconciliation.[7] The new law grants amnesty to state-armed militias and those members of armed groups who surrender. Human rights activists are suggesting that this evades international obligations. Victims associations, many headed by women and including those in the Algerian diaspora, have organized to seek truth about the disappearance and abduction of relatives.[8] Most victims whose husbands or brothers were kidnapped know the names of the men who kidnapped them. These women do not have the status of widow because the body has not been found, thus it is impossible for them to come to an emotional acceptance of the truth. In such a context, the new Charter seems to pass over this trauma in silence. Many women have taken up the challenge to struggle for urgent social reform. Fatima Oussedik writes, 'the transition is deep and painful because we have lived through so much violence. We need to deal with that before we can have any sort of amnesty: it is directly linked to truth and justice' (in Kristianasen 2006). Oussedik's fear is that without this debate, Algeria will remain an authoritarian society. It is only in understanding the context that outsiders can understand why women may be in opposition to the President's Charter for Peace and Reconciliation. A reconciliation that slides over truth and justice will be only superficial and thus fragile.

Apology and forgiveness

I have clarified some understandings of reconciliation as an ideal and a process and have advocated the importance of creating open, reconciliatory spaces. It is now important to explore the roles that apology and forgiveness have in furthering reconciliation. In this section, I make four key points. First, in order to understand the rich dimensions to forgiveness, I offer a range of understandings and suggest that it is meaningful within moral boundaries where there is a continuum of degrees of wrongdoing from minor offences to evil. A reluctance to forgive and a desire for revenge is complex and must be explained in the context of the gravity of harm suffered. Second, I explain how, in order for there to be a chance to forgive, generally an apology precedes forgiveness. Third, forgiveness is not required for healing to occur, but certainly assists the process. The examples used will concern individuals, so fourth, I explore the relational aspects to political forgiveness.

While it is often assumed that the concept of forgiveness is Christian, it is also present in Hebrew, Islamic, Confucian and Buddhist traditions. Each culture and religious tradition has varied rituals for confession, apology, acknowledging forgiveness and absolving wrongdoers. For example, Christian sources still call on suffering and the redemptive power of forgiveness, Jewish sources look to Talmudic restoration and repair, in Africa, traditional variations of community repair build on some variation of *ubuntu* and indigenous cultures rely on variations of restorative justice to renounce the harmful act but not the offender. The concept of boundaries of forgiveness has crucial moral implications in defining cultural norms and shared expectations of protection against harm and security. I argue that the boundaries delineate what can be forgiven and what should be forgiven, but they are shifting boundaries, dependent on the nature of the wrong, the person wronged and the social, cultural, religious and political moment of harm. To extend my argument, they also indicate areas where reconciliatory spaces are unlikely to open and where they surprisingly open.

Where do the boundaries of forgiveness lie? We examined evil in the previous chapter and I maintained the need to respond to evil without doing evil. War is an evil, qualified often controversially, as the lesser of evils.[9] To explore the moral boundaries, I begin with a woman's complicity in war rape, an act that is almost incomprehensible. At the time of writing Pauline Nyiramasuhuko, the former National Minister of Family and Women's Affairs in Rwanda, is on trial for genocide. She was 'reported to have ordered soldiers to rape before killing' (Schott 2004: 206). In such a horrific instance, who can forgive such acts? Some suggest that 'there are wrongs suffered that can never be put right' (Elshtain 2003b: 49), particularly when people have been hurt so badly that they cannot bring themselves to consider forgiveness. It may be easy for those of us who have not suffered grave torment to pass judgement and expect others to forgive, particularly if an apology has been given. But we should be cautious in judging others and consider how we would respond if we too suffered dreadfully. The empathy of a politics of compassion may illuminate our response. Wrongs must be acknowledged with explicit articulation of awful details. Elsthain draws on Hannah Arendt's account of how young Germans who were infants in Hitler's time could not be held accountable for what occurred in their lifetimes, 'but they were obliged to remember in order that they could be free to act in other ways' (Elshtain 2003b: 51). Elshtain explains that this 'knowing forgetting' is to avoid Albert Camus' executioner or victim option and to posit instead 'an accountable human agent' (2003b: 51), responsible for evil but capable of transforming and reconciling relationships. I am sympathetic to this argument.

I argue that only those who have been harmed can set the boundaries of forgiveness. Anything else suggests patronization and fails to grasp the enormity of inner hurt. There are many astonishing instances of victims thrusting these boundaries aside, breaking down the barriers of the unimaginable and choosing, against all odds, to forgive. In doing so, the victim is transformed into a survivor, a moral agent with some self-dignity restored, willing to explore reconciliatory spaces. I provide examples of individual forgiveness then expand the nature of apology.

We have discussed the boundaries of forgiveness and I have suggested that there are exceptional examples of people willing to break through the rigidity of moral boundaries. It is humbling to consider some of these examples. On 8 November 1987, Gordon Wilson's daughter Marie was killed in Northern Ireland by an IRA bomb. After her death, he was forgiving of his daughter's killers and conciliatory in response and frequently is upheld as a moral beacon. Such an act of forgiveness is a peace offering, what some call a gift. It is also a sign of resilience allowing those who suffer to continue everyday mundane tasks with dignity. Jo Berry was the daughter of Sir Anthony Berry, who died when a bomb planted by an IRA member, Patrick Magee, hit the Grand Hotel in Brighton on 12 October 1984, where the Conservative Party conference was being held. Its prime target was Prime Minister Margaret Thatcher. Jo Berry befriended Magee, seeking to understand his motives. On the first meeting Berry recalls:

> Patrick opened up and became a real human being. We shared a lot of his struggles and how he felt and the cost to him of taking a violent stand. He wanted to know the kind of man my father was. My 7-year-old daughter got me to ask him why he killed her grandad, and he was shaken.
>
> (in Smith 2004: 10)

When asked to reflect on the nature of forgiveness, Berry criticized any notion of forgiveness implying closure, saying that she wanted 'to be able to feel angry – so I prefer to say I can understand' (in Smith 2000: 10).[10] To restate, it is often anger that drives men and women to pursue justice, or in this instance, understanding.

In 2006, Archbishop Desmond Tutu hosted encounters between British soldiers and paramilitaries in Northern Ireland and the families of victims in a BBC television programme called *Facing the Truth*. The family of Dermot Hackett sat crying waiting for the appearance of former loyalist gunman, Michael Stone, who was committed for Hackett's murder. Stone did not apologize nor express feelings of remorse, but as he talked of his own grandchildren, he recognized that the man he killed did not get a chance to meet his own grandchildren. Clifford Burridge was a young soldier in Belfast who shot and killed Michael McLarnon. Michael's sister Mary explained what the death had meant to her family. Burridge asked for forgiveness but Mary McLarnon did not feel able to oblige. The programmes were controversial: some thought that it was inappropriate reality TV, highly emotive and very private. Others thought that the confrontation between killer and victims' loved ones was a powerful means of moving closer to healing through reconciliation. Some thought that Tutu was brilliant in facilitating healing. Others thought that Tutu was unhelpful in always assuming a Christian forgiveness.

There are other remarkable examples. Marie-Claire, a Rwandan genocide survivor, said: 'I have already forgiven the killers. God forgives, therefore we must forgive ... There is no one pressuring me to forgive the people who killed my family' (in Clark 2005: 182). Phil Clark argues that such notions of forgiveness 'should be understood as a gift which survivors bestow upon perpetrators' (2005: 277). It is an incredible gift. Clark's argument mirrors Jacques Derrida's ideas of the paradox of forgiveness, whereby 'forgiveness forgives only the unforgivable' (2002: 32). Derrida writes profoundly that 'the concept of the "crime against humanity" remains on the horizon of the entire geopolitics of forgiveness. It furnishes it with its discourse and legitimation' (2002: 30). Derrida emphasizes that forgiveness '*should* remain exceptional and extraordinary, in the face of the impossible' (2002: 32; emphasis in original). The boundaries of forgiveness are moral structures, albeit flexible ones. What Derrida is indicating is that 'monstrous crimes', those crimes that we would have classified as 'unforgivable', are becoming increasingly 'visible, known, recounted, named, archived by a "universal conscience" better informed than ever' (Derrida 2002: 33). I argued in the previous chapter that naming evil for what it is and claiming responsibility for evil is part of owning the truth of the past. In this chapter, I am maintaining that those who have been harmed can make choices to resist, to leap over or set their own boundaries of forgiveness. I argue that if a person is ready, forgiveness aids healing.

Apology

My first point made in this section is that there is a spectrum of wrongdoing and while forgiveness may depend on the gravity of harm, individuals may disrupt typical moral boundaries and forgive the seemingly unforgivable. Second, what constitutes a reasonable apology is enormously contentious and dependent to some degree on whether one is a victim, relative of a victim, the wrongdoer or a political regime. Apology requires much more than simply saying, 'I'm sorry.' Such a statement can be made easily without it having real consequence. Also, one can accept an apology without feeling compassion or a desire to reconcile. An apology is a moral act, but it is no simple solution for alleviating victims' sense of moral injury or restoring the damaged self-worth of the wronged person. 'The apology will never be genuine unless the apologizer understands the harm that has been done, recognizes her or his culpability in bringing about that harm, and actually feels sorrow for having done what she or he did' (Spelman 2003: 247). Elizabeth Spelman raises the important issue that it is important to learn what sort of 'harms to one's self entitle one to ask for or expect an apology' (2003: 247). This view is consistent with the boundaries of forgiveness outlined above. Spelman cites 'Aristotle's view that among the moral virtues young people must acquire is learning to be angry at the right people, in the right amount, at the right time, and in the right way' (2003: 251). As explained, anger need not be a negative or destructive emotion. Anger often is the passionate driver for a search for justice and restoration of dignity.

One well-documented case of apology is that of Winnie Madikizela-Mandela's exchanges in the TRC in South Africa where she was giving testimony that linked her to the kidnapping and murder of Stompie Seipei, a 14-year-old activist, and also to the murder of Abubaker Asvat, the doctor who treated Stompie. Initially, she was intransigent, denying all allegations of human rights abuses made against her, responding by saying that the accusations were 'ludicrous' and 'ridiculous' and that she had 'fought a just war' (in Krog 1998: 257). Tutu placed his plea to her firmly within the language of morality and the need to struggle 'to establish a new, a different dispensation characterized by a new morality, where integrity, truthfulness and accountability were the order of the day' (1999: 134). Tutu acknowledged her role in the history of the African struggle and reminded her 'that something went wrong, horribly, badly wrong' (1999: 134). Tutu pleaded with her to be more cooperative, particularly to acknowledge that something went wrong. Tutu begged her to apologize, to ask for forgiveness and looked at her directly for the first time. Madikizela-Mandela's response was:

> I will take this opportunity to say to the family of Dr (Abubaker) Asvat, how deeply sorry I am; to Stompie's mother, how deeply sorry I am – I have said so to her before a few years back, when the heat was very hot. I am saying it is true, things went horribly wrong. I fully agree with that and for that part of those painful years when things went horribly wrong and we were aware of the fact that there were factors that led to that, for that I am deeply sorry.
>
> (in Tutu 1999: 135; see also Digeser 2001: 144–145)

After this response, Tutu adjourned the hearing. It was a highly emotionally charged moment. Digeser (2001: 145) points out three significant things with her statement: it shows an element of taking responsibility, some willingness to show humility and it meets the minimal threshold of justice. Whether the family and friends of the two murdered people perceived this as such is another matter. Krog points to the importance of Tutu instinctively latching onto her 'culture of clan honour and shame'; by begging her publicly, he was honouring her as an equal because 'in the culture of honour, you are answerable for your honour only to your social equals' (1998: 260).

Forgiveness and healing

So far, I have explored some different ways to understand forgiveness and the role of apology. The third aim of this section is to clarify further the degree to which forgiveness assists healing. Before doing so, it is pertinent to ask, 'why forgive?', particularly in times of what Elshtain calls, 'contrition chic' (2003b: 45) where public figures offer forgiveness for acts committed in history. Elshtain explains that forgiveness implies a relationship, that it is 'about the creation of a new relationship or order of things, the restoration of an order of things, or the healing of a relationship that has been broken apart or torn by violence, cruelty, or indifference' (2003b: 47). So what happens in forgiveness? How does forgiveness assist healing? When there is personal injury, forgiveness allows the chance 'to reconnect and recognize the common humanity of the other' (Minow 1998: 14). Minow reiterates that forgiveness does not take the place of punishment, neither is it a substitute for justice, but 'in practice forgiveness often produces exemption from punishment' (1998: 15). The relationship dimension of forgiveness is central to healing within a politics of compassion.

Forgiveness is complex. Claudia Card suggests that a paradigmatic case of forgiveness has five features:

• renunciation of hostility;
• compassionate concern for the offender;
• acceptance of the offender's apology and contrition;
• remission of punishment; and
• renewal of a relationship or acceptance of the other.

(2004: 213; 2002)

If each feature is realized, forgiveness leads to healing. Yet 'most atrocity perpetrators will not become contrite, apologize, and seek or even welcome forgiveness' (Card 2004: 213). The act of forgiveness does not justify the wrongful action. We are referring here to gross violations. In order to be meaningful, forgiveness must be sincere. Hence, 'forgiving is morally justified only if it is done in a way that preserves the conditions for the possibility of universal respect for any person as a moral agent' (Babic 2000: 90). Thus, Jovan Babic (2000: 93) separates forgiveness from mercy, suggesting that we can forgive without the wrongdoer being absolved. Tutu's book is aptly titled, *No Future Without Forgiveness,* where he argues that 'confession, forgiveness and reparation, wherever feasible, form part of a continuum' (1999: 221). Some ask if Tutu's emphasis on redemption and reconciliation, forgiveness and healing undermines justice and retribution. Minow's response is pertinent: 'Between vengeance and forgiveness lies the path of recollection and affirmation of the path of facing who we are, and what we could become' (Minow 1998: 147). We have the capacity for harming others and for healing.

Not everyone can or should forgive. The expectation that people will forgive is a form of cultural pressure and provokes duress. Victims struggling with the emotional confusion of hurt, bitterness, terror and anger brought about by conflict traumas can find an appeal to forgive the aggressor as untimely. 'Expecting a victim to cease resentment and condemnation can even be damaging and dehumanizing in the sense of adding the burden of guilt to one already carrying a heavy yoke' (Montiel 2000: 96 – 97). This can have the effect of further silencing oppressed people under the pretext of forgiveness. Robin Dillon argues persuasively that 'self-respect issues are at the heart of both not forgiving and forgiving oneself' (2001: 53). Where there is damaged self-respect, such as with a woman who has been raped in war, there is an understandable tendency toward deep shame, which often underlies the reluctance of raped women to testify. Dillon defends the Kantian ideal that all persons have equal intrinsic worth and thus 'are always worthy of respect, no matter what they have done. The recognition of this worth is the central moral value of self-forgiveness' (2001: 54). By 'forgiving oneself', Dillon implies that one can reach the state whereby one is no longer crippled by damning conceptions of oneself.[11] Sometimes forgiveness is warranted, particularly when it frees one from entrapment and self-dignity is restored. Sometimes, the evil of an act is so horrible that understandably, forgiveness is constrained. It is important to remember that forgiveness is not an automatic right, it is a gift from those who have been victimized. Only those who have been harmed seriously can offer the gift, and the motivation is sometimes simply a release, letting go of bitter hatred. Minow claims further that 'to forgive is to let go of vengeance; to avenge is to resist forgiving' (1998: 21).

Robin Schott suggests that empirical accounts of how victims move on do not necessarily indicate that forgiveness is primary to recovery. Other factors that may be more important include forming safe networks of interpersonal relations that allow the victim's 'remembrance, mourning, reconnection with the world' (Schott 2004: 207). Again, Schott is not undervaluing the importance of forgiveness in certain contexts, such as the woman who 'might need to forgive the child whom she gave birth to as a result of rape' in order to break the cycle of hostility and care for her child (Schott 2004: 208). This is a classic case of the ambiguity of moral relations. Rape, whether in Bosnia, Guatemala, Haiti, Nicaragua and Rwanda or elsewhere, destroys the sense of self-integrity and trust in fellow human beings. Forgiveness in this instance is curious, forgiving an 'innocent baby' for being the 'wrong ethnicity' or the 'wrong skin colour' may be necessary for a healing acceptance of her child.

Sharon Lamb (2006) is critical of forgiveness therapies that concentrate on the individualized psychological view of being a victim and erase the gendered context of politics and sexism which underlie the acts. Further, while many people who have suffered during times of war and violent conflict talk of themselves as being survivors, Lamb is critical of this notion of 'survivor', because she thinks it degrades the enormity involved in being a 'victim' (2006: 49). Like Thomas Brudholm, she argues that while 'anger can be self-destructive and paralyzing, it also can motivate and engage victims in struggles for justice' (2006: 55). Often it is justice rather than forgiveness that is the driving force toward healing. Instead of an individualized notion that victims should let go and unemotionally move on, Lamb calls for victims to surround themselves with other victims and sympathizers who provide warmth and understanding and whose support and solidarity give strength to fight further injustices within whatever group she belongs. Apology generally precedes forgiveness. As with so many other writers, Marina Warner places the potential of apology to 'restore dignity and spread forgiveness, by recognizing, as in *ubuntu*, the dignity and presence of the oppressed' (2002: 16). The key aspect to forgiveness that is relevant to the overall argument of this book is that it enables self-respect to be restored. It allows the raped woman, the tortured child, the grieving mother, the angry grandmother to come to the stage where they refuse to let their lives be dominated by victimhood, negativity, destructive thoughts and excruciating memories. The emotional release can allow people to move on. This is not a 'forgive and forget', a deliberate amnesia, but a 'forgive and be restored'.

Political forgiveness

The forgiveness discussed above is mainly personal, but there are many recent examples of political apologies. Warner (2002) writes about 'the apologist', the person who accepts responsibility for wrongdoing, takes the blame for injury caused and speaks of regret and all that is implied in this. There are many public apologies that have occurred. Ronald Reagan signed the Japanese–American Internment compensation Bill in August 1988; George Bush senior signed subsequent letters of apology and the cheques. In May 1997, Bill Clinton apologized for racism to African American men when treatment was withheld for syphilis; he apologized to victims of the conflict in Rwanda and to the people of El Salvador for American policies that were not his responsibility. Queen Elizabeth of the UK apologized to Maoris for the dispossession of land in New Zealand and in India for the massacre of Amrits in 1919. Tony Blair apologized for his country's role in the Irish potato famine of 1845–1851. The Japanese Prime Minister Tomiichi Murayama apologized for the suffering inflicted in the Second World War and there was a conditional apology for utilizing 'comfort women' in the Second World War. East German lawmakers apologized for the Holocaust. Pope John Paul II apologized for violence during the counter-reformation and offered partial apology for his church's role in the Second World War. The Canadian government apologized to the native aboriginal population for past government actions that suppressed language, cultures and spiritual practices. John Howard refuses to apologize in Australia to the indigenous people for dispossession of land and for creating a stolen generation of indigenous children despite Australians instigating and practising an annual Sorry Day.[12] Warner stresses the powerful point that 'in several languages, the word apology does not exist independently of the word for forgiveness' (2002: 4).

It is useful to assess the significance of political forgiveness. Donald Schriver writes, 'precisely because it attends at once to moral truth, history, and the human benefits that flow from the conquest of enmity', forgiveness has political ramifications (1995: x). Digeser (2001) develops useful ideas on the notion of political forgiveness as dependent on the demands of justice being minimally satisfied. He acknowledges the shortcomings of forgiveness in that while it releases us from the burdens of the past, it risks 'not taking seriously harms done' (2001: 12). He explains the potential of political forgiveness to be both 'part of a *process* of reconciliation that involves the restoration of trust and civility' and also part 'of a *state* of reconciliation' (Digeser 2001: 33; emphasis in original). As both process and state of reconciliation, forgiveness incorporates a shared account of responsibility, otherwise it risks being interpreted as an insult. Further, this account needs to be public, based on accessible evidence which can be defended and, if necessary, contested. The relationship between forgiveness

and reconciliation is reciprocal. Forgiveness may facilitate reconciliatory relations between parties that once destroyed each other, and reconciliatory political
acts may accelerate collective forgiveness (Montiel 2000: 99).

Yet, political forgiveness, like reconciliation, is undoubtedly a demanding
ethic. Political actors should confront their culpability, acknowledge the suffering caused and the truth of their acts, express remorse, be willing to offer reparations and accept punishment; and victims should refrain from vengeance,
express empathy and respond to forgiveness 'by reducing or eliminating the
offenders' debts or the deserved punishment or both' (Amstutz 2005: 5). This
relational aspect to political forgiveness is central to agency. Even wrongdoers
are 'morally responsible agents who are capable of change' (Amstutz 2005: 11).
Given the enormity of the issues of violence central to this book, this point is
worth stressing. Perpetrators of violence can change. To continue to call people
'terrorists' for activities engaged in the past hinders reconciliation. An apology
is meaningless without a social context. The power of apology enfolds through
the collective nature of the process of apologizing. As Minow (1998) explains,
the ways in which an apology is offered and accepted reflects and constitutes a
moral community. When Monica McWilliams was leader of the NIWC, she was
asked by some victims to approach combatants on their behalf. One woman
came to her office who 'simply wanted to know the last words of her husband
who was murdered in a case of mistaken identity by the IRA' (McWilliams
2006: 76). McWilliams facilitated an introduction to the political spokesperson
for the IRA who could not identify the perpetrator but was able to 'issue a
further apology on behalf of the organization' (2006: 76). She argues that structured processes could take cases such as this much further.

Again, the relational aspects of political forgiveness are crucial. 'Unilateral
forgiveness takes an unconditional form, an unsolicited gift given to the
offender. It does not require anything from the offending side, such as an
apology, remorse, or plea for forgiveness' (Kim 2005, 155). Sung Hee Kim
rightly warns that, while this might promote healing in the victim, it does not
guarantee 'healing in the *relationship* between the victim and the victimizer'
(Kim 2005: 156; emphasis in original) which is crucial for reconciliation. This is
important where it concerns tribes, clans or nations. In most areas where inter-
group conflict exists, antagonists live side-by-side and hence the practicality of
unilateral forgiveness is limited. In contrast, 'bilateral forgiveness is an interactive process that involves an exchange between the victim and the offender;
that is, the victim forgives in exchange for genuine contrition by the offender'
(Kim 2005: 156). This is the ideal space for apology and forgiveness to meet.
The victim can be freed from the desire for revenge and the offender freed from
shame and guilt. Where both parties are culpable, contrition is needed from both
sides. Similarly, Hannah Arendt argues that 'without being forgiven, released
from the consequences of what we have done, our capacity to act would, as it
were, be confined to one single deed from which we could never recover' (1974:
237). The relationship established between the one who forgives and one who is
forgiven is personal, although not necessarily private, 'in which *what* was done

is forgiven for the sake of *who* did it' (Arendt 1974: 241; emphasis in original).
Arendt's point is that forgiveness can break repetitive cycles of vengeance.

Practising reconciliation

I have established the significance of apology and forgiveness for reconciliation.
I have suggested the ideal is where both the perpetrator of violence and the
victim are freed through the interactive power of an accepted apology and forgiveness. It is useful now to turn to some practical examples of reconciliation. A
conspicuous feature of peacebuilding and reconciliation is novel, traditional
initiatives by women. For example, in the Pacific region in Bougainville, there is
a matrilineal tradition. The Inter-Church Women's Forum, along with NGOs,[13]
worked to address the impact of the conflict on women and this was instrumen-
tal in kick-starting the peace negotiations in the mid-1990s.[14] 'Mothers went into
the bush to attempt to bring their sons home' (Böge and Garasu 2004: 573). In
the Solomon Islands, women initiated a reconciliation and peace committee in
1999. As Sharon Bhagwan Rolls writes, in the Solomon Islands, 'a woman can
stand between two warring parties and challenge them by uttering words such as:
"Enough is enough. Stop fighting. If you continue to fight after my words, you
have worked over my legs"', which clearly is forbidden and thus fighting must
stop in order for negotiations to begin (in Shoemaker with Conaway 2005: 37).
This is very similar to the *Bangwe* project in the Great Lakes sub-region of Africa,
in Burundi, Democratic Republic of Congo and Rwanda, where the role of conflict
arbitration and families and village communities is left to women. 'Women have
the right to stand between the disputing brothers shouting *"bangwe"*, stopping the
fight and forcing the men to resolve the dispute peacefully' (Vlachová and Biason
2005: 211).[15] In Fiji after the May 2000 coup, women from the National Council
of Women maintained a vigil and provided a secure venue for dialogue. In Pacific
cultures, the public expression of peace and reconciliation is a central element of
conflict resolution and customarily women are seen as responsible for acting as the
go-betweens that lead to such resolution. Despite these important roles, the
significant contribution from the sidelines and discreet lobbying, women continue
to struggle to participate directly in formal peace processes.

Other novel examples succeed in creating reconciliatory spaces. *Athwaas* is
a group of Kashmiri Muslim, Sikh and Hindu women. *Athwaas* is a Kashmiri
word which means a handshake or holding hands as an expression of solidarity
and trust. The project is facilitated by the Delhi-based WISCOMP and grew
from the need to search for creative, inclusive approaches for conflict transformation in Kashmir. Kashmir is one of the most militarized regions in the
world. Manjrika Sewak, Programme Officer, WISCOMP tells how the journey
of this group began with a deconstruction of stereotypes of what it means to
be Muslim, Sikh and Hindu women. The *Athwaas* women first engaged 'in
extensive dialogues with one another to understand each other's contrasting
realities and divergent political perspectives' and then with 'conceptualized
peacebuilding initiatives following an intensive process of active listening with

a cross-section of Kashmiri society' (Sewak in Schirch and Sewak 2005a: 11). This is a practical example of the politics of compassion. The focus of its work lies at the interface of education, reconciliation and development. The work builds trusting friendships, cooperation and understanding through sustained dialogue. One of the most significant initiatives undertaken by *Athwaas* is the establishment of *Samanbals* in different parts of Jammu and Kashmir, sharing centres for women to express their trauma and hopes for the future. While the centres have practical activities such as literacy campaigns, income generation, capacity-building and trauma counselling, their main goal is the creation of a safe space for contemplation and reconciliation. Sewak stresses that the work of these women demonstrates an understanding of peace as more than the ending of violence; it includes the importance of listening to different perspectives, building a culture of coexistence and addressing the centrality of justice to social change (2005a: 12).

In 2000, the second Palestinian *intifada* had been raging when a young Israeli woman, Natalia Wiesteltier, telephoned the wrong number and started talking with an Arab living in Gaza. A tenuous bridge established and a project, 'Hello Shalom/Hallo Salaam', to encourage dialogue between Israelis and Palestinians developed. This grew into Families Forum, an organization of Palestinians and Israelis who have lost family members in the conflict. Their view of reconciliation is that it 'allows each side to transform precisely those views about the other side that lead to a self-perpetuating cycle of violence. This transformation creates trust between the two sides' (Barnea and Shinar 2005: 497). Underlying the transformation of beliefs is empathy for victims from the opposing side. Taking responsibility to rebuild society after conflict is enormous.

> How do you accept a son or daughter who may have tortured or killed? How do you deal with going back to your village when your neighbour fought on the side that killed your husband or raped your daughter?
>
> (Bennett *et al.* 1995: 16)

Rosaura from Nicaragua says, 'I almost didn't want to talk to the mothers of the other side because at times you feel afraid or remember your sons. I sometimes thought it could be this woman's son who killed my boy and I'd feel bad' (in Bennett *et al.* 1995: 16). Reconciliation is necessary because of terrible mistakes committed in the past, but it is possible because of the capacity of moral agents to transform.

Rwanda and Burundi

Rwanda provides insights into the connections between security and gender justice and provides useful examples of peacebuilding and reconciliation. Between April and July 1994, Rwanda experienced one of the most shocking genocides in modern history where 'nearly three-quarters of the total Tutsi population were murdered and hundreds of thousands were exiled to neighbour-ing countries' (Clark 2005: 11–12). Rwandans murdered Rwandans. Atrocious rapes occurred, sometimes by a man who had murdered a woman's husband and children. Almost every survivor of the genocide has a dramatic story. Victims were Tutsis or Hutu moderates seen as Tutsi co-conspirators. Women were victims of systematic violence during the genocide and faced rape, torture, cruelty, loss of livelihood, displacement, separation from family, food insecu-rity, destroyed social structures, severed traditional networks and psychological trauma. In the immediate aftermath of genocide, the population was 70 per cent women and girls who had to assume 'roles as heads of household, community leaders and financial providers, meeting the needs of devastated families and communities' (Powley 2005: 146). By the end of 1996, more than 1 million returnees had come back to Rwanda. Relief work transferred from the refugee camps to programmes to rebuild civil society. Humanitarian assistance was structured on the lessons learned in previous complex emergency responses. Rwandan women organized to form networks and local associations to support each other, and in their search for rights, challenged traditional gender roles and began to rebuild the country. By 1999, Rwandan women's organizations exceeded 15,000. The reasons for the growth are various, but after 1994 there was extra international support.[16]

For example, the 'UNHCR deployed the Rwanda Women's Initiative (RWI), modelling it on the Bosnia Women's Initiative, with the aim of mainstreaming gender perspectives while helping to rehabilitate a post-genocide nation' (Women's Commission for Refugee Women and Children 2000: 4). The initi-ative took strategic and practical holistic approaches to income, agriculture, land title, childcare and gender-related violence. The RWI adopted a holistic approach, strategic in combating discrimination and practical in attempting to meet basic needs. It worked across the country in partnership with grass roots women's associations and the Ministry for Gender and Women in Development (MIGEPROFE). The achievements of the RWI include: providing food, shelter and income to rural women; contributing to the development of Women's Com-munal Funds; developing responses to acts of violence against women; provid-ing a focus for adolescent girls; increasing the visibility of gender concerns; and promoting the role of women in politics (Baines 2001: 8–11). However, while there was a large injection of funds in 1997 primarily from the USA, by 2000 these funds had shrunk. While there had been a focus on capacity-building and working with local organizations, many grass roots groups were unable to manage their projects. The RWI was 'folded into the Imagine Coexistence Initi-ative', a project between the UNHCR and Harvard Law School, which 'seeks to promote coexistence among returning and local populations, rather than the more distant goal of reconciliation' (Baines 2001: 26). When Erin Baines asked a Rwandan woman if the initiative had made a difference in her life, she replied, 'you cannot dance if you cannot stand' (2001).

Suzanne Ruboneka is responsible for peace programmes in Pro-Femmes, the umbrella organization of women's groups which mobilizes women around issues of peace, tolerance and non-violence. It had to confront the consequences of genocide. Ruboneka acknowledged:

> We urged women to come together in spite of their differences ... in order to build our collective on what we had in common as mothers and citizens, rather than looking at what kept us apart. This way we could rebuild the country for our children.
>
> (Ruboneka in Omaar and Ibreck 2004: 15)

The post-genocide conditions fostered women's leadership roles, particularly as women-headed households. While some of these organizations are ethnically defined, many involve both Hutu and Tutsi groups, concentrating on what unites rather than divides. As one Rwandan woman said, 'boundaries do not separate the commonalities women face everywhere in this region such as poverty, violence against women, feeding their children and shelter' (in Baines 2001: 32). Boundaries do not prevent women from working together for common concerns. Elizabeth Powley (2003) suggests there is the perception among survivors of both sexes that, because fewer women perpetrated the killings, were jailed or viewed as corrupt women were more ready to forgive and begin the route to reconciliation. For many women, being agents of change in a country pursuing reconciliation means very practical things. 'They were the ones who picked up the pieces of a literally decimated society and began to rebuild. They buried the dead, found homes for nearly 500,000 orphans, and built shelters (Powley 2003: 13). Significant examples include those 'women whose relatives perpetrated genocide teamed up with women whose families were victimized' (Louise Mushikiwaboo in Enda 2003: 2). Many women have taken in orphaned children, including children whose parents had murdered their loved ones. This is an incredible gesture. It stretches moral boundaries. It makes what Norman Porter (2003) calls 'strong reconciliation' possible.

Democratic processes are necessary for sustainable peace that includes all voices in society. Such processes 'are not just philosophical ideals but are necessary mechanisms for reconciliation and the prevention of future violence' (Powley 2003: 14). The support of the UN, NGOs and other members of the international community has been crucial in empowering Rwandan women to push for political and legal reforms to increase their rights and access to land and inheritance, increase their participation in the legislature and judiciary and bring attention to women's needs in mechanisms for justice and reconciliation. Berthe Muukamusoni's life was shattered in 1994 but she asked, 'How long could I remain traumatized?', knowing that the survival of her eight children depended on her to earn a living. She became President of the National Women's Council in 2000 and then a parliamentarian (Women for Women International 2004: 11). Women such as Berthe in political and civic groups saw the window of opportunity in the drawing up of the 2003 Constitution, which integrated gender, provides full institutional mechanisms for women's political participation and to secure rights for women in matrimony and inheritance.

A pyramid system starting from the grass roots and winding its way up to the national level brings women into political processes and provides opportunities through which women can move.

Reconciliation after genocide requires the reconstruction of the moral and social basis to the nation. However, there are multiple divisions in Rwandan society: not simply Hutu versus Tutsi; there are divisions within these ethnic groups, between moderates and extremists, old and new refugees, urban and rural Rwandans and between intellectuals and grass roots policymakers (Hamilton 2000). The government established a National Unity and Reconciliation Commission (NURC) in 1999 to coordinate government efforts on reconciliation. At the age of 26, Aloisea Inyumba was the first Women's Minister after the genocide, the Minister of Gender, Family and Social Affairs, creating programmes for advanced coexistence and peace and directing a national adoption campaign for children orphaned by genocide. She later served as Executive Secretary of the NURC. She acknowledged the 'real resistance to the idea of reconciliation' (Women's Commission for Refugee Women and Children 2000: 3), defined 'in terms of political structures and poverty alleviation' (2000: 18), again, a broader practical definition than merely reconciling ethnic differences and healing antagonistic relationships. The NURC holds workshops, seminars and 'solidarity camps' to discuss attitudes towards ethnicity and traditional gender roles and to share personal stories. Her leadership was significant in giving women ownership of democratic processes. From the outset, NURC staff worked with MIGEPROFE to understand gender roles in development and peacebuilding. The NURC shaped its plan through grass roots meetings. These consultations then led to programmes in civic education, conflict resolution and community support.

The entrenched sectarianism and patterns of exclusion, which culminated in the horrors of the genocide, were so deep that western models of reconciliation that worked elsewhere simply were not feasible. Fatuma Ndangiza, Executive Secretary of the NURC said, 'for us, perpetrators and survivors had to continue living side-by-side ... Formalized, legalistic and elite driven' mechanisms would have had little relevance to the grass roots (in Nantulya 2006: 45–46). Consequently, 'Rwanda is one of the few African countries that has integrated traditional and modern peace mechanisms practically and holistically' (Nantulya 2006: 45). Paul Nantulya[17] lead an evaluation and impact assessment of the NURC. Unlike other post-war reconciliation commissions, the NURC does not have a strict mandate or a limited timeframe. Rather, its remit is to motivate reconciliation at the grass roots level, eventually transferring ownership to communities. Inyumba summarizes the Commission's role: 'in our experience, we found out that the people had to come first. The only thing they need is an enabling environment ... and once that is in place ... they will take up the reconciliation agenda on their own' (in Nantulya 2006: 47). The process adapted is *gacaca*.

Gacaca (literally 'grassy space'), in pre-colonial times was the traditional dispute resolution mechanism conducted outdoors, mediated by members of the community (*Inyangamugayo*) who exhibited exemplary virtues of courage, honour, justice and truth. *Gacaca* reflects the need for justice and reconciliation to be linked to accepted traditions. The *Inyangamugayo* are selected by the community on the basis of their leadership and adherence to truth, fairness and justice. During the *gacaca* service, there is an insistence on 'unhindered and participatory dialogue in seeking out truth' (Nantulya 2006: 47). Nantulya explains the traditional tools adopted by the NURC. *Ingando* refers to the attempt to halt normal activities in order to find solutions to national challenges, and the NURC uses it as problem-solving retreats for different groups of people such as refugees, demobilized soldiers, youth, traders, prisoners, those with disabilities, community leaders and survivors. Mediation committee members (*Abunzi*) mediate conflict between parties and only when this fails are disputes brought before the courts. *Abakangurambaga* are peace volunteers who are selected from within communities to solve basic problems, and address wider social conflicts which are not part of the remit of the *Abunzi*. *Ubudehe* is again based on traditional practices of encouraging communities to be involved in their own welfare through consultation and dialogue. Community-based reconciliation associations are emerging, with one of their prime motivations addressing 'poverty as one of the impediments to meaningful reconciliation' (Nantulya 2006: 48). Today's *gacaca* courts, while controversial for fear that the guilty will be freed, 'is a participatory model of restorative justice designed not only to accelerate the judicial process, but also to further reconciliation at the community level' (Powley 2003: 25). While women traditionally were not *Inyangamugayo*, women's participation as judges has been promoted. UNIFEM have facilitated the training of judges on issues of gender justice.

In modern use, 'in the face of extreme individual and social devastation, *gacaca* represents a brave attempt to involve the entire population in the processes of justice, reconciliation and post-genocide reconstruction' (Clark 2005: 4). Philip Clark's fieldwork in Rwanda is one of the first detailed accounts of how *gacaca* operates based on his 'personal observations of *gacaca* hearings, focusing on the population's active involvement in the institution and the key external social, cultural, legal and political factors that influence it' (2005: 6). He argues that the six key concepts which embody the main aims of *gacaca*, are 'reconciliation, peace, justice, healing, forgiveness and truth' (Clark 2005: 26). Clark suggests that reconciliation is crucial to the rebuilding of social relationships and is foundational for the positive reconstruction of social relations of conflict. He argues that contrary to dominant defences of *gacaca*, its primary objective is not to punish perpetrators but to reconcile perpetrators and survivors (2005: 78). He reflects on women's participation:

> My observations from *gacaca* hearings show that women in particular have participated readily in *gacaca*, which few critics predicted given the lowly social and political status afforded to women in most communities before *gacaca* and the fear that the level of violence, particularly sexual, against women during the genocide would deter many women from participating in

gacaca. Women drive much of the discourse in the General Assembly; in the majority of hearings which I observed, women were the first to speak, often without prompting from the judges, and actively encouraged others to participate. Many women survivors told me that they were surprised at how freely they could participate at *gacaca* and how much they had benefited from communal discussions.

(Clark 2005: 368)[18]

At a trial in Kanombe, on the outskirts of Kigali, Nantulya 'was told of a case of a woman survivor who adopted the person who killed her family members and offered to pay his bride price as a gesture of reconciliation' (2006: 47). The generosity of the human spirit knows no bounds.

Despite these positive reflections on women's involvement in *gacaca,* the prosecution of the crime of rape is outstanding. As explained in earlier chapters, evidence of widespread sexual violence used as a weapon of conflict in the former Yugoslavia and genocide in Rwanda led to the establishment of the ICTY and the ICTR. Binaifer Nowrojee[19] talks of failures in that 'on the tenth anniversary of the Rwandan genocide, the ICTR had handed down 21 sentences: 18 convictions and 3 acquittals. An overwhelming 90 per cent of those judgments contained no rape convictions' (2005: iv). This is disturbing. Nowrojee interviewed Rwandan rape survivors, including some who testified as witnesses before the ICTR, to listen to the voices of the victims. To summarize, Nowrojee says that the women talked about the process of justice, their desire for information to make informed decisions on testifying, an enabling environment and following testimony, safety and protection from reprisal and stigma as well as access to AIDS medications (2005: 4).[20] Nowrojee's report shows that 'punishment and vengeance were astonishingly the least articulated reasons for why Rwandan women wanted and valued ICTR prosecutions of rape' (2005: 5). One young woman living on the outskirts of Kigali had been raped during the 1994 genocide, had contracted HIV and had made arrangements to care for her three young children following her death. When asked about her thoughts on justice and the ICTR, she responded:

For those of us on the road to death, this justice will be too slow. We will be dead and no one will know our story. Our families have been killed and our remaining children are too young to know. What happened to us will be buried with us. The people for whom this tribunal was set up for are facing extinction – we are dying. We will be dead before we see any justice.

(in Nowrojee 2005: 5)

As we have seen in previous chapters, the recognition of the wrongness of violation acknowledges the humanity of victims. Nowrojee's warning is strong: 'A reader of the ICTR jurisprudence will be left mistakenly believing that the mass rapes had little or nothing to do with the genocidal policies of their leaders. This is indeed a serious miscarriage of justice' (2005: 7). Again, I make the point that for many victims or survivors, the need for justice precedes reconciliation. For others, an understanding of reconciliation is not about forgiveness or even reconciling the perpetrator of violence and the victim but, as Rose Rwabuhihi, a Rwandan woman working with the UN asked, 'is there a way such that we can live together?' (in Hamilton 2000: 10). The promotion of national reconciliation or Rwandan unity (*Banyarwanda*) is complicated where 'the dilemma is that to be a Hutu in contemporary Rwanda is to be presumed a perpetrator' (Mamdami 2001: 267).

Reconciliation is disorderly. That is, 'in the wake of violence, on a societal scale, finding the right balance between justice and healing, retribution and forgiveness, tribunals and truth commissions, remembering and "moving on" is a messy' goal (Zorbas 2004: 30). As Tutu expresses it, 'reconciliation exposes the awfulness, the abuse, the pain, the degradation, the truth. ... It is a risky undertaking' (1999: 218). The messy risks of reconciliation involve compromises and going outside of personal comfort zones. A widowed Rwandan woman asked the question, 'how can I forgive, when my livelihood was destroyed and I cannot even pay for the schooling of my children?' (in Zorbas 2004: 37). Rwanda ranked 162 out of 173 in the UNDP's 2002 Human Development Index and thus 'poverty reduction is a key part of the answer to this' (Zorbas 2004: 37). The justice needed for many is practical – attention to everyday basic needs.

It is quite remarkable that in October 2003, Rwandan women won 48.8 per cent of seats in the National Assembly and nine out of 28 Ministerial posts and thus 'now ranks first among all countries of the world in terms of the number of women elected to parliament' (Powley 2005: 142). These gains for women are not a coincidence, they have arrived because of the specific mechanisms used to increase women's political participation, including the constitutional guarantee, the quota system and an innovative electoral structure. The Inter-Parliamentary Union assisted Rwandans on writing a 'gender-sensitive' Constitution. In 2000, a 12-member Constitutional Commission included three women. Judith Kankuze, one of these Commissioners, was allocated the role of 'gender expert', with her main constituency being the women's movement in Rwanda. The Constitution enshrines the commitment to gender equality, and the quota of at least 30 per cent of posts in decision-making positions. Funding from the Netherlands trained women in decision-making and political awareness. UNIFEM distributed an illustrated brochure on the 22 articles of the Constitution, which include references to women's rights and gender equality. In the Chamber of Deputies, the lower house of the Rwandan Parliament, there are 24 seats reserved for women to be contested in women-only ballots where women compete against women rather than feeling uncomfortable challenging men directly. A series of women's councils at grass roots level are elected at the cellular level by women only and this continues through sector, district, province to national level.

There is a Ministry for Gender and Women in Development and gender posts in other government structures. A Forum for Rwandan Women Parliamentarians brings together women from the country's eight political parties. The Forum reviews laws, amends discriminatory legislation, gender proofs proposed laws, liaises with the women's movement 'and conducts meetings and training with women's organizations to sensitize the population to and advise about legal issues' (Powley 2005: 148). One of the biggest spurs was the need to campaign for gender equity in new laws and, from 2000, the Law on Succession of Property allows women to inherit land. Interestingly, female ex-combatants from Rwanda sought a role in regional peacekeeping, highlighting their experience of warfare and its impact on women as a major advantage in efforts to bring stability to Africa. Since SCR 1325, Rwanda has moved into a developmental approach to peacebuilding, where gender equality is an important focus. UNIFEM is proactive in furthering security, gender justice and reconciliation. Yet there are enormous challenges with the *gacaca* process, where some women are reluctant to expose the truth of their rapes or try to protect relatives. Intense poverty remains, as does illiteracy, child mortality, patriarchal traditions, spousal abuse and minimal freedom to criticize the government, whatever one's sex. The lesson that local and international peacebuilders can take from this is the ongoing nature of the task, that peacebuilding needs to be continuous in order to heal deep wounds. Other lessons include the need to be attuned to early warnings of crises recurring and the urgency to develop local capacity for conflict prevention work.

Across the border from Rwanda in Burundi, women's organizations play a vital part in promoting reconciliation within their communities. These women's groups range from small cooperatives in local communities to state-registered NGOs. Again, the strategies used to build peace and reconciliation are practical issues that revolve around providing the basic needs of conflict-affected populations. In order to survive and organize for these needs to be met, central aspects to reconciliation are needed, such as building trust through cross-community dialogue, gaining legitimacy through networking and advocacy, building capacity and local knowledge on how to meet basic needs and mobilize resources to support peace work. Reconciliation within women's organizations is grounded in everyday experiences of communities recovering from conflict. As referred to in earlier chapters, women's organizations came together during the Arusha peace process to advocate for the inclusion of women's needs and interests, despite not being included as active participants at the peace table. The All-Party Burundi Women's Peace Conference in 2000 was held in parallel with the formal negotiations. The new Constitution passed in 2005 now requires 30 per cent of all decision-making posts within the government, parliament and the senate to be for women, and consequently women have made crucial gains in participation at high levels of decision-making (NGOWG 2006: 36).

The promotion of reconciliation within communities sits alongside this political participation. Dealing with divisive tensions between the Hutu and Tutsi communities is a major emphasis of many women's organizations. Additionally, these organizations work with refugee and displaced populations and ex-combatants on reconciliation issues. A woman's organization called *Dushire-hamwe* ('Let's Reconcile') aims to rebuild trust among communities and works towards fostering sustainable social integration of the victims of conflict.

Women exchange views and train leaders to act as community mediators. Dialogue breaks down divisive barriers. In telling personal stories, different understandings of the root causes of conflict emerge, as does the awareness of shared priorities that promote reconciliation. None of this is easy work. What remains are the traumas from past experiences, the lack of trust, ethnic tension and fear of reprisal in the community, particularly for ex-combatants and returnees. *Dushirehamwe,* in partnership with International Alert and Women Waging Peace, began as a training of trainers project in gender and conflict transformation in 1996. In 2002, *Dushirehamwe* strengthened its strategic value by establishing itself as an independent local women's peacebuilding association. '*Dushirehamwe* now works with 238 affiliated women's groups and community level, with 5,022 members based in 80 of the 129 districts throughout 13 of the 17 provinces in Burundi', reaching more than 10,000 women at the community level, linking the community and national political levels (NGOWG 2006: 38).

It is interesting to note that in September 2006, Burundi President Pierre Nkurunziza called on the UN and the Peacebuilding Commission (PBC) in particular 'to make gender equality a priority, emphasizing that his government regarded this as crucial to alleviating poverty' (NGOWG 2006: 39). What is significant about this plea is that it reflects the message made by women continually that peace, security and reconciliation must translate to provide basic needs. Women as prime carers within the community have the responsibility to meet needs heavily placed on their shoulders. Reconciliation is most certainly about restoring relationships; in many instances it is about building new relationships that have never existed. These relationships cannot happen on an empty stomach or when one's children are crying for food. There can be no reconciliation or the fulfilment of SCR 1325 where physical security and well-being is in jeopardy.

Embracing difference

It is antagonistic difference that underlies conflict. I end this chapter on a positive note. In reconciliation, embrace of difference humanizes the enemy, contributing to healing of self-dignity and national civility. For the idea of embrace, I draw on Miroslav Volf, a Croatian theologian who writes from his own experiences of the war in the former Yugoslavia. The metaphor of embrace is expressive.[21]

> *The will to give ourselves to others and 'welcome' them, to readjust our identities to make space for them, is prior to any judgment about others, except that of identifying them in their humanity.* The *will to embrace* precedes any 'truth' about others and any construction of their 'justice'.
>
> (Volf 1996: 29; emphasis in original)

Volf argues that *'the embrace itself –* full reconciliation – cannot take place until the truth has been said and justice done' (1996: 29; emphasis in original). Consider the symbolic importance of a gesture as a significant part of this embrace, such as the handshake between Yitzhak Rabin and Yasser Arafat at Jamal in

2000, or David Trimble's refusal to shake Gerry Adam's hand in Northern Ireland. Norman Porter also draws on the embrace, which 'primarily implies a mode of response to the fact that we inhabit a world of apparently ineliminable differences, one that signifies welcoming acceptance of, and participation in, this world' (2003: 104). The embrace signifies being open and viewing plurality as potential enrichment rather than threat. The embrace opens reconciliatory spaces.

The embrace affirms humanity, the global recognition of human rights. The UN Charter uses strong moral language reaffirming fundamental human rights, the dignity and worth of the human person, equal gender rights, justice obligations, tolerance, the need to live in peace and the importance of being good neighbours. Whether it is Auschwitz, Baghdad, Coventry, Dafur, Dresden, Free Town, Hiroshima, Kabul, Kigali, Phnom Penh, Pristina, Sarajevo, Soweto or the West Bank, there have been horrific occurrences that make us wonder how it is possible for humans to commit such acts of horror, torture, rape, violent assault and murder. Given such incredible inhuman acts, sometimes it is difficult to see the perpetrators of violence as human. The term 'crimes against humanity' is significant. Such crimes have their 'origins in the denial of the full humanity of the stranger, the nonrecognition of the other as a human being' (Rigby 2001: 190). How, then, is it possible to embrace the humanity of the seemingly inhumane?

Humanizing the enemy

We have seen that dehumanization is critical to war rape, ethnic cleansing, genocide and terrorism. However, recognizing humanity in the 'enemy', the 'other', provides a check to destructive ways of relating, it prioritizes a concern for welfare and security. It rarely comes easily. For there to be reconciliation between former enemies, some development of empathy must occur. Empathy involves the imagining of others' situations in order to understand the perspective of another person. In Chapter 4, I argued that empathy is a crucial feature of a politics of compassion where there is attentiveness to others' suffering, active listening to others' stories and wise judgements in response. Specifically, in facing the humanity of the 'former enemy', 'the major function of empathy is to individualize and particularize and thereby to challenge the major aspects of dehumanization' (Halpern and Weinstein 2004: 568). With this empathy, one is curious about others. 'Finding commonality through identification with a former enemy is a first step' (Halpern and Weinstein 2004: 567), such as recognition of mutual suffering, despite different reasons for grief or mutual anger, despite different explanations of injustices suffered. Jodi Halpern and Harvey Weinstein conducted extensive interviews[22] with people in Bosnia-Herzegovina and Croatia who were working together and living as neighbours, but they came to the disturbing conclusion that they 'could not find a single example of what we could term empathy' (2004: 570). This led them to ask whether people should be satisfied with coexistence. At least with coexistence, the killing ceases. To the contrary, they maintain that 'coexistence without empathy is both superficial and fragile, just below the surface is mistrust, resentment, and even hatred' (2004: 570). A Bosnian woman in a focus group in Mostar, 2002, says: 'We are all pretending to be nice and to love each other. But, be it known that I hate them and that they hate me. It will be like that forever, what we are now pretending' (in Halpern and Weinstein 2004: 570). However, not all stories are so negative. Dobrinka, a Serb, and Marija, a Croat, are both mothers who lost sons during war and hated each other during initial meetings in 1997. They were involved in a project trying to find those who went missing during the war in the former Yugoslavia. By 2002, Dobrinka says, 'We have come to a point of interpersonal tolerance. We can now get together and have conversations without hatred ... We are in the same because of our common tragedy' (in Halpern and Weinstein 2004: 578). Marija remains sceptical of friendship. Nevertheless, what enables these women to work together is what enables many people to work together, namely seeing enough humanity in the 'other' to recognize shared values and commitment to similar goals. The potential barriers to empathy are fear of the 'other', mistrust, dangerous stereotypes, feelings of betrayal, ongoing discrimination and yielding to pressure of an ethnic group, paramilitaries, warlords or terrorist leaders.

In testifying to the South African TRC, Cynthia Ngewu, the mother of Christopher Piet who was murdered brutally by the apartheid police, said:

> This thing called reconciliation ... if I am understanding it correctly ... if it means this perpetrator, this man who has killed Christopher Piet, if it means he becomes human again, this man, so that I, so that all of us, gets our humanity back ... then I agree, then I support it all.
>
> (in Krog 1998: 109)

As argued previously, those who have been harmed deeply sometimes find incredible inner strength to defy bitterness and forgive the unforgiveable, humanize the inhumane, confirming a common humanity. Ngewu explained her position as a mother:

> Anger comes and goes, but there's a point where you feel: this is another woman's child. What if he were my son? What would I have wanted his mother to do were my son in his shoes and he in my son's?
>
> (in Gobodo-Madikizela 2005: 22)

This empathy captures the full significance of *ubuntu*. There is little doubt that Desmond Tutu's reconciliation theology had a massive impact on emphasizing the need to humanize the enemy. Tutu says, 'you can only be human in a humane society. If you live with hatred and revenge in your heart, you dehumanize not only yourself, but your community' (in Krog 1998: 110). A visible example of the refusal to live with revenge was presented in Father Michael Lapsley, who laid responsibility for the bomb that caused his hands to be amputated and an eye to be lost on F.W. de Klerk. Krog writes that during Lapsley's testimony:

Several times the pincers move towards his face in a reflex action – as if he wants to cover his face with his hands – and every movement flashes the inhumanity of South Africa's past into the hall ... hard, shiny and sterile.

(1998: 133)

Yet somehow Lapsley could say, 'I do not see myself as a victim, but as a survivor of apartheid' (in Krog 1998: 133). Tutu drew continually on the idea of *ubuntu*. 'In the African *Weltanschauung* a person is not basically an independent, solitary entity. A person is human precisely in being enveloped in the community of other human beings, in being caught up in the bundle of life' (Tutu in Krog 1998: 110). *Ubuntu* encapsulates the essence of humanity. To praise someone as having *ubuntu* 'means they are generous, hospitable, friendly, caring and compassionate. They share what they have. It also means my humanity is caught up, is inextricably bound up, in theirs' (Tutu 1999: 34–35). A person with *ubuntu* does not need to feel threatened by others and knows that they are diminished when others are humiliated, tortured, oppressed or treated as if they are not human. This philosophy appeals to ancient African concepts of the relationship between individuals and the community and it has much to teach peacebuilders everywhere.

Humanization is a crucial part of reconciliation processes. While it is true that transforming gender roles is important everywhere, the goal takes on particular dimensions in societies coming out of conflict, where masculinized success is defined by force, power, domination, conquest and success in war. Alternative values such as consensus, persuasion, equality, cooperation and the peaceful resolution of difference seem foreign. Within war-affected areas, almost every group in society may be affected by trauma, either directly as combatants, having been injured or having lost loved ones; or indirectly through witnessing violence and transmitting hatred and an urge for revenge to the younger generation. The need for healing involves making 'bearable what has been unbearable' (Humphrey 2002: 9). Healing for many is a lengthy process. Brandon Hamber stresses that after extensive violence, healing is not merely about assisting individuals but also about repairing communities and 'restoring a normalized everyday life that can recreate and confirm people's sense of being and belonging' (2003a: 77). He suggests three broad principles to guide strategies that are aimed at healing. First, context is not an incidental variable, but 'should be the starting point when developing the healing strategy' (2003a: 80). Second, 'localized coping mechanisms and models of social and emotional resilience should be identified, supported and built upon where possible' (2003a: 81). Third, healing is part of broader reconstruction programmes and hence intimately associated with truth, acknowledgement, justice and socio-economic and cultural reconstruction. Hamber rightly emphasizes 'individual and collective processes of healing' (2003b: 162) so that there may be healing of individuals but not the healing of the nation, as is the case in many transitional societies moving from a violent conflict to a new future.

What does healing mean for girls and women who have been subject to sexual abuse during violence, forced to resort to prostitution when refugees or displaced persons, taken as girl soldiers or jungle brides or raped during armed conflict? Indeed, who wants to be reconciled with a rapist even if they were a former neighbour or teacher, such as occurred in the former Yugoslavia? Recognition is crucial and for many women, having their offences acknowledged, recognized as hurtful, as destroying self-esteem, and having resources allocated to deal with the psychological consequences of trauma are important dimensions toward healing. Practical assistance restores self-dignity, the humanization process generates new possibilities. For women who bear children through war rape, being accepted in the community and having their child recognized as a family member with full human rights may contribute more meaningfully to long-term reconciliation than having to initiate relationships with one's former enemies. These relationships might or might not come later. That is, the search for truth and justice may be more immediate than living alongside one's former enemies. For women-headed households and war widows, the practical aspects of inheritance of land and ways to fulfil their obligations as family providers assist reconciliation. However, in political processes, former enemies need to humanize each other to begin, maintain and sustain a new political era. Also, exceptional individuals demonstrate incredible instances of creating reconciliatory spaces where no one would have dreamed it possible – except for the unlimited nature of our moral capacities.

In this chapter, I have explained a range of differing understandings of reconciliation as an ideal and a process. I have highlighted the role of apology and forgiveness in facilitating reconciliation. I have argued that ultimately, it is those who have been harmed who can set the boundaries of forgiveness. This means that for some traumatized victims, forgiving the unforgivable seems impossible, while others are freed to offer this gift. The gift comes easier when a sincere apology is offered and is as valuable. Rwanda shows incredible examples of reconciliation. I conclude with suggesting that an embrace of difference can extend to humanizing enemies, but restoration of self-dignity is the first step. All this seems remarkably idealistic – and it is. When political compassion comes into play and the moral imagination is unleashed within us, we begin to create reconciliatory spaces that sustain peaceful security.

Conclusion
Peace with justice and security

> One of today's greatest development challenges is turning policy into practice.
> This is especially the case in the realm of women's rights and gender equality,
> where the commitments made at the international and national levels remain far
> from the day-to-day realities of women's lives.
>
> (Valasek 2006: i)

In this book, I have sought to articulate many of the theories that underlie the
concept of peacebuilding. What really is important are the practices of peacebuilding. Throughout the book I have provided examples of significant concrete
short-term and long-term programmes, policies and practices that build and
sustain meaningful peace. Women contribute to all the foundations on which
sustainable peace lies: security, governance, processes of justice, social and
community development, economic redevelopment and reconciliation. Importantly, women are crucial to conflict prevention strategies also. While it is true
that much more remains to be done to ensure women's peace with justice and
security, there has been significant progress in understanding the need for gender
equality and in advancing women's empowerment. In this conclusion, I return to
the merits of SCR 1325, assess its progress, particularly in increasing women's
political representation, provide an update on Afghanistan, East Timor and Iraq
and conclude with the remaining challenges.

This book is situated around the historical context of SCR 1325 (2000). Five
years on, NGOWG recommended the need to establish a Security Council
working group to integrate the resolution into the daily work of the Council
(Lynes and Torry 2005: 2). Few women know about this resolution, or know how
to use it to leverage change. Progress in some places is evident. What we have
seen is that, while women are absent from formal Track 1 (negotiations), they are
very active in Track 2 (civil society diplomacy) and Track 3 (grass roots
activities).[1] As demonstrated in the International Alert and Women Waging Peace
toolkit (2004) and in the stories of *1000 Peace Women* (Association 1000
Women for the Nobel Peace Prize 2005), peacebuilding often begins in civil
society groups where political skills are learned and could be transferred to
formal peace negotiations. There are countless examples of women's courage
across the globe.[2]

In 2006, in areas likely to experience violent conflict, there are women heads of state.[3] Gloria Macapagal-Arroyo is President of the Philippines, Khaleda Zia is Prime Minister of Bangladesh, Portia Simpson-Miller is Prime Minister of Jamaica, Luisa Diogo is Prime Minister of Mozambique and South Africa's Deputy President is Phumzile Mlambo-Ngcuka. Michelle Bachelet is Chile's first woman President, yet Chile has the highest rate of domestic violence. Ellen Johnson-Sirleaf is the first female President of Liberia and Africa, sometimes called 'Mama Africa'. Some campaign banners read: 'Ellen – She's Our Man'. For both Bachelet and Johnson-Sirleaf, a key to their victory 'was the power of maternal symbolism – the hope that a woman could best close wounds left on their societies by war and dictatorship' (Polgreen and Rohter 2006: 4). Unlike Margaret Thatcher and Golda Meir, these new leaders have embraced traditional feminine qualities and offer them as exactly what countries emerging from the heartbreak of oppression and strife need.

> On January 16, 2006 when Ellen Johnson-Sirleaf stepped up to the podium to deliver her acceptance speech as Liberia's President, she was not only making history as Africa's first elected female head of state, but she was to become the only elected African President of the country emerging from civil war to expressly recognize, in her inaugural address, the role women had played as transformers of conflict.
>
> (Williams 2006: 30)

Resolution 1325 'calls on all actors to incorporate a gender perspective into peacekeeping operations, and to ensure that where feasible, field operations should contain a gender component'.[4] Gender concerns are now raised in all new peacekeeping mandates and in 2005 there were full-time gender adviser positions in peacekeeping operations in Afghanistan, Burundi, Côte d'Ivoire, Democratic Republic of Congo, Kosovo (Serbia and Montenegro), Haiti, Liberia, Sierra Leone, Sudan and Timor-Leste. Security Council resolutions on peacekeeping operations exhibit strong condemnation of the violations of human rights in the Darfur region in the Sudan and express grave concern at the allegations of sexual exploitation and misconduct by UN personnel. In Burundi, the Council condemns the increasing incidents of rape and reaffirms a determination to bring perpetrators of such acts to justice by the rule of law.

Resolution 1325 encourages 'all those involved in the planning for DDR to consider the different needs of female and male ex-combatants and to take into account the needs of their dependents'. In Liberia, calls for the need to address violence against women and girls as a tool of warfare led to an induction training programme provided by the Office of Gender Affairs to peacekeepers to teach employees about the different concepts related to gender and effects of war on gender relations. In September 2003, the Security Council called for a DDR programme in Liberia that specifically included attention to the special needs of children and women. Additionally, some progress has been made in incorporating gender perspectives and age-appropriate DDR programmes to cater for the special needs of child ex-combatants, especially for counsel in the Democratic Republic of Congo, Sierra Leone and Sudan.

Resolution 1325 'calls on all States to end impunity and to prosecute those responsible for genocide, crimes against humanity and war crimes including those relating to sexual and other violence against women and girls'. In 2001, Peru established its TRC with the mandate to analyse the political context which allowed violence to take place. With UNIFEM's support, the Commission investigated the sexual violations of women during the armed conflict. In 2003, the Commission recommended that persons who were violated during the armed conflict and children born as a result of such violation should be entitled to compensation. This recognition restores human dignity. Similarly, in Sierra Leone, the TRC gave special attention to sexual abuse and again UNIFEM successfully lobbied for gender initiatives. A witness protection programme encouraged women to disclose gender-based violence.

There are many positive examples of SCR 1325 making a difference. The resolution 'calls for increased representation of women at all levels of decision-making'. In July 2003, the African Union adopted a number of successful milestones in the advancement of women's rights. It welcomed the election of five women commissioners; it adopted the Protocol on the Rights of Women in Africa to the African Charter on Human Rights and formulated policies to manage gender mainstreaming. The resolution also 'calls on all actors to ensure the full participation of women in peace processes and to adopt gender perspectives when negotiating peace agreements'. In June 2002 in Sri Lanka, the government and the Liberation Tigers of Tamil Eelam (Tamil Tigers), established a subcommittee on gender issues to elaborate gender-sensitive guidelines for the peace process, supported by Norway. In addition to calling for the full implementation of SCR 1325, women also recommended that both the government and the Tamil Tigers pay attention to:

- the substantive issues of violence and sexual violence;
- refugees and internally displaced women;
- the protection of the rights of women during resettlement;
- rights in the possession of homes, land and title;
- war widows;
- the families of detainees;
- the families of the disappeared;
- the families of soldiers;
- combatants;
- provision of food;
- housing;
- clean water;
- health care;
- education;
- trauma counselling;

- the economic and social rights of women; and
- trafficking.

Peace and security are multifaceted.

Resolution 1325 also 'urges Member States to ensure increased representation of women at all decision-making levels in national, regional and international institutions and mechanisms for the prevention, management, and resolution of conflict'. The proportion of women in national assemblies increased from 9 per cent in 1995 to almost 16 per cent in 2004, which is far short of the Beijing call for equality (UNRISD 2005: 147). In 2005, the top 15 countries reaching the 30 per cent critical mass of women in parliament were:

- Rwanda – 48.8 per cent;
- Sweden – 45.3 per cent;
- Denmark – 38 per cent;
- Finland – 37.5 per cent;
- Netherlands – 36.7 per cent;
- Norway – 36.4 per cent;
- Cuba – 36 per cent;
- Spain – 36 per cent;
- Costa Rica – 35.1 per cent;
- Belgium – 34.7 per cent;
- Austria – 33.9 per cent;
- Argentina – 33.6 per cent;
- Germany – 32.8 per cent;
- South Africa – 32.8 per cent; and
- Iceland – 30.2 per cent.[5]

There are no women in parliament in Bahrain, Guinea-Bissau, Kuwait, Micronesia, Nauru, Palau, Saint Kitts and Nevis, Saudi Arabia, Solomon Islands, Tonga, Tuvalu and the United Arab Emirates (in Zeitlin 2005: 17).

If we concentrate on the conflict situations, the proportion of women in national parliaments that have witnessed the biggest increase are in Bangladesh, Bosnia-Herzegovina, Cambodia, Croatia, the Democratic Republic of Congo, Ethiopia, Mozambique, Peru, Rwanda, Sierra Leone, South Africa, and Zimbabwe (UNRISD 2005: 252).[6] Inter-Parliamentary Union[7] figures from January 2006 have Rwanda topping the chart for women's representation at 48.8 per cent, with Mozambique at 34.8 per cent, South Africa at 32.8 per cent and Burundi at 30.5 per cent (in Williams 2006: 320). Eritrea, Namibia, Timor-Leste, and Uganda all have more than 22 per cent of women representatives. The statistics are not accidental. The percentage of women now active has occurred in the process of democratization with extensive practical support from the international community. Indeed, the constitutional drafting process introduced reserve seats in Rwanda, while in Mozambique and South Africa, political parties insured quota mechanisms. These political moves are significant in recognizing the importance of including women in reconstruction processes in transitional democracies through cementing women's participation as active citizens.

UNIFEM conducted extensive reviews of peace processes in Africa, Asia, Europe, Latin America and the Middle East in order to identify the key factors necessary to guarantee women's participation at the peace table and integrate gender perspectives into peace accords. Key factors include 'building a constituency of women with a gender-sensitive agenda', fostering an enabling environment with structures and strategies to support women and addressing women's priorities in peace agreements to encourage gender-sensitive implementation (Banaszak *et al.* 2005: 3). UNIFEM's work continues to provide practical assistance to different groups across the full range of gender equality issues in policymaking processes, which include gender-sensitive DDR programmes, support for women's special needs in economic, physical and psychosocial support, education and skills training and reproductive health care, and collaborating to end sexual violence in situations of conflict and displacement. Practical workshops emphasize the capacity-building of local women and the role of the international community and foster local leadership. While UNIFEM's support for women involved in peace processes translates into greater access for women in their respective transitional governments and provides avenues for constitutional reform, such interventions require sustained, long-term support. When support is removed or where the UN moves peacekeepers out too quickly, disorder may result and conflict erupts. Much of the positive work that has been built in reconstructive stages is lost. Sustained international support is indispensable.[8]

What, then, has happened in Afghanistan and Iraq since the terrible invasion and preemptive strike of the 'war on terrorism'? Resolution 1325 'calls on all actors to incorporate gender perspectives in post-conflict reconstruction efforts and to take into consideration the special needs of women and girls'. In December 2001, international organizations helped to host the Afghan Women's summit for democracy in Brussels. Forty women participated in a round table hosted by UNIFEM and the Belgian government. The Brussels Action Plan included recommendations on education, media and culture, health, refugees and internally displaced persons, human rights and the Constitution and informed the UN Transitional Assistance Programme for Afghanistan in 2002 (Rehn and Johnson-Sirleaf 2002: 80). In Afghanistan, women were involved in the drafting of the new Constitution. The Afghan Constitution was adopted on 4 January 2004 and provides for equal rights before the law. This explicit recognition of the rights for women and men is a major advance, given the efforts by Islamic fundamentalists to dismiss international treaties and laws. However, serious obstacles to equality remain. In the September 2005 elections in Afghanistan, Afghani women made up 43 per cent of voters. There were more than 600 women candidates for the 68 seats (from a total of 249) guaranteed to women under the Afghan Constitution. President Hamid Karzai appointed three women Ministers to his Cabinet, including a Minister of Women's Affairs. Women's representation seems very positive, but decades of repression have left Afghanistan scarred. Particularly within rural areas, there is an enormous challenge in making it possible for women to participate as equals to men while not radically altering tribal traditions. Many women remain confined to their homes, are often kept out of school and pressured to have their children marry while still very young.

In Iraq, in 2004, as the UN supported preparations for national elections, UNIFEM acted as a broker between local women's groups and the UN, including a special advisor to the Secretary-General, Lakhdar Brahimi and for the DPA elections advisory team. The purpose of this brokerage was to ensure that women's concerns could be taken into account in establishing the transitional governing structures and to progress the nomination of qualified female candidates to positions within the structures. The women who came to present the demands to Brahimi invoked SCR 1325. In June 2004, six women were among 30 Ministers named to the new Iraq interim government. In the elections for the Transitional National Assembly in Iraq, January 2005, 31 per cent of the total seats went to women. This Assembly established a constitutional committee, with eight of the seats going to women. After successful lobbying of Iraqi women's groups and the international community, the Constitution created by the transitional government contains prohibitions on tribal customs that violate human rights, such as domestic violence, and includes equal rights for women. In the elections of December 2005, the Independent Electoral Commission reported that women would fill the constitutionally mandated 25 per cent of the Council of Representatives. However, both the US-led Transitional Governing Authority and its successor, the Iraqi Governing Council, have excluded Iraqi women. Instability hampers Iraqi women's efforts to contribute to a changed society, while Iraq hovers on the brink of civil war.

East Timor was held up by the UN and donor nations as a post-conflict success story, given that political stability and peace marked the first four years of the nation. East Timor has been called a possible model for peacekeeping missions in terms of the Gender Affairs Unit established. Few successes can be taken for granted. In May 2006, violence again hit the streets of East Timor, resulting in deaths, pain, loss and displaced people floundering in convents converted into refugee camps. Kirsty Sword Gusmao, the wife of President Xanana Gusmao, asks pertinent questions as to why things went wrong when the nation-building process seemed to be proceeding so well. Sword Gusmao reflects on her status as the first lady of the world's newest nation, where her Alola Foundation[9] and the women's movement in East Timor are working to elevate the status of women and create the conditions for a healthier, more dignified life for poor women. She reminds us of the intense poverty of the women, with more than half of them illiterate and many still struggling to heal the wounds of more than 25 years of military occupation. Gains have been significant, with one of the highest levels of women's representation in South-East Asia, but many still feel ill-equipped to be legislators and representatives of constituencies. 'They also claim to face discrimination and prejudice, and struggle to combine public duties with motherhood and onerous family obligations' (Sword Gusmao 2006: 29).

During the 2006 crisis, where four years of gain almost evaporated, Sword Gusmao experienced 'a moment of truth':

> In the face of physical danger and political upheaval, women were again relegated to the roles of caregivers and victims. It is telling that not a single East Timorese woman solicited an audience with my husband, or had her views sought, on solutions to the crisis at the height of the turmoil. It wasn't a deliberate act of exclusion. It just didn't occur to anyone, in this intensely patriarchal society, that women may have something important and useful to contribute to the delicate and vital processes of disarmament, reconciliation and peacebuilding.
>
> (Sword Gusmao 2006: 29)

Yet women are left with the responsibility of the mess of conflict, the continuing struggle to provide for families' shelter, food, basic needs and coping with insecurity. Peace is foundational for progress and women are uniquely placed to build peace with security. Sword Gusmao reiterates the direction in this book that 'they are virtually absent from discussions on reform of the security sector' (2006: 29).

Despite the significance of SCR 1325, women remain disturbingly absent or marginalized from negotiating tables, political decision-making opportunities and senior policy and judicial advisory positions. Indeed, these problems exist within the UN itself. 'Until the year 2000, only four women have ever served as Special Representatives of the Secretary-General (SRSG). Out of 27 peace support operations (peacekeeping and political and peacebuilding missions), there currently are no women serving as SRSG' (NGOWG 2006: 32). In 2007, an all-female Indian UN police unit went to Liberia as a landmark deployment, a specialized women's police unit assisting peacekeeping operations. Inclusion matters: without plural inclusivity extended to all significant groups, there is no peace with justice and equality. SCR 1325 calls on all actors involved in peace processes to adopt a gender perspective. Certainly, there are tensions between gender mainstreaming and having the sound judgement to know when women-specific provisions are necessary.

So much has been achieved, but so much more needs to be done. Despite the amazing initiatives around the world regarding women, peace and security, the mandates explicit in SCR 1325 are not being systematically implemented. The creation of national action plans provides a space for detailed analysis and consultation with stakeholders. Action plans lead to increased 'comprehensiveness, coordination, awareness-raising, ownership, accountability, monitoring and evaluation' (Valasek 2006: i–ii). Kristin Valasek (2006: ii) notes some interesting responses to this call to create national plans of action on SCR 1325 created in Canada, Denmark, Norway, Sweden, Switzerland and the UK, and integrated into legislation in Colombia, Fiji and Israel (2006: ii). Valasek is right to stress that there is no 'one size fits all' planning process, or one action plan for the perfect implementation of strategies. However, she does stress three core methodologies that are foundational to adequate implementation: 'strategic planning, participatory planning and gender/socio-economic analysis' (2006: ii). The challenges remaining are enormous, given the lack of funding and political will. Investing in raising awareness of these issues is the first step, but capacity-building, monitoring and evaluation are essential to implement strategies.

The PBC is the UN body advising on peacebuilding, development and reconstruction strategies. It recognizes that there are many different actors in peace-building processes. Its main purposes are to integrate strategies for peacebuilding and recovery, provide financial assistance in recovery stages, extend the period of attention by the international community and develop best practices on those issues that require collaboration among political, military, humanitarian and development actors. To date, there are no structural or institutionalized mechanisms to ensure that women's needs and interests are addressed in the work of the PBC, despite the pressure mounted by NGOWG.[10] The NGOWG reiterates how shortsighted it is to think that 'in the midst of pressing reconstruction needs, the imperative to address the political, economic and social status of women is often treated as a separate and lesser priority' (NGOWG 2006: 18). It provides the example of elections. Not to take into account gender is to ignore the practicalities of whether men and women get different forms of information in different locations from different media, whether women are willing to stand in line and vote next to men, or whether provisions are made for the care of young children when women have to stand for hours in the hot sun. As I have repeated throughout this book, the experience in many countries 'suggests that the achievement of sustainable peace is far more likely when gender equality and women's rights issues are made a central aspect of reconstruction' (NGOWG 2006: 19). Equality requires the participation of all citizens in shaping the justice framework that addresses violations of human rights and reforms discriminatory laws which impede equal participation in political, social and economic matters and access to available resources for all members of society. Throughout the book, I have offered positive examples of women's activities that build sustainable peace.

Sustaining peace is an ongoing task. Within our own families, friendships and collegial networks, we work to sustain harmonious relationships. As I have argued, peacebuilding involves all processes that build positive relationships, heal wounds, reconcile antagonistic differences, restore esteem, respect rights, meet basic needs, enhance equality, instil feelings of security, empower moral agency and are democratic, inclusive and just. Peace processes take time – there is the gradual building of relationships through trust, storytelling, sharing experiences, agreeing or amicably disagreeing on goals and cooperating on shared aspirations. Peacebuilding is contextual, grounded and shaped by the particular conflict and the historical, religious, economic, political, cultural, ethnic and regional factors that contribute to hostilities. Peacebuilding is multilayered. Yet, antagonism can be deep and mechanisms of political and structural peacebuilding do not necessarily develop a culture of peace.[11] To include women in political decision-making in transitional societies is to take seriously gender justice, gender equality, women's human rights and the rebuilding of relationships in demilitarized societies. Peacebuilding is an informal and formal ongoing process. It involves all actors working to further peace and reconciliation. For reconciliation to be more than a fashionable slogan, all stages of peacebuilding must be inclusive of women and men from all branches of life. Through embracing the rich diversity of humanity we can practise a politics of compassion that creates unimaginable reconciliatory spaces of mutual respect for equal dignity.

Notes

Introduction

1 It is important to note that of the countries most at risk, there are 17 African nations south of the Sahara plus Algeria on the North Africa coast and a further 19 in the next vulnerable category south of the Sahara plus Egypt, Libya, Morocco and Tunisia in the North. Only Benin, Botswana, Malawi, Mali, Mauritius, Namibia, South Africa, Swaziland and Zimbabwe are classified as being able to manage conflict without breaking out into armed conflict and providing reasonable levels of security. At the time of writing, countries with ongoing armed conflict include Afghanistan, Algeria, Burundi, Colombia, Democratic Republic of Congo, India, Indonesia, Iraq, Israel, Ivory Coast, Myanmar (Burma), Nepal, Nigeria, Philippines, Russia, Somalia, Sudan and Uganda.

2 This book refers primarily to the following PFA Objectives: Strategic Objective E.3, to 'promote non-violent forms of conflict resolution', and Objective E.4, to 'promote women's contribution to fostering a culture of peace'. I also examine Strategic Objective G.1, to 'take measures to ensure women's equal access to and full participation in power structures and decision-making', and Objective G.2, to 'increase women's capacity to participate in decision-making and leadership'. See DAW (2000). For a review of the PFA, see Anderlini (2000a).

3 See WILPF, the official UN website for Beijing +10: www.peacewomen.org/un/ Beijing10%20/beijing10index.html.

4 Fukuyama's (1998) argument that violence, power, status and military involvement are rooted in biology rather than being products of patriarchal culture mocks the feminist explanations for how international politics is gendered. See Tickner's response, where she maintains that 'rather than joining debates about aggressive men and peaceful women, IR feminists are striving to better understand unequal social hierarchies, including gender hierarchies, which contribute to conflict, inequality, and oppression' (1999: 11).

5 This statement does not justify the benefits of war. Rather, in looking at the horrors of war, Turshen (1998: 20) searched desperately for positive meanings, looking at examples such as changed gender relations in Chad, women gaining land in Rwanda, women in Mozambique having more control over finances and displacement in the Sudan changing women's status to breadwinners.

6 See in particular, McKay and Mazurana (2002), Rehn and Johnson-Sirleaf (2002), Anderlini (2000b), International Alert and Women Waging Peace (1999), Mazurana and McKay (1999), and Pankhurst (1999a) for general accounts of women and peacebuilding.

7 In Chapter 1, I explain the reasons behind my reluctance to use the term 'post-conflict'.

8 See UNRISD (2005) for a detailed outline of global trends of gender equality, well-being, work and politics, post-Beijing. In particular, section 4 deals with gender, armed conflict and the search for peace.

9 A 2003 United Nations High Commission for Refugees (UNHCR) analysis of refugee and internally displaced persons suggests that women and children constitute 70.5 per cent of this group (Mack 2005: 101).

10 See also the Windhoek Declaration, 31 May 2000, 'Mainstreaming a Gender Perspective in Multidimensional Peace Support Operations'.

11 'Underage girls have been present in the armed forces of 55 countries; in 27 of these countries, girls were abducted to serve and in 34 of them, the girls saw combat' (Mack 2005: 35). Those girls who join armed groups are usually fleeing abusive situations.

12 See Ellsberg and Heise (2005) for a very useful manual on *Researching Violence Against Women,* which suggests ways to develop a research strategy and the ethical considerations of fieldwork.

13 See UN OSAGI (2004b) for the *Inventory of UN Resources on Women, Peace and Security.* This includes guidelines, training materials, manuals and reports. The online inventory is updated as new UN resources become available. See INSTRAW (2006) for a guide that concentrates on the creation of action plans on women, peace and security. There is an ever-growing range of useful materials available so it is troubling that, given the resources available and the constructive suggestions for change, gender inequalities are prevalent.

14 This is typical for feminist IR theorists. See Peterson (2000: 200), Jabri (1999) and Tickner (1997: 615).

15 See Youngs (2004) for an excellent overview on the current direction of debates within feminist approaches to IR and her listing of specialist journals that cover feminist IR topics as well as the key feminist IR theorists. Peterson (2000) also includes a vast summary of literature within feminist IR theory. Steans (1998: 184–185, 193) includes many references to gender in IR and to the important differences between feminist approaches to IR.

16 I read Lederach's book after I had conducted the majority of my own research and indeed had written the substantial part of this book.

17 See Paris (2004), where he scrutinizes the assumptions underpinning the design and conduct of peacebuilding operations, such as occurred in Namibia 1989, Nicaragua 1989, Angola 1991, Cambodia 1991, El Salvador 1991, Mozambique 1992, Liberia 1993, Rwanda 1993, Bosnia 1995, Croatia 1995, Guatemala 1997, East Timor 1999, Kosovo 1999 and Sierra Leone 1999.

18 I accept Garcia's (2004: 26) plea for a rethinking in the field of conflict prevention and transformation to overcome artificial boundaries between official/unofficial, governmental/non-governmental and regional/global.

19 These are no longer considered solely theological tools.

1 Peacebuilding as process: United Nations Security Council Resolution 1325

1 Enloe talks of 'militarized peace' (1993: 73).

2 Their web portal is very useful: www.WomenWarPeace.org.

3 On 9 November 2006, the Secretary-General's High Level Panel (2000) on System-Wide Coherence released a report, 'Delivering as One'. With regard to gender equality, a key recommendation is to consolidate UN OSAGI, DAW and UNIFEM into one gender entity headed by an Undersecretary-General.

4 See Ekiyor (2004) for the examples of WIPNET in West Africa.

5 See paras 122 and 124 for women's participation at all levels of decision-making in conflict prevention, resolution, peacekeeping, peacebuilding and post-conflict

recovery; para 128 for education for conflict resolution skills; para 130 for gender-sensitive training to peacekeepers; para 122 for gender-sensitive strategies in humanitarian crisis; and para 133 for equal benefit for refugees and displaced women.

6 See Report of the Secretary-General (2000).

7 Resolution adopted by the General Assembly, 2000, S-23/s 'Further actions and initiatives to implement the Beijing Declaration and PFA', 10 June 2000, A/RES/S-23/3.

8 Femmes Africa Soldarité (FAS) Women's Action for New Directions, Women's Division of the United Methodist Church and Women's Environment and Development Organization have also been part of the Group for various reports and activities.

9 These meetings are held outside the Council chambers and are unofficial discussions that prompt follow-up bilateral communication between NGOs and Council members.

10 The Global Partnership for the Prevention of Armed Conflict was launched 'to enhance the role of civil society in conflict prevention and peacebuilding by strengthening civil-society networks' (van Tongeren *et al.* 2005: 84–85).

11 In particular, it recalls resolutions 1208 (1998), 1261 (1999), 1265 (1999), 1296 (2000) and 1314 (2000). It recalls the Beijing Declaration and PFA and the Outcomes Document of the 23rd Special Session of the UN General Assembly on Women 2000: Gender Equality, Development and Peace for the Twenty-First Century (A/S-23/10/Rev.1). It notes the Windhoek Declaration and the Namibia Plan of Action on Mainstreaming a Gender Perspective in Multidimensional Peace Support Operations (S/2000/693) of 2000, which calls on women and men to be equal participating partners and beneficiaries in all aspects of the peace process. It calls on all parties to abide by the Geneva Conventions 1949, the Additional Protocols of 1977, the Refugee Convention 1951 and Protocol of 1967, CEDAW 1979 and the Optional Protocol of 1999, the BPA 1995, the UN Convention on the Rights of the Child 1989 and the two Optional Protocols of 2000 and to bear in mind the Rome Statute of the ICC.

12 See Inter-Action-CAW and IIRR (2004) for concrete, successful examples of gender mainstreaming and the promotion of gender equity in the Asia Pacific region through examples such as media, politics, community theatre, health services, sustainable economic development, crop diversification and leadership.

13 See www.genderandpeacekeeping.org for these resources.

14 Johnson-Sirleaf was elected President of Liberia in 2006, the first woman President of an African nation.

15 The Best Practices Unit in DPKO is the focal point for gender mainstreaming in peacekeeping missions. Both the Canadian Department of Foreign Affairs and International Trade and the UK's Department for International Development have written materials on 'Gender and Peace Support Operation' (see www.dfait-maeci.gc.ca/genderandpeacekeeping/ for course materials).

16 In particular OSAGI cites SCR 1325 (2000); the Windhoek Declaration and the Namibia Plan of Action (2000); the UN General Assembly Resolution, 'Further Actions and Initiatives to Implement the Beijing Declaration and PFA' (2000); the European Parliament resolution on Participation of Women in Peaceful Conflict Resolution (2000); the G8 Roma initiative on Strengthening the Role of Women in Conflict Prevention (2001); and the CSW Agreed Conclusions on Women's Equal Participation in Conflict Prevention, Management and Conflict Resolution and Post-Conflict Peacebuilding (2004). See UN OSAGI (2004: 3) for web details of these documents.

17 See UNIFEM's site (www.womenwarpeace.org) and WILPF (www.peacewomen.org).

18 For an analysis on *An Agenda for Peace Ten Years On,* see the UN Association of

the UK, Global Policy Forum at: www.globalpolicy.org/reform/initiatives/ghlai/2002/0203ten.htm.

19 The peacebuilding tools include: relief and humanitarian assistance; food aid; water and sanitation; health; mine clearance; logistics; securing financial resources; rebuilding governmental administrative apparatus; the DDR of ex-combatants; refugee reintegration; strengthening human rights; strengthening democratic governmental systems; elections; crime prevention; the administration of justice; reconstructing transport and energy systems; and the rehabilitation of civil society (UNDP 1996). This list reflects the typical duties of peacekeepers.

20 The DPA is also the lead department for early warning, preventive diplomacy, peacemaking, electoral assistance and counter-terrorism.

21 Bendaña (2004) develops a strong argument that under the auspices of 'peacebuilding', 'state-building' becomes a way of imposing western liberal, market-oriented governance. The rebuilding of institutions and keeping order is to stimulate a market economy. See also Hippler (2005) for a critique of the way 'nation-building' has been used to justify military interventions in Afghanistan, Iraq and Somalia. Where there are 'failed' states, the concept can legitimize foreign powers' control and reshaping of countries in conflict.

22 There is a clear link between liberal democratic societies with their expectation of shared values and non-violent ways to deal with conflict, and this notion of stable peace.

23 Maiese (2003) does not refer to women. However, the article provides a useful annotated bibliography on the topic of peacebuilding.

24 See for example, the CSW's 48th session, 1–12 March 2004: 'Women's equal participation in conflict prevention, management and conflict resolution and in post-conflict peacebuilding. Agreed conclusion'.

25 For example, despite a peace agreement, economic growth and extensive funding in Northern Ireland, sectarianism and segregation is high.

26 The surveys maintain that 'half of the world's countries have serious weaknesses that call for international scrutiny and engagement', and the countries at greatest risk of escalating violence and government instability include 17 African countries (Marshall and Gurr 2005: 2).

27 This discussion is summarized in CSW (2000b).

28 I am not exploring the new security regimes that have emerged in western countries post-9/11. See Young for an excellent interpretation of the US through 'a gender lens of masculinist protection' (2003: 225). Young explains a security regime as one where 'the state and its officials assume the role of protector towards its citizens, and the citizens become positioned as subordinates, grateful for the protection afforded them' (2003: 225). Patriotism plays a crucial 'emotive function', dissent is seen as 'ungrateful' and subordinate citizens consent to limitation on freedom in exchange for a promise of security' (2003: 227).

29 'Nearly half of all peace agreements collapse within five years. ... In the life of almost every peace process, there comes a time – usually three to seven years out – when disillusionment is high' (UN Secretary-General 2004b: 4).

30 Some parties were absent, so seven women from 72 persons participated in the 1998 Assembly from a potential of 14 women out of 108.

2 Overcoming the harm of polarization

1 I use polarization in the sense of antagonistic views and I use dichotomy, dualism and binaries synonymously.

2 For my previous accounts of dualism in books, see Porter (1999 and 1991, chapter 2). The account of dualism in this chapter closely resembles my article, 'The Harm of Dualism' (Porter 2005a).

3 Lloyd's (1984) influential work, *The Man of Reason*, was an early inspiration on my ideas when I began working on my doctorate in the mid-1980s on the critique of a male bias in conceptions of moral identity (Porter 1991).

4 I refer here to all forms of fundamentalism, ideological and sectarian, particularly Christian and Islamic versions.

5 For a critique of how just war theory was used in Australia, the UK and USA, see Porter (2006b).

6 Elshtain argues that within the Christian just war tradition, 'all notions of moral absolutism smack of triumphalism and a crusading mentality of war without limits and must therefore be repudiated' (2003a: 134).

7 There was also the bombing of the Marriott Hotel in Jakarta, in 2003, the Australian embassy bombing in 2004 and the bombing in Bali of tourist areas in 2005, which killed 26 and injured others.

8 The concept of *ubuntu* will be explained in more detail in later chapters. It reflects our interconnectedness and the unity of human beings.

9 As Rose (1993: 5, 10), a psychoanalytic feminist, maintains, fear and loathing may have roots in the unconscious but they are manifest in intentional ways, making the unconscious political.

10 Some of the key organizations providing training and support are UNIFEM, Search for Common Ground, International Alert and Women Waging Peace and the US Institute for Peace.

11 Paez is viewed as a defector from FARC and sought rehabilitation to unlearn how to kill.

12 See Porter (1999) for an extended outline of what constitutes feminist ethics.

13 See in particular Sevenhuijsen (1998), Held (1995), Larabee (1993), Tronto (1993, 1995), Porter (1991), Kittay and Meyers (1987).

14 In particular, they relate to the relationships that pertain to families, childcare, custody, health, welfare, aged care or disability rights. These are extremely important areas that require an ethics of care, but I am expanding the political domain in which care is appropriate.

15 In particular, those who build on the formative work of Gilligan, whose ethic of care is 'tied to feelings of empathy and compassion' (1983: 69).

16 Jabri maintains that 'the justice–care dualism parallels in form the normative project in international relations' (1999: 41–42) and she too argues against the inevitability of this dualism.

17 This blame translates readily to taking 'our' jobs, moving into 'our' neighbourhoods and being so 'strange', that 'we' need to know 'they' are not welcome.

18 Tickner avoids using the label of 'idealist', which she claims is a realist label 'that has contributed to the delegitimization of the idealist tradition' (1997: 617), a rich tradition that includes communitarian, liberal and cosmopolitan thought.

19 Their project covered Angola, Brazil, Canada, East Timor, Israel, Liberia, Macedonia, Mozambique, Nepal, Northern Ireland, Papua New Guinea, Sierra Leone, Somalia, South Africa and the USA.

20 These responses were developed initially in my earlier work (Porter 2005a).

3 Recognition and inclusion

1 See Toppinen (2005) for a comparison between Fraser's and Honneth's (2003) views on recognition, where Fraser's emphasis is on context, social equality and democratic participation, and Honneth deals with redistribution as derivative from the moral category of recognition.

2 Other groups include indigenous groups, gay and lesbian activists, political dissidents, human rights advocates, older marginalized people, welfare recipients and physically and mentally disabled groups.

3 For works on the relationship between security and gender identity, see Hoogensen and Rottem (2004) and Jabri and O'Gorman (1999).
4 Graça Machel was married to the President of Mozambique, who was killed in 1986. She played a powerful role in assisting the education of women and girls in Mozambique and chaired an Expert Study on the Impact of Armed Conflict on Children. She is now married to Nelson Mandela.
5 Again, it is important to note that this does not happen without substantial help from the international community. UNIFEM and UNDP particularly provided essential support to Somalian women to meet and learn from prominent women from Burundi and South Africa, who have been part of their own country's peace processes.
6 *Sati* is the traditional Hindu practice of a widow immolating herself on her husband's funeral pyre.
7 Here I adopt Hage's (1998: 83) qualifier that the ideology of multiculturalism is both descriptive in stating the existence of cultural diversity and prescriptive in promoting positive attitudes to diversity.
8 The notion of 'peaceful coexistence' became associated with calls for a less antagonistic relationship between the Soviet Union and the West. Under Lenin, the notion was an ideological cover for aggression and deception.
9 Crocker *et al.* (2005) write of some of the most obstinate conflicts, including Angola, the Balkans, Cambodia, Central America, Colombia, Cyprus, Iraq, Indonesia, Kashmir, Korea, the Middle East, Nigeria, the Philippines, Somalia, Southern Africa, Sri Lanka and Sudan.
10 This project is an initiative by UNHCR and funded by the Japanese government to encourage the use of public spaces to draw members of conflicting groups together.
11 D'Estrée and Babbitt (1998: 206) qualify their comments by saying that women exhibited these skills in relationships with other women, but dilution of the strength of these skills occurs when men are present, reinforcing the critical mass thesis that at least 30 per cent of women is necessary to bring out the best in women.
12 Cockburn (2004) acknowledges that these are contested terms.
13 As John Marks, the founder of Search for Common Ground, Washington, DC puts it, this organization adapts methods to each case and the methodology is based on the principle *'understanding the differences; act on the commonalities'* (2005: 186; emphasis in original).
14 REDE is an umbrella organization encompassing 18 women's NGOs.
15 Statistics from 2006 suggest 7.8 children per woman (ReliefWeb: www.reliefweb.int/).

4 Justice and compassion

1 I build here on some of my earlier arguments (Porter 2006a).
2 Admittedly, the immediate trauma of rape, poverty, disease or being displaced from one's homeland leaves people bewildered, shamed and distressed beyond all realms of thinking clearly. My point is that giving support is important to assist people to articulate what they need in order to overcome their suffering, rather than to assume we know what is best.
3 For a critical appraisal of this view, see Huyse (2005).
4 Goldstone was Justice of the Constitutional Court of South Africa and former prosecutor for the Yugoslav and Rwanda Tribunals when he wrote this.
5 Conventions that address women include CEDAW (1979), the Beijing Declaration and PFA (1995), the Optional Protocol to CEDAW (1999), the Windhoek Declaration (2000) and UN SCR 1325 (2000).
6 Nowrojee suggests that sexual violence crimes at the ICTR were never incorporated consistently into prosecution strategies, whereas they were incorporated and followed through in Sierra Leone, where prosecutor David Crane addressed people in

every province with his mandate to provide justice to his client, the people of Sierra Leone (in Nowrojee 2005: 8, 11).

7 See Frazer and Lacey (1993) for their feminist critique of the liberal–communitarian debate.

8 Women have been party to official negotiations in Afghanistan (2001–2002), Burundi (2000), Northern Ireland (1996–1998), the Inter-Congolese Dialogues (2001–2002) and elsewhere.

9 Chinkin notes 'the tension between gender mainstreaming and women-specific provisions' in the content and implementation of peace agreements (2003: 9).

10 This work of Benhabib's looks particularly at the need to 'render the distinctions between "citizens" and "aliens", "us" and "them" fluid and negotiable through democratic iterations' (2005: 21).

11 This is contentious, it assumes consensus on the capabilities.

12 The capacities include: life; bodily health and integrity; bodily integrity; senses, imagination, thought; emotions; practical reason; affiliation; other species; play; and control over one's environment (Nussbaum 2000: 78–80; 1999: 41–42). Later, she calls the second capability 'bodily health' (Nussbaum 2000: 78).

13 For elaboration on gender mainstreaming, see the special edition of *International Feminist Journal of Politics*, 7(4) (2005) and Porter (2005b).

14 See McNairn (2005) for an analysis of security programmes in Rwanda.

15 See Huyse (2003b: 57) for different official definitions of what constitutes a victim.

16 The Greek origin of the word trauma is wound, so psychologically, trauma is a 'wound to the soul' (Kleck 2006: 344).

17 In 1997, the British government appointed Sir Kenneth Bloomfield as Victims Commissioner to establish a Victims Liaison Unit. In the devolved Northern Ireland Assembly, a Victims Unit was set up in 2002. In 2005, Bertha McDougall, a widow of a murdered policeman, was appointed as interim Victims Commissioner until the legislation on victims is finalized.

18 MONUC was the first to create an office to address allegations of sexual abuse of some of their civilian and military personnel in the Democratic Republic of Congo.

19 As of September 2005, gender advisors were in peacekeeping and political missions in Afghanistan, Burundi, Côte d'Ivoire, Democratic Republic of the Congo, Haiti, Kosovo, Liberia, Sierra Leone, Sudan and Timor-Leste while the other missions have gender focal points, staff assigned gender-related responsibilities.

20 Havel was President of the Czech and Slovak Federative Republic, December 1989–July 1992.

21 See Huyse (2003c: 113) for examples of restorative justice in Sudan and Bougainville.

22 In chairing the TRC, Tutu talked frequently about the overlap between the values of restorative justice, truth and reconciliation.

23 'Restorative justice also shares important ground with retributive justice. Both insist that wrongs must be *put right*' (Acorn 2004: 20–21; emphasis in orginal).

24 The issue of compensation is fraught with complexities 'where some of the alleged participants in human rights abuses are in government and may well be in a position to influence the outcome of the judgment' Muchenga Chicuecue (1997: 484).

5 Memory and truth

1 Cady Stanton (1815–1902) was a US suffragist. This was a public statement.

2 She explains that what is considered as basic is shared cross-culturally in much the same way as Nussbaum's (2000, 1999) capabilities approach.

3 I accept that this is a difficult moral position to defend in view of the enormity of violations committed in war, but it is a reminder that there is a moral duty to treat even the worst criminals with dignity.

4 Walzer (1977: 298) also argues that the degree of responsibility for government and official wrongdoing varies according to degrees of freedom and possession of information.

5 Govier's examples in this context address the treatment of Canadian people with regard to the humanity of Aboriginal peoples in Canada.

6 One hundred and eighteen submissions were received. See www.healingthroughremembering.org. See also House of Commons Northern Ireland Affairs Committee (2005).

7 Sometimes, repressed memory permits victims to 'forget' the act of violence committed against them, for a measure of time. Often, something deep in the subconscious haunts a victim and bizarre, disconnected activities or items trigger the memory. This seems a common pattern with victims of sexual abuse in their youth.

8 See Freeman and Hayner (2003) for an account of truth commissions, with Guatemala and South Africa having had considerable attention, commissions having been underway in East Timor, Nigeria, Panama, Peru, Uruguay, the Federal Republic of Yugoslavia and more recently in Ghana and Sierra Leone. In Northern Ireland there is a Victim's Commissioner appointed in the late 1990s, commissions on the disappeared in Sri Lanka and Uganda; truth and justice commissions in Ecuador and Haiti; TRCs in Chile, Sierra Leone, South Africa, the Federal Republic of Yugoslavia and a Commission for Reception, Truth and Reconciliation in East Timor.

9 Rigby suggests that after General Franco's death in 1975 there was a form of 'collective amnesia' in the desire to subordinate everything 'to the peaceful transition to democratic rule' (2001: 2).

10 The text of these truth commissions can be found at the website of the US Institute of Peace: www.usip.org.

11 Some suggest that limiting the mandate to investigating disappearances and unlawful killings is a weakness, 'too little justice, too little truth, and hence...no solid foundation for reconciliation' (Rigby 2001: 126).

12 Amnesty is not limited to truth commissions. In Czechoslovakia after taking office, Havel quickly tried to counter a legacy of the communist regime in releasing more than 20,000 political prisoners (Rigby 2001: 100).

13 This could also be said for the unionist community in Northern Ireland.

14 Risk factors that leave countries susceptible to further genocide include: a prior history of genocide/politicide, previous upheavals, and minority elite such as Tutsi domination in Burundi and Rwanda or Tigreans dominant in Ethiopia; or an exclusionary ideology, such as Islamists in Sudan, Hutu militants in Burundi and Rwanda, the Taliban in Afghanistan, Marxists in China, Maoists in Nepal, Tamil separatists in Sri Lanka, Sunni Islamists in Iraq or conflict between secular nationalists and Islamists in Algeria (Marshall and Gurr 2005: 60).

15 Foča was a Bosnian-Serb run concentration camp named after the nearby Bosnian town.

16 For Drakulic's account, see Drakulic (2001).

17 Nyiramasuhuko's defence case started in 2005 and has been given until mid-2007 to complete.

18 Verwoerd, a member of the ANC and a researcher for the TRC, is the grandson of the architect of apartheid, Dr H.F. Verwoerd.

19 Yvonne Khutwane was 'the first woman to include a description of sexual violation in her public testimony' (in Ross 2003: 80) and there were diverse interpretations of her testimony.

20 Minow supports the importance of the presence of sympathetic witnesses; she argues that therapists who work with survivors of traumatic violence maintain 'how crucial a moral, sympathetic, and politically attentive statement is to the therapeutic relationship' (1998: 71).

21 After Lapsley was exiled by the South African government in 1976, he joined the ANC and became one of their chaplains. While living in exile in Zimbabwe he discovered he was on the government hit list, and in 1990 he received a letter bomb in the post. He lost both hands and an eye but realized that if he was filled with hatred and revenge, he would remain a victim forever.

22 The first phase of the project began with a meeting of experts in New York in December 2004. In June 2005 the authors of the country reports met to choose the case studies on Guatemala, Peru, Rwanda, Sierra Leone, South Africa and Timor-Leste. At the time of writing, the edited volume (Rubio-Marín 2006) was not available and I am reliant on executive summaries of the case studies. The case study on gender reparations in Timor-Leste was written by Galuh Wandita, Karen Campbell-Nelson and Manuela Leong Pereira; in Guatemala by Claudia Paz y Paz Bailey; in Peru by Julie Guillerot; in Rwanda by Heidy Rombouts; in Sierra Leone by Jamesina King; and in South Africa by Beth Goldblatt. The summaries were taken from the ICTJ websites: www.ictj.org/en/research/projects/gender/index.html (accessed 19/04/2006).

6 Reconciliation and difference

1 See Sarkin and Daly (2004: 662–663) where they write of legislation in Guatemala, Namibia, Nicaragua and South Africa; truth commissions in East Timor, Nigeria, Peru and Sierra Leone; ministries in the Fiji, Rwanda and Solomon Islands; and Australia and Canada pursuing reconciliation with indigenous populations.

2 Hermann elaborates Lederach's ideas of reconciliation as a 'locus' where truth, mercy, justice and peace meet by explaining truth as 'acknowledgement, transparency, revelation, and clarity', mercy as 'acceptance, forgiveness, support, compassion, and healing', justice as 'equality, right relationships, rectification, and restitution' and peace as 'harmony, unity, well-being, security, and respect' (2004: 45–46).

3 Between 1910 and 1970, there was a forcible removal of indigenous children from their families and communities. The children were placed in institutions, church missions or adopted or fostered to white families, where Australia's assimilation policies left generations bereft of their own culture and language.

4 See Prager (2003: 24–25) for a list of significant studies on reconciliation as well as the themes of restorative justice, acknowledgement, forgiveness, restitution and reparations.

5 The contribution of the international community has been particularly significant in Bosnia, El Salvador, Nicaragua and Northern Ireland.

6 The Bill can be found at www.fijitimes.com/unitybill.html#I.

7 Also, the Family Code was amended in 2005. It retains the need for women to have a guardian, contraception is available only for married women, polygamy is practised and inheritance laws leave two-thirds to sons and one-third to daughters.

8 There are similarities with this instance of women demanding information about their loved ones who had disappeared with the *Madres de Plaza de Mayo* in Argentina and the Tamil Mothers' Front in Sri Lanka, which was independent of the Tamil Tigers. This front disbanded when the demands of the women for the return of their children was used by the opposition parties to campaign against the ruling party.

9 For an analysis of just war theory, see Porter (2006b).

10 For elaboration of Berry's ideas, see her website at: www.buildingbridgesforpeace.org.

11 In addition to women who have been raped or sexually assaulted, this concept is pertinent to ex-combatants and returnees.

12 Many reconciliation groups and institutions supportive of indigenous peoples demonstrate solidarity on a 'Sorry Day'.

13 These include the Bougainville Community-Based Integrated Humanitarian Programme and the Leitana Neihan Women's Development Agency.

14 Despite women's successful efforts to implement a permanent ceasefire, they were left out of national level negotiations. In June 2005 there was the first autonomous government of Bougainville. 'Women were involved in the Bougainville Constituent Assembly that formulated the new Constitution', whereby three regional seats have been set aside for women and women can contest other seats (Shoemaker and Conaway 2005: 39).

15 The support committee for this project is in Geneva.

16 The international community played a key supportive role and the UNDP Trust Fund for Women, the US Agency for International Development's Women in Development Programme and UNHCR for RWI. RWI worked in partnership with MIGEPROFE.

17 Nantulya is Head of Political Engagement at the Institute for Justice and Reconciliation in the Great Lakes region.

18 This is based on fieldwork with survivors in May 2003.

19 Nowrojee is a member of the Coalition for Women's Human Rights in Conflict Situations and directs the Open Society Institute's Initiative in East Africa.

20 The Tribunal currently provides HIV/AIDS medications to defendants in custody but not necessarily to the women who are rape victims (Nowrojee 2005: 4).

21 Volf refers to the apostle Paul's injunction in the *Bible* to 'Welcome one another, therefore, just as Christ has welcomed you' (Romans 15:7). He acknowledges that there are cultural differences in identification with such a metaphor. For example, an African bishop defended the metaphor, while a north European theologian considered it to be too intimate (Volf 1996: 29).

22 This involved 90 key informant interviews, 24 focus groups, a survey of 800 people in Mostar, Bosnia-Herzegovina, and 400 people in Vukovar, Croatia and 400 in Prijedor, Bosnia-Herzegovina (Halpern and Weinstein 2004: 569).

Conclusion: peace with justice and security

1 A Swiss initiative launched in 2003 gained international support in nominating 1000 women from 150 different countries for the joint 2005 Nobel Peace Prize. These women are making a significant contribution to reconciliation and reconstruction, rights, democracy, indigenous women, justice, health, education, economics, politics and cultural conceptions of peace. The 1000th woman was named 'Anonyma' for all the nameless women whose work continues to be overlooked (Association 1000 Women for the Nobel Peace Prize 2005: 2005, see also www.1000peacewomen.org).

2 See International Alert and Women Waging Peace (www.international-alert.org/women), UNIFEM (www.unifem.org/), UN Inter-Agency Network on Women and Gender Equality (www.un.org/womenwatch), WILPF (www.peacewomen.org/un/sc/1325.html).

3 There are women Vice-Presidents too: Aisatou N'Jie Saidy in Gambia, Annette Lu in Taiwan, Sandra Sumang Pierantozzi in Palau, Lineth Saborio Chaverri in Costa Rica and Ana Vilma de Escobar in El Salvador. Aung San Suu Kyi has been leader of the National League for Democracy in Burma since 1988.

4 All quotations are from SCR 1325 (S/RES/1325 2000).

5 UNRISD (2005) include Mozambique with 30 per cent and claim that all of the successful countries except Cuba, Denmark and Finland have quotas.

6 There had previously been none in Bangladesh, Cambodia, Ethiopia, and Sierra Leone (UNRISD 2005: 252).

7 The Inter-Parliamentary Union assisted Rwandans on writing a 'gender-sensitive' Constitution.

8 For example, FAS supports the peace processes in West Africa. FAS has been supporting training of MARWOPNET members on conflict transformation, conflict resolution, peacebuilding and techniques of negotiation to build their capacities as

peace advocates. The Ford Foundation, Government of Finland, the Government of Norway and UN branches support FAS programmes.

9 The Foundation works on maternal and child health, education and economic empowerment.

10 This included the Boston Consortium on Gender, Security and Human Rights; International Alert and Women Waging Peace; International Women's Tribunal Centre, FAS; Women's Action for New Directions; Women's Commission for Refugee Women and Children; DAW, General Board of Global Ministries of the United Methodist Church; and WILPF.

11 In Northern Ireland after the 1998 Peace Agreement, there have been major steps forward in establishing equality, human rights, parades and victim and survivor commissions, a criminal justice review, policing board, a reformed police service and racial equality strategy, but sectarianism and racism continue.

Bibliography

Abdela, Lesley (2005) '1325: Deeds Not Words', *openDemocracy*, 17 October 2005, Online, available at: www.opendemocracy.net/xml/xtml/articles/2929.html (accessed 25 October 2005).

Abu-Saba, Mary (1999) 'Human Needs and Women's Peacebuilding in Lebanon', *Peace and Conflict: Journal of Peace Psychology*, 5(1): 37–51.

Acorn, Annalise (2004) *Compulsory Compassion: A Critique of Restorative Justice*, Vancouver, BC: University of British Columbia Press.

Afkhami, Mahnaz (ed.) (2002) *Toward a Compassionate Society*, Bethesda, MD: Women's Learning Partnership.

Afzali, Aneelah and Colleton, Laura (2003) 'Constructing Coexistence. A Survey of Coexistence Projects in Areas of Ethnic Conflict', in Antonia Chayes and Martha Minow (eds) *Imagine Coexistence. Restoring Humanity After Violent Ethnic Conflict*, San Francisco, CA: Jossey-Bass, pp. 3–20.

Ahmed, Sara (2005) 'Sustaining Peace, Rebuilding Livelihoods: The Gujarat Harmony Project', in Caroline Sweetman (ed.) *Gender, Peacebuilding and Reconstruction*, Oxford: Oxfam, pp. 94–102.

al-Hibri, Azizah (2001) 'Standing at the Precipice: Faith in the Age of Science and Technology', in Azizah Y. al-Hibri, Jean Bethke Elshtain and Charles C. Haynes (eds) *Religion in American Public Life. Living with Our Deepest Differences*, New York and London: W. W. Norton and Co., pp. 62–95.

Alison, Miranda Helen (2006) *Women and Political Violence. Female Combatants in Ethno-national Conflict*, London and New York: Routledge.

Allison, Juliann Emmons (2001) 'Peace Among Friends: A Feminist Interpretation of the "Democratic Peace"', *Peace and Change*, 26(2): 204–222.

Amstutz, Mark R. (2005) *The Healing of Nations, The Promise and Limits of Political Forgiveness*, Lanham, MD: Rowman & Littlefield Publishers.

Anderlini, Sanam Naraghi (2005) 'Women and Peace through Justice', *Development*, 48(3): 103–110.

—— (2000a) *Women, Peace and Security. A Preliminary Audit. From the Beijing Platform to Security Council Resolution 1325 and Beyond. Achievements and Emerging Challenges*, London: International Alert and Women Waging Peace. Online, available at: www.international-alert.org/pdf/background.pdf (accessed 1 February 2001).

—— (2000b) *Women at the Peace Table. Making a Difference*, New York: UNIFEM.

Anderlini, Sanam Naraghi and Stanski, Victoria (2004) 'Conflict Prevention, Resolution and Reconstruction', in International Alert and Women Waging Peace (eds) *Inclusive*

Security, Sustainable Peace: A Toolkit for Advocacy and Action, London and Washington, DC: International Alert and Women Waging Peace.

Anderlini, Sanam Naraghi, Manchanda, Rita and Karmali, Shereen (eds) (1999) *Women, Violent Conflict and Peace-Building: Global Perspectives. International Conference, London, May 1999*, London: International Alert and Women Waging Peace.

Annan, Kofi (2000) 'The Secretary-General's Remarks to Security Council Meeting on Women and Peace and Security'. Online, available at: www.un.org/womenwatch/news/articles/kasc.htm (accessed 21 August 2001).

Arendt, Hannah (1974) *The Human Condition*, Chicago: University of Chicago Press.

—— (1973) *On Revolution*, Harmondsworth: Penguin Books.

Association 1000 Women for the Nobel Peace Prize 2005 (2005) *1000 Peace Women Across the Globe*, Zurich: Kuntrast.

Aziz, Razia (1992) 'Feminism and the Challenge of Racism', in Helen Crowley and Susan Himmelweit (eds) *Knowing Women, Feminism and Knowledge*, Cambridge: Polity Press, pp. 291–305.

Babic, Jovan (2000) 'Justifying Forgiveness', *Peace Review*, 12(1): 87–93.

Baines, Erin K. (2005) 'Gender Research in Violently Divided Societies: Methods and Ethics of "International" Researchers in Rwanda', in Elisabeth Porter, Gillian Robinson, Marie Smyth, Albrecht Schnabel and Eghosa Osaghae (eds) *Research in Conflict in Africa. Insights and experiences*, Tokyo: UN University Press, pp. 140–155.

—— (2004) *Vulnerable Bodies. Gender, the UN and the Global Refugee Crisis*, Aldershot and Burlington, VT: Ashgate.

—— (2001) *You Cannot Dance if You Cannot Stand. A Review of the Rwanda Women's Initiative and the UN High Commissioner for Refugees' Commitment to Gender Equality in Post-conflict Societies*, New York: Women's Commission for Refugee Women and Children.

Banaszak, Klara, Conaway, Camille Pampell, Goetz, Anne Marie, Iiyanmbo, Aina and Muna, Maha (2005) *Securing the Peace. Guiding the International Community towards Women's Effective Participation Throughout Peace Processes*, New York: UNIFEM.

Barnea, Aaron and Shinar, Ofer (2005) 'Building Trust, Promoting Hope: The Families Forum Hello Peace Project in Israel and Palestine', in Paul van Tongeren, Malin Brenk, Marte Hellema and Juliette Verhoeven (eds) *People Building Peace II. Successful Stories of Civil Society*, Boulder, CO: Lynne Rienner Publishers, pp. 495–500.

Bar-Tal, Daniel and Bennink, Gemma H. (2004) 'The Nature of Reconciliation as an Outcome and as a Process', in Yaacov Bar-Siman-Tov (ed.) *From Conflict Resolution to Reconciliation*, Oxford: Oxford University Press, pp. 11–38.

Basch, Linda (2004) 'Human Security, Globalization, and Feminist Visions', *Peace Review*, 16(1): 5–12.

Bassiouni, M. Cherif (1997) 'Searching for Peace and Achieving Justice: The Need for Accountability', *Law and Contemporary Problems*, 59(4): 9–28.

Baxi, Upendra (1999) 'Voices of Suffering, Fragmented Universality, and the Future of Human Rights', in Burns Weston and Stephen Marks (ed.) *The Future of International Human Rights*, New York: Transnational Publishers, pp. 101–156.

Bell, Christine, Campbell, Colm and Ní Aoláin, Fionnuala (2004) 'Justice Discourses in Transition', *Social and Legal Studies*, 13(3): 305–328.

Bell, Diane (2002) 'Good and Evil: At Home and Abroad', in Susan Hawthorne and Bronwyn Winter (eds) *September 11, 2001: Feminist Perspectives*, Melbourne: Spinifex, pp. 432–449.

Bendaña, Alejandro (2004) 'From Peace-Building to State-Building: One Step Forward and Two Backwards?', *Nation-Building, State-Building and International Intervention: Between 'Liberation' and Symptom Relief*, presented at CERI, Paris, 15 October 2004. Online, available at: www.transcend.org/t_database/printarticle. php?ida=506 (accessed 3 February 2005).

Benhabib, Seyla (2005) *The Rights of Others. Aliens, Residents, and Citizens*, Cambridge: Cambridge University Press.

—— (1992) *Situating the Self. Gender, Community and Postmodernism in Contemporary Ethics*, Cambridge: Polity Press.

Bennett, Olivia, Bexley, Jo and Warnock, Kitty (1995) 'Introduction', in Olivia Bennett, Jo Bexley and Kitty Warnock (eds) *Arms to Fight, Arms to Protect. Women Speak Out about Conflict*, London: Panos Publications, pp. 1–25.

Bickford, Susan (1996) *The Dissonance of Democracy. Listening, Conflict, and Citizenship*, Ithaca, NY: Cornell University Press.

Biggar, Nigel (2003) 'Making Peace or Doing Justice: Must We Choose?', in Nigel Biggar (ed.) *Burying the Past. Making Peace and Doing Justice after Civil Conflict*, Washington, DC: Georgetown University Bell, pp. 3–24.

Blanchard, Eric M. (2003) 'Gender, International Relations and the Development of Feminist Security Theory', *Signs* 28(4): 1289–1312.

Bloomfield, David (2003) 'Reconciliation: An Introduction', in David Bloomfield, Teresa Barnes and Luc Huyse (eds) *Reconciliation after Violent Conflict. A Handbook*, Stockholm: International Institute for Democracy and Electoral Assistance, pp. 10–18.

Bloomfield, David, Barnes, Teresa and Huyse, Luc (eds) (2003) *Reconciliation After Violent Conflict. A Handbook*, Stockholm: International Institute for Democracy and Electoral Assistance.

Böge, Volker and Garasu, Lorraine (2004) 'Papua New Guinea: A Success Story of Post-conflict Peacebuilding in Bougainville', in Annelies Heijmans, Nicola Simmonds and Hans van de Veen (eds) *Searching for Peace in Asia Pacific. An Overview of Conflict Prevention and Peacebuilding Activities*, Boulder, CO: Lynne Rienner Publishers, pp. 564–580.

Boulding, Elise (2002) 'Peace Culture', in Hahnaz Afkhami (ed.) *Toward a Compassionate Society*, Bethesda, MD: Women's Learning Partnership, pp. 8–15.

Boulding, Kenneth (1978) *Stable Peace*, Austin, TX: University of Texas Press.

Bouraine, Alex (2005) 'Transitional Justice', in Simon Chesterman, Michael Ignatieff and Ramesh Thakur (eds) *Making States Work: State Failure and the Crisis of Governance*, Tokyo: UN University Press, pp. 318–338.

Bouta, Tsjeard (2005) *Gender and Disarmament, Demobilization and Reintegration*, The Hague: Netherlands Institute of International Relations.

Boutros-Ghali, Boutros (1995) *Supplement to An Agenda for Peace: Position Paper of the Secretary-General on the Occasion of the Fiftieth Anniversary of the United Nations* A/50/60/-S/1995/1, 3 January, New York: UN Publications.

—— (1992) *An Agenda for Peace: Preventive Democracy, Peacemaking and Peacekeeping: Report of the Secretary-General* A/47/277-S/24111, 17 June, New York: UN.

Brahimi, Lakhdar (2000) 'Report on Peace Operations', A/55/305-A/2000/809. Online, available at: www.un.org/peace/reports/peace.operations (accessed 1 December 2000).

Brahm, Eric (2003) 'Conflict Stages', *Beyond Intractability*. Online, available at: www.beyondintractability.org/m/conflict_stages.jsp (accessed 1 December 2005).

Braithwaite, John (1996) 'Restorative Justice and a Better Future', *Dalhousie Review*, 76(1): 9–32.

Brett, Rachel and Specht, Irma (2004) *Young Soldiers. Why They Choose to Fight,* Boulder, CO: Lynne Rienner.

Brudholm, Thomas (2006) 'Revisiting Resentments: Jean Améry and the Dark Side of Forgiveness and Reconciliation', *Journal of Human Rights,* 5(1): 7–26.

Bunch, Charlotte (2004) 'A Feminist Human Rights Lens', *Peace Review,* 16(1): 29–34.

—— (2002) 'Human Rights as the Foundation for a Compassionate Society', in Mahnaz Afkhami (ed.) *Toward a Compassionate Society,* Bethesda, MD: Women's Learning Partnership, pp. 16–20.

Burnell, Peter (2004) 'The Coherence of Democratic Peace-building', UN WIDER Conference on making Peace Work, Helsinki, Finland, 4–5 June. Online, available at: www.wider.unu.edu/conference/conference-2004-1/conference-2004-1-menu.htm (accessed 5 August 2004).

Burton, Mary (1998) 'The South African Truth and Reconciliation Commission: Looking Back, Moving Forward – Revisiting Conflicts, Striving for Peace', in Brandon Hamber (ed.) *Past Imperfect. Dealing with the Past in Northern Ireland and Societies in Transition,* Derry/Londonderry: INCORE, pp. 13–24.

Butler, Judith (1996) 'Universality in Culture', in Joshua Cohen (ed.) *Debating the Limits of Patriotism: For Love of Country. Martha C. Nussbaum with Respondents,* Boston, MA: Beacon Press, pp. 45–52.

Caprioli, Mary (2004) 'Democracy and Human Rights versus Women's Security: A Contradiction?' *Security Dialogue,* 35(4): 411–428.

Cabrera, Roberto (1998) 'Should We Remember? Recovering Historical Memory Guatemala', in Brandon Hamber (ed.) *Past Imperfect. Dealing with the Past in Northern Ireland and Societies in Transition,* Derry/Londonderry: INCORE, pp. 25–30.

Card, Claudia (2004) '*The Atrocity Paradigm* Revisited', *Hypatia,* 19(4): 212–222.

—— (2002) *The Atrocity Paradigm: A Theory of Evil,* Oxford: Oxford University Press.

Chigas, Diana and Ganson, Brian (2003) 'Grand Visions and Small Projects. Coexistence Efforts in Southeastern Europe', in Antonia Chayes and Martha Minow (eds) *Imagine Coexistence. Restoring Humanity after Violent Ethnic Conflict,* San Franscisco, CA: Jossey-Bass, pp. 59–84.

Chinkin, Christine (2003) 'Peace Agreements as a Means for Promoting Gender Equality and Ensuring Participation of Women', *Expert Group Meeting on Peace Agreements as a Means for Promoting Gender Equality and Ensuring Participation of Women,* 10–13 November, EGM/PEACE/2003/BP.1, Ottawa: DAW.

—— (1999) 'Gender Inequality and International Human Rights Law', in Andrew Hurrell and Ngaire Woods (eds) *Inequality, Globalization, and World Politics,* Oxford: Oxford University Press, pp. 95–121.

Clark, Philip (2005) 'Justice without Lawyers. The Gacaca Courts and Post-Genocide Justice and Reconciliation in Rwanda', unpublished DPhil thesis, Balliol College, University of Oxford.

Clement, Grace (1996) *Care, Autonomy and Justice. Feminism and the Ethic of Care,* Boulder, CO: Westview Press.

Clements, Kevin (2005) 'The War on Terror: Effects on Civil-Society Actors in the Field of Conflict Prevention and Peacebuilding', in Paul van Tongeren, Malin Brenk, Marte Hellema and Juliette Verhoeven (eds) *People Building Peace II. Successful Stories of Civil Society,* Boulder, CO: Lynnne Rienner Publishers, pp. 71–82.

Cobb, Sara (2003) 'Fostering Coexistence in Identity-Based Conflicts. Toward a Narrative Approach', in Antonia Chayes and Martha Minow (eds) *Imagine Coexistence. Restoring Humanity After Violent Ethnic Conflict,* San Francisco, CA: Jossey-Bass, pp. 294–310.

Cockburn, Cynthia (2004) *The Line. Women, Partition and the Gender Order in Cyprus*, London: Zed Books.

—— (2002) 'Women's Organization in the Rebuilding of Bosnia-Herzegovina', in Cynthia Cockburn and Dubravka Zarkov (eds) *The Post-War Moment: Militaries, Masculinities and International Peacekeeping*, London: Lawrence and Wishart, pp. 68–84.

—— (1998) *The Space between Us. Negotiating Gender and National Identities in Conflict*, London: Zed Books.

Cockburn, Cynthia and Zarkov, Dubravka (eds) (2002) *The Post-War Moment: Militaries, Masculinities and International Peacekeeping*, London: Lawrence and Wishart.

Coomeraswamy, Radhika (ed.) (2004) *Women, Peace-making and Constitutions*, New Delhi: Women Unlimited.

Copelon, Rhonda (2000) 'Gender Crimes as War Crimes: Integrating Crimes Against Women into International Criminal Law', *McGill Law Journal*, 46: 217–240.

Corrin, Chris (2004) 'International and Local Interventions to Reduce Gender-Based Violence Against Women in Post-Conflict Situations', paper presented to the UN WIDER Conference on Making Peace Work, Helsinki, Finland, 4–5 June. Online, available at: www.wider.unu.edu/conference/conference-2004–1/conference-2004–1-menu.htm (accessed 5 August 2004).

Crocker, Chester A., Osler Hampson, Fen and Aall, Pamela (eds) (2005) *Grasping the Nettle. Analyzing Cases of Intractable Conflict*, Washington, DC: US Institute of Peace Press.

Crocker, David A. (2003) 'Reckoning with Past Wrongs: A Normative Framework', in Carol A. L. Prager and Trudy Govier (eds) *Dilemmas of Reconciliation. Cases and Concepts*, Waterloo, Ontario: Wilfred Laurier University Press, pp. 39–64.

D'Costa, Bina (2006) 'Marginalized Identity: New Frontiers of Research for International Relations?' in Brooke A. Ackerly, Maria Stern and Jacqui True (eds) *Feminist Methodologies for International Relations*, Cambridge: Cambridge University Press, pp. 129–152.

D'Estrée, Tamra Pearson and Babbitt, Eileen F. (1998) 'Women and the Art of Peacemaking: Data from Israeli–Palestinian Interactive Problem-Solving Workshops', *Political Psychology*, 19(1): 185–209.

Danbolt, Iselin, Gumbonzvanda, Nyaradzai and Karamé, Kari (2005) *Towards Achieving the MDGs in Sudan: Centrality of Women's Leadership and Gender Equality*, Oslo: Norwegian Ministry of Foreign Affairs.

Das, Veena (1996) 'Language and Body: Transactions in the Construction of Pain', *Daedalus*, 125(1): 67–92.

DasGupta, Sumona and Gopinath, Meenakshi (2005) 'Women Breaking the Silence: The *Athwaas* Initiative in Kashmir', in Paul van Tongeren, Malin Brenk, Marte Hellema and Juliette Verhoeven (eds) *People Building Peace II. Successful Stories of Civil Society*, Boulder, CO: Lynne Rienner Publishers, pp. 111–116.

Date-Bah, Eugenia (2003) 'Women and Other Gender Concerns in Post-Conflict Reconstruction and Job Promotion Efforts', in Eugenia Date-Bah (ed.) *Jobs after War. A Critical Challenge in the Peace and Reconstruction Puzzle*, Geneva: International Labour Office, pp. 111–149.

de la Rey, Cheryl and McKay, Susan (2006) 'Peacebuilding as a Gendered Process', *Journal of Social Issues*, 62(1): 141–153.

Derrida, Jacques (2002) *On Cosmopolitanism and Forgiveness*, trans. M. Dooley and M. Hughes, London: Routledge.

Diamond, Louise and MacDonald, John (1996) *A Systems Approach to Peace*, 3rd edn, West Hartford, CT: Kumarian Press.

Digeser, P. E. (2001) *Political Forgiveness*, Ithaca, NY: Cornell University Press.

Dillon, Robin S. (2001) 'Self-Forgiveness and Self-Respect', *Ethics*, 112(1): 53–83.

Drakulic, Slavenka (2001) 'Foča's Everyday Rapists', *Institute for War and Peace Reporting Tribunal Update*, TU 226, 18–23 June. Online, available at: www.iwpr.net/index.pl?archive/tri/tri_226_2_eng.txt (accessed 1 March 2005).

Dwyer, Susan (1999) 'Reconciliation for Realists', *Ethics and International Affairs*, 13(1): 81–98.

Eisenstein, Zillah (1996) *Hatreds. Racialized and Sexualized Conflicts in the 21st Century*, London: Routledge.

Ekiyor, Thelma Arimiebi (2004) 'Women's Empowerment in Peacebuilding; A Platform for Involvement in Decision Making. The WIPNET Experience'. Online, available at: http://awdf.org/lib/pdf/awdf%20paper.pdf (accessed 1 February 2005).

El-Bushra, Judy (2003) *Women Building Peace. Sharing Know-how*, London: International Alert and Women Waging Peace.

—— (2000) 'Transforming Conflict: Some Thoughts on a Gendered Understanding of Conflict Processes', in Susie Jacobs, Ruth Jacobsen and Jennifer Marchbank (eds) *States of Conflict, Gender, Violence and Resistance*, London: Zed Books, pp. 66–86.

El-Bushra, Judy, with Adrain-Paul, Ancil and Olson, Maria (2005) *Women Building Peace: Sharing Know-How. Assessing Impact: Planning for Miracles*, London: International Alert and Women Waging Peace.

El Jack, Amani (2003) *Gender and Armed Conflict. Overview Report*, University of Sussex: BRIDGE Institute of Development Studies. Online, available at: www.ids.ac.uk/bridge.

Ellsberg, Mary and Heise, Lori (2005) *Researching Violence Against Women: A Practical Guide for Researchers and Activists*, Washington, DC: World Health Organization/PATH.

Elshtain, Jean-Bethke (2003a) *Just War Against Terror*, New York: Basic Books.

—— (2003b) 'Politics and Forgiveness', in Nigel Biggar (ed.) *Burying the Past. Making Peace and Doing Justice after Civil Conflict*, Washington, DC: Georgetown University Bell, pp. 45–64.

—— (1987) *Women and War*, London: Harvester Press.

Enda, Jodi (2003) 'Women Take Lead in Reconstruction of Rwanda', *Women's e-News*, 16 November. Online, available at: www.globalpolicy.org/socecon/inequal/gender/2003/1116womenrwanda.htm (accessed 11 March 2005).

Enloe, Cynthia (2002) 'Demilitarization – or More of the Same? Feminist Questions to Ask in the Postwar Moment', in Dubravka Zarkov and Cynthia Cockburn (eds) *The Post-War Moment: Militaries, Masculinities and International Peacekeeping*, London: Lawrence and Wishart, pp. 22–32.

—— (1993) *The Morning After: Sexual Politics at the End of the Cold War*, Berkeley, CA: University of California Press.

—— (1990) *Bananas, Beaches and Bases: Making Feminist Sense of International Politics*, Berkeley, CA: University of California Press.

—— (1988) *Does Khaki Become You? The Militarization of Women's Lives*, London: Pandora Press/HarperCollins.

Farah, Ahmed Yusuf and Lewis, Ioan Myrddin (1995) *Somalia: The Roots of Reconciliation*, London: Action Aid.

Fast, Larissa and Neufeldt, Reina C. (2005) 'Envisioning Success: Building Blocks for Strategic and Comprehensive Peacebuilding Impact Evalution, *Journal of Peacebuilding and Development*, 2(2): 24–41.

Flax, Jane (1993) *Disrupted Subjects, Essays on Psychoanalysis, Politics and Philosophy*, New York: Routledge.

—— (1998) 'Displacing Woman. Toward an Ethics of Multiplicity', in Bat-Ami Bar On and Ann Ferguson (eds) *Daring to Be Good. Essays in Feminist Ethico-Politics*, New York and London: Routledge, pp. 143–155.

Forget, Marc (2003) 'Crime and Interpersonal Conflict: Reconciliation between Victim and Offender', in Carol A. L. Prager and Trudy Govier (eds) *Dilemmas of Reconciliation. Cases and Concepts*, Waterloo, Ontario: Wilfred Laurier University Press, pp. 111–136.

Forsberg, Tuomas (2003) 'The Philosophy and Practice of Dealing with the Past: Some Conceptual and Normative Issues', in Nigel Biggar (ed.) *Burying the Past. Making Peace and Doing Justice after Civil Conflict*, Washington, DC: Georgetown University Bell, pp. 65–84.

Fox, Mary Jane (2004) 'Girl Soldiers: Human Security and Gendered Insecurity', *Security Dialogue*, 35(4): 465–479.

Fraser, Nancy (2003) *Redistribution or Recognition? A Political–Philosophical Exchange*, London: Verso.

—— (2002) 'Recognition without Ethics?' in Scott Lash and Mike Featherstone (eds) *Recognition and Difference. Politics, Identity, Multiculture*, London: Sage, pp. 21–42.

Fraser, Nancy and Honneth, Axel (2003) *Redistribution or Recognition? A Political–Philosophical Exchange*, trans. Joel Solg, James Ingram and Christine Wilke. London: Verso.

Frazer, Elizabeth and Lacey, Nicole (1993) *The Politics of Community. A Feminist Critique of the Liberal–Communitarian Divide*, Toronto: University of Toronto Press.

Freeman, Mark and Hayner, Priscilla B. (2003) 'Truth-Telling', in David Bloomfield, Teresa Barnes and Luc Huyse (eds) *Reconciliation after Violent Conflict. A Handbook*, Stockholm: International Institute for Democracy and Electoral Assistance, pp. 122–139.

Fukuyama, Francis (1998) 'Women and the Evolution of World Politics', *Foreign Affairs*, 77(5): 24–40.

Galtung, Johan (2004a) 'The Security Approach and the Peace Approach: Some Cultural Factors Conditioning the Choice'. Paper presented at the World Culture Open, UN Meeting, Building Peace Through Harmonious Diversity, 9 October: Online, available at: www.transcend.org/t_database/printarticle.php?ida=491 (accessed 3 March 2005).

—— (2004b) 'Human Needs, Humanitarian Intervention, Human Security – and the War in Iraq', Keynote address at Sophia University/ICU, Tokyo, 14 December 2003. Online, available at: www.transcend.org/t_database/printarticle.php?ida=262 (accessed 3 March 2005).

Garcia, Ed (2005) 'Bridging Memory and Hope', in Gráinne Kelly and Brandon Hamber (eds) *Reconciliation: Rhetoric or Relevant?*, report 17, Belfast: Democratic Dialogue, pp. 36–41.

—— (2004) 'Empowering People to Build a Just Peace in the Asian Arena', in Annelies Heijmans, Nicola Simmonds and Hans van de Veen (eds) *Searching for Peace in Asia Pacific. An Overview of Conflict Prevention and Peacebuilding Activities*, Boulder, CO: Lynne Rienner Publishers, pp. 23–36.

Gardner, Judith and El-Bushra, Judy (eds) (2004) *Somalia – the Untold Story. The War Through the Eyes of Somali Women*, London: Pluto Press.

Gardner, Judith with Warsame, Amina Mohamoud (2004) 'Women, Clan Identity and Peace-building', in Judith Gardner and Judy El Bushra (eds) *Somalia – the Untold Story. The War Through the Eyes of Somali Women*, London: Pluto Press, pp. 153–165.

Gilligan, Carol (1987) 'Moral Orientation and Moral Development', in Eva Feder Kittay and Diana T. Meyers (eds) *Women and Moral Theory*, Totowa, NJ: Rowman & Littlefield, pp. 19–33.

—— (1983) *In a Different Voice*, Cambridge, MA: Harvard University Press.

Gobodo-Madikizela, Pumla (2003) *The Human Being Died that Night: A South African Story of Forgiveness*, New York: Houghton Mifflin.

Gobodo-Madikizela, Pumla (2005) *Women's Contribution to South Africa's Truth and Reconciliation Commission*, New York: Hunt Alternatives Fund.

Goldblatt, Beth and Meintjes, Sheila (1998) 'South African Women Demand the Truth', in Meredith Turshen and Clotilde Twagiramariya (eds) *What Women Do In Wartime. Gender and Conflict in Africa*, London: Zed Books, pp. 27–61.

Goldstone, Richard J. (1996) 'Justice as a Tool for Peace-Making: Truth Commissions and International Criminal Tribunals', *New York University Journal of International Law and Politics*, 28(3): 485–503.

Goodhand, Jonathan and Hulme, David (1999) 'From Wars to Complex Political Emergencies: Understanding Conflict and Peace-Building in the New World Disorder', *Third World Quarterly*, 20(1): 13–26.

Gopinath, Meenakshi and DasGupta, Sumona (2006) 'Structural Challenges, Enabling Spaces: Gender and Non-Traditional Formulations of Security in South Asia', in Ralf Emmers, Mely Caballero-Anthony and Amitabh Acharya (eds) *Studying Non-Traditional Security in Asia. Trend and Issues*, Singapore: Marshall Cavendish Academic, pp. 192–209.

Gordon, Michael (2001) *Reconciliation. A Journey*, Sydney: University of New South Wales Press.

Gould, Carol (2004) *Globalizing Democracy and Human Rights*, Cambridge: Cambridge University Press.

—— (1996) 'Diversity and Democracy: Representing Differences', in Seyla Benhabib (ed.) *Democracy and Difference. Contesting the Boundaries of the Political*, Princeton, NJ: Princeton University Press, pp. 171–186.

Govier, Trudy (2003) 'What Is Acknowledgement and Why Is It Important?', in Carol A. L. Prager and Trudy Govier (eds) *Dilemmas of Reconciliation. Cases and Concepts*, Waterloo, Ontario: Wilfred Laurier University Press, pp. 65–90.

—— (1999) 'Forgiveness and the Unforgivable', *American Philosophical Quarterly*, 36(1): 59–76.

Govier, Trudy and Verwoerd, Wilhelm (2004) 'How Not to Polarize "Victims" and "Perpetrators"', *Peace Review*, 16(3): 371–377.

Grosz, Elizabeth (1994) 'Sexual Difference and the Problem of Essentialism', in Naomi Schor and Elizabeth Weed (eds) *The Essential Difference*, Bloomington, IN: Indiana University Press, pp. 82–97.

Guillerot, Julie (2006) 'Linking Gender and Reparations in Peru: A Failed Opportunity', in Ruth Rubio-Marín (ed.) *Engendering Reparations: Recognizing and Compensating Women Victims of Human Rights Violations*, New York: International Centre for Transitional Justice, pp. 136–193.

Gutmann, Amy (1992) 'Introduction', in Charles Taylor (ed.) *Multiculturalism and 'The Politics of Recognition'*, Princeton, NJ: Princeton University Press, pp. 3–24.

Gutmann, Amy and Thompson, Dennis (1996) *Democracy and Disagreement*, Cambridge, MA: Belknap Press.

Habel, Norman C. (1999) *Reconciliation. Searching for Australia's Soul*, Sydney: HarperCollins Publishers.

Hafner-Burton, Emilie and Pollack, Mark, A. (2002) 'Mainstreaming Gender in Global Governance', *European Journal of International Relations*, 8(3): 339–373.

Hage, Ghassan (1998) *White Nation. Fantasies of White Supremacy in a Multicultural Society*, Annandale, NSW: Pluto Press.

Halpern, Jodi and Weinstein, Harvey, M. (2004) 'Rehumanizing the Other: Empathy and Reconciliation', *Human Rights Quarterly*, 26(3): 561–583.

Hamber, Brandon (2003a) 'Healing', in David Bloomfield, Teresa Barnes and Luc Huyse (eds) *Reconciliation after Violent Conflict. A Handbook*, Stockholm: International Institute for Democracy and Electoral Assistance, pp. 77–88.

—— (2003b) 'Does the Truth Heal? A Psychological Perspective on Political Strategies for Dealing with the Legacy of Political Violence', in Nigel Biggar (ed.) *Burying the Past. Making Peace and Doing Justice after Civil Conflict*, Washington, DC: Georgetown University Bell, pp. 155–174.

Hamber, Brandon and Kelly, Gráinne (2005a) *A Place for Reconciliation? Conflict and Locality in Northern Ireland*, report 18, September, Belfast: Democratic Dialogue.

—— (2005b) 'The Challenge of Reconciliation in Post-Conflict Societies: Definitions, Problems and Proposals', in Ian O'Flynn and David Russell (eds) *Power Sharing. New Challenges for Divided Societies*, London: Pluto Press, pp. 188–203.

Hamilton, Heather B. (2000) 'Rwanda's Women: The Key to Reconstruction', *Journal of Humanitarian Assistance*, 10 May. Online, available at: www.jha.ac/greatlakes/b001.htm (accessed 26 April 2005).

Handrahan, Lori (2004) 'Conflict, Gender, Ethnicity and Post-Conflict Reconstruction', *Security Dialogue*, 35(4): 429–445.

Hayner, Priscilla (1999) 'In Pursuit of Justice and Reconciliation: Contributions of Truth Telling', in C. J. Arnson (ed.) *Comparative Peace Processes in Latin America*, Stanford, CA: Stanford University Press, pp. 363–383.

Healing Through Remembering (2002) *The Report of the Healing Through Remembering Project*, June, Belfast: Healing Through Remembering.

Held, Virginia (ed.) (1995) *Justice and Care. Essential Readings in Feminist Ethics*, Oxford: Westview Press.

Hermann, Tamar (2004) 'Reconciliation: Reflections on the Theoretical and Practical Utility of the Term', in Yaacov Bar-Siman-Tov (ed.) *From Conflict Resolution to Reconciliation*, Oxford: Oxford University Press, pp. 39–60.

Heyzer, Noeleen (2000) 'Statement by Noeleen Heyzer', *Security Council Open Debate on Women, Peace and Security*. Online, available at: www.unifem.undp.org (accessed 24 January 2001).

Hippler, Jochen (ed.) (2005) *Nation-Building. A Key Concept for Peaceful Conflict Transformation?* London: Pluto Press.

Hoogensen, Gunhild and Rottem, Svein Vigeland (2004) 'Gender Identity and the Subject of Security', *Security Dialogue*, 35(2): 155–171.

Hoogensen, Gunhild and Stuvøy, Kirsti (2006) 'Gender, Resistance and Human Security', *Security Dialogue*, 37(2): 207–228.

House of Commons Northern Ireland Affairs Committee (2005) *'Ways of Dealing with Northern Ireland's Past: Interim Report – Victims and Survivors*, vols I and II, London: The Stationery Office.

Hudson, Heidi (2005) '"Doing" Security as Though Humans Matter: A Feminist Perspective on Gender and the Politics of Human Security', *Security Dialogue*, 36(2): 155–174.

Human Rights Watch (2001) 'World Report 2001: Women's Human Rights'. Online, at: www.hrw.org/wr2k1/women (accessed 31 May 2007).

Humphrey, Michael (2002) *The Politics of Atrocity and Reconciliation. From Terror to Trauma*. London: Routledge.

Hunt, Swanee and Posa, Christina (2001) 'Women Waging Peace', *Foreign Policy Magazine*, (May–June): 1–7. Online, available at: www.foreignpolicy.com/issue_mayjune_2001/huntprint.html (accessed 6 September 2001).

Hutchings, Kimberley (2001) 'Ethics, Feminism, and International Affairs', in Jean-Marc Coicaud and Daniel Warner (eds) *Ethics and International Affairs: Extent and Limits*, Tokyo: UN University Press, pp. 194–216.

Huyse, Luc (2005) 'Justice after Transition: On the Choices Successor Elites Make in Dealing with the Past', *Law and Social Inquiry*, 20(1): 51–78.

—— (2003a) 'The Process of Reconciliation', in David Bloomfield, Teresa Barnes and Luc Huyse (eds) *Reconciliation after Violent Conflict. A Handbook*, Stockholm: International Institute for Democracy and Electoral Assistance, pp. 19–33.

—— (2003b) 'Victims', in David Bloomfield, Teresa Barnes and Luc Huyse (eds) *Reconciliation after Violent Conflict. A Handbook*, Stockholm: International Institute for Democracy and Electoral Assistance, pp. 54–66.

—— (2003c) 'Justice', in David Bloomfield, Teresa Barnes and Luc Huyse (eds) *Reconciliation after Violent Conflict. A Handbook*, Stockholm: International Institute for Democracy and Electoral Assistance, pp. 97–115.

Ignatieff, Michael (2003) 'Afterword. Reflections on Coexistence', in Antonia Chayes and Martha Minow (eds) *Imagine Coexistence. Restoring Humanity after Violent Ethnic Conflict*, San Francisco, CA: Jossey-Bass, pp. 325–333.

—— (1993) *Blood and Belonging. Journeys into the New Nationalism*, London: Chatto and Windus.

InterAction-Commission on the Advancement of Women (CAW) and International Institute of Rural Reconstruction (IIRR) (2004) *Gender Mainstreaming in Action: Successful Innovations from Asia and the Pacific*, Washington, DC and Cavite, the Philippines: CAW and IIRR.

International Alert and Women Waging Peace (2004) *Inclusive Security, Sustainable Peace: A Toolkit for Advocacy and Action*, London and Washington DC: International Alert and Women Waging Peace.

International Women's Tribune Center (2002) 'Facts for PeaceWomen: A Fact Sheet on Women and Armed Conflict', *1325 PeaceWomen E-News (12th ed.)*, 1 November. Online, available at: listserv@peacewomen.org (accessed 1 November 2002).

Jabri, Vivienne (2001) 'Restyling the Subject of Responsibility in International Relations', in Hakan Seckinelgin and Hideaki Shinoda (eds) *Ethics and International Relations*, Basingstoke: Palgrave, pp. 161–184.

—— (1999) 'Explorations of Difference in Normative International Relations', in Vivienne Jabri and Eleanor O'Gorman (eds) *Women, Culture and International Relations*, London: Lynne Rienner Publishers, pp. 39–59.

Jabri, Vivienne and O'Gorman, Eleanor (eds) (1999) *Women, Culture and International Relations*, London: Lynne Rienner Publishers.

Jaggar, Alison M. (1998) 'Globalizing Feminist Ethics', *Hypatia*, 13(2): 7–31.

Jakobsen, Janet (1998) *Working Alliances and the Politics of Difference*, Bloomington, IN: Indiana University Press.

Junne, Gerd and Verkoren, Willemijn (2005) 'The Challenges of Postconflict Development', in Gerd Junne and Willemijn Verkoren (eds) *Postconflict Development. Meeting New Challenges*, Boulder, CO: Lynne Rienner Publishers, pp. 1–18.

Kaldor, Mary (2003) *Global Civil Society: An Answer to War*, Cambridge: Polity Press.

Kandiyoti, Deniz (2005) 'The Politics of Gender Reconstruction in Afghanistan', *Occasional Paper*, 4, February, Geneva: UNRISD.

Karam, Azza (2001) 'Women in War and Peace-building. The Roads Transversed, The Challenges Ahead', *International Feminist Journal of Politics*, 3(1): 1–25.

Karamé, Kari (2001) *Gendering Human Security. From Marginalization to the Integration of Women in Peace-building,* NUPI report no. 261, Oslo: Norwegian Institute of International Affairs.

Kašić, Biljana (ed.) (1997) *Women and the Politics of Peace. Contributors to a Culture of Women's Resistance*, Zagreb: Centre for Women's Studies.

Kateb, George (1992) *The Inner Ocean: Individualism and Democratic Culture*, Ithaca, NY: Cornell University Press.

Kegley, Charles W. and Wittkopf, Eugene R. (2004) *World Politics. Trend and Transformation*, 9th edn, Belmont, CA: Thomson Wadsworth.

Kelly, Gráinne and Hamber, Brandon (2005) 'Views in Northern Ireland', in Gráinne Kelly and Brandon Hamber (eds) *Reconciliation: Rhetoric or Relevant?*, report 17, Belfast: Democratic Dialogue, pp. 21–33.

Khoo, Tseen (2004) 'Fortress Australia', *Signs*, 29(2): 584–586.

Kim, Sung Hee (2005) 'The Role of vengeance in Conflict Escalation', in I. William Zartman and Guy Olivier Faure (eds) *Escalation and Negotiation in International Conflicts*, Cambridge: Cambridge University Press, 141–162.

King, Angela (2000) 'Statement by Angela King', *Security Council Open Debate on Women, Peace and Security*. Online, available at: www.un.org/womenwatch/news/articles/aksc.html (accessed 24 January 2001).

Kittay, Eva Feder and Meyers, Diana Tietjens (eds) (1987) *Women and Moral Theory*, Totowa, NJ: Rowman & Littlefield.

Kleck, Monika (2006) 'Working with Traumatized Women', in Martina Fischer (ed.) *Peacebuilding a Civil Society in Bosnia-Herzegovina. Ten Years after Dayton*, Berlin: LIT VERLAG, pp. 343–355.

Knight, W. Andy (2004) 'Conclusion. Peacebuilding Theory and Praxis', in Tom Keating and W. Andy Knight (eds) *Building Sustainable Peace*, Tokyo: United Nations University Press, pp. 355–387.

Kriesberg, Louis (2000) 'Coexistence and the Reconciliation of Communal Conflicts', in Eugene Weiner (ed.) *The Handbook of Interethnic Coexistence*, New York: Continuum, pp. 182–198.

Kristeva, Julia, (1993) *Nations without Nationalism*, trans. L. S Roudiez, New York: Columbia University Press.

Kristianasen, Wendy (2006) 'Algeria: The Women Speak', *Le Monde diplomatique*, April. Online, available at: http://mondediplo.com/2006/04/07algeria (accessed 26 November 2006).

Krog, Antjie (2001) 'Locked into Loss and Silence. Testimonies of Gender and Violence at the South African Truth Commission', in Carolyn Moser and Fiona Clark (eds) *Victims, the Perpetrators or Actors? Gender, Armed Conflict and Political Violence*, London: Zed Books, pp. 203–216.

—— (1998) *Country of My Skull*, London: Jonathan Cape.

Lamb, Sharon (2006) 'Forgiveness, Women, and Responsibility to the Group', *Journal of Human Rights*, 5(1): 45–60.

Lapsley, Michael (1998) 'Confronting the Past and Creating the Future: The Redemptive Value of Truth Telling', *Social Research*, 65(4): 741–758.

Larrabee, Mary Jeanne (ed.) (1993) *An Ethic of Care. Feminism and Interdisciplinary Perspectives*, London: Routledge.

Lederach, John Paul (2005) *The Moral Imagination. The Art and Soul of Building Peace*, Oxford: Oxford University Press.

—— (2004) *Building Peace. Sustainable Reconciliation in Divided Societies*, Washington, DC: United States Institute of Peace Press.

Lloyd, Genevieve (1984) *The Man of Reason. 'Male' and 'Female' in Western Philosophy*, London: Methuen.

Lorentzen, Lois Ann and Turpin, Jennifer (eds) *The Women and War Reader*, New York: New York University Press.

Lynes, Krista and Torry, Gina (eds) (2005) 'From Local to Global: Making Peace Work for Women'. *NGO Working Group on Women, Peace and Security. Security Council Resolution 1325 – Five Years on Report*, October, New York: NGO Working Group on Women, Peace and Security.

McKay, Susan (2000) 'Gender Justice and Reconciliation', *Women's Studies International Forum*, 23(5): 561–570.

McKay, Susan and Mazurana, Dyan (2002) *Raising Women's Voices for Peacebuilding: Vision, Impact, and Limitations of Media Technologies*, London: International Alert and Women Waging Peace.

McNairn, Rosemarie (2005) 'Building Capacity to Resolve Conflict in Communities: Oxfam Experience in Rwanda', in Caroline Sweetman (ed) *Gender, Peacebuilding and Reconstruction*, Oxford: Oxfam, pp. 83–93.

McWilliams, Monica (2006) 'Human Rights and Conflict Resolution: Are They Mutually Dependant in a Divided Society?', in Elisabeth Porter and Baden Offord (eds) *Activating Human Rights*, Oxford: Peter Lang, pp. 67–86.

—— (2002) 'Collective Effort is Our Success', Speech to the Northern Ireland Women's Coalition. Online, available at: www.niwc.org/monicaspeech.asp (accessed 11 March 2005).

MacIntyre, Alasdair (1981) *After Virtue. A Study in Moral Theory*, London: Duckworth.

Machel, Graça (1996) 'The Impact of Armed Conflict on Children', New York: UNICEF. Online, available at: www.unicef.org/graca/ (accessed 1 September 2000).

Mack Andrew (ed.) (2005) *Human Security Report 2005. War and Peace in the 21st Century*, New York: Oxford University Press.

Maclellan, Nic (2004) 'Regional Introduction: Creating Peace in the Pacific – Conflict Resolution, Reconciliation, and Restorative Justice', in Annelies Heijmans, Nicola Simmonds and Hans van de Veen (eds) *Searching for Peace in Asia Pacific. An Overview of Conflict Prevention and Peacebuilding Activities*, Boulder, CO: Lynne Rienner Publishers, pp. 526–542.

Maiese, Michelle (2003) 'What it Means to Build a Lasting Peace', in Guy Burgess and Heidi Burgess (eds) *Beyond Intractability*. Online, available at: www2.beyond intractability.org/m/peacebuilding.jsp (accessed 5 December 2005).

Maiguashca, Bice (2000) 'Theorising Politics in "No Man's Land": Feminist Theory and the Fourth Debate', in Michi Ebata and Beverly Neufeld (eds) *Confronting the Political in International Relations*, London: Macmillan, pp. 123–150.

Mamdani, M. (2001) *When Victims become Killers: Colonialism, Nativism and the Genocide in Rwanda*, Princeton, NJ: Princeton University Press.

Mani, Rama (2005) 'Balancing Peace with Justice in the Aftermath of Violent Conflict', *Development*, 48(3): 25–34.

Mansbridge, Jane (1996) 'Reconstructing Democracy', in Nancy Hirschmann and Christine Di Stefano (eds) *Revisioning the Political*, Boulder, CO: Westview Press, pp. 117–138.

Mantilla, Julissa (2006) *Gender, Justice, and Truth Commissions*, Washington, DC: The World Bank.

Marks, John (2005) 'Understand the Differences, Act on the Commonalities', in Paul van Tongeren, Malin Brenk, Marte Hellema and Juliette Verhoeven (eds) *People Building Peace II. Successful Stories of Civil Society*, Boulder, CO: Lynnne Rienner Publishers, pp. 185–186.

Marshall, Monty G. and Gurr, Ted Robert (2005) *Peace and Conflict. A Global Survey of Armed Conflicts, Self-Determination Movements, and Democracy*, College Park, MD: Center for International Development and Conflict Management, University of Maryland.

Mazurana, Dyan (2004) *Women in Armed Opposition Groups Speak on War, Protection, and Operations under International Humanitarian and Human Rights Law*, Geneva: Geneva Call.

—— (2002) 'International Peacekeeping Operations: To Neglect Gender Is to Risk Peacekeeping Failure', in Cynthia Cockburn and Dubravka Zarkov (eds) *The Postwar Moment: Militaries, Masculinities and International Peacekeeping*, London: Lawrence and Wishart, pp. 41–50.

Mazurana, Dyan E. and McKay, Susan R. (1999) *Women and Peacebuilding*, Montreal: International Centre for Human Rights and Democratic Development.

Mazurana, Dyan, McKay, Susan, Carlson, Khristopher and Kasper, Janel (2002) 'Girls in Fighting Forces: Their Recruitment, Participation, Demobilization, and Reintegration', *Peace and Conflict*, 8(2): 97–123.

Meintjes, Sheila, Pillay, Anu and Turshen, Meredeth (2001) 'There Is No Aftermath for Women', in Sheila Meintjes, Anu Pillay and Meredeth Turhsen (eds) *The Aftermath. Women in Post-Conflict Transformation*, London: Zed Books, pp. 3–18.

Méndez, Juan E. (2001) 'National Reconciliation, Transnational Justice, and the International Criminal Court', *Ethics and International Affairs*, 15(1): 25–44.

Michnik, Adam and Havel, Václav (1993) 'Confronting the Past. Justice or Revenge?' *Journal of Democracy*, 4(1): 20–27.

Midgley, Mary (1999) 'Toward an Ethic of Global Responsibility', in Tim Dunne and Nicholas Wheeler (eds) *Human Rights in Global Politics*, Cambridge: Cambridge University Press, pp. 160–176.

Miller, David (1997) *On Nationality*, Oxford: Clarendon Press.

Mindry, Deborah (2001) 'Nongovernmental Organizations, "Grassroots", and the Politics of Virtue', *Signs: Journal of Women in Culture and Society*, 26(4): 1187–1211.

Minow, Martha (2003) 'Education for Coexistence', in Antonia Chayes and Martha Minow (eds) *Imagine Coexistence. Restoring Humanity after Violent Ethnic Conflict*, San Francisco, CA: Jossey-Bass, pp. 213–234.

—— (1998) *Between Vengeance and Forgiveness: Facing History after Genocide and Mass Violence*, Boston, MA: Beacon.

—— (1997) *Not Only for Myself. Identity, Politics and the Law*, New York: The New Press.

Montiel, Cristina Jayme (2000) 'Constructive and Destructive Post-Conflict Forgiveness', *Peace Review*, 12(1): 95–101.

Muchenga Chicuecue, Noel (1997) 'Reconciliation: The Role of Truth Commission and Alternative Ways of Healing', *Development in Practice*, 7(4): 483–486.

Nakaya, Sumie (2004) 'Women and Gender Equality in Somalia and Mozambique', in Tom Keating and W. Andy Knight (eds) *Building Sustainable Peace*, Tokyo: UN University Press, pp. 142–166.

Nantulya, Paul (2006) 'African Nation-building and Reconstruction: Lessons from Rwanda', *Accord. Conflict Trends*, 1: 45–50. Online, available at: www.accord.org.za/ct/2006–1.htm (accessed 19 June 2006).

Narayan, Uma (1995) 'Colonialism and its Others: Considerations on Rights and Care Discourses', *Hypatia*, 10(2): 133–40.

Näslund, Emma (1999) 'Looking at Peace through Women's Eyes: Gender-Based Discrimination in the Salvadorean Peace Process', *Journal of Public and International Affairs*, 10: 16–32.

Nemeh, Norma (2001) 'The Female Element in the Security Equation', *Jordan Times*, 16 December.

NGO Working Group on Women and International Peace and Security (NGOWG) (2006) *SCR 1325 and the Peacebuilding Commission. Security Council Resolution 1325 on Women, Peace and Security – Six Years on Report*, October, New York: NGO Working Group on Women, Peace and Security.

—— (2004) *Four Years On: An Alternative Report and Progress Check on the Implementation of Security Council Resolution 1325 – Findings and Recommendations for UN Member States and UN Entities from Women's Civil Society Organizations*. Online, available at: www.peacewomen.org.un/ngo/ngopub/FourYearsOnOct04.pdf (accessed 7 February 2005).

—— (2001) *Security Council Resolution 1325 – One Year On*. Online, available at: www.international-alert.org/women/oneyron.PDF (accessed 6 September 2002).

Notter, James and Diamond, Louise (1996) *Building Peace and Transforming Conflict: Multi-Track Diplomacy in Practice. Occasional Paper No 7*. Washington, DC: Institute of Multi-Track Diplomacy.

Nowrojee, Binaifer (2005) '"Your Justice is Too Slow". Will the ICTR Fail Rwanda's Rape Victims?' *Occasional Paper 10*, Geneva: UNRISD.

Nussbaum, Martha C. (2000) *Women and Human Development. The Capabilities Approach*, Cambridge: Cambridge University Press.

—— (1999) *Sex and Social Justice*, Oxford: Oxford University Press.

—— (1996) 'Compassion: The Basic Social Emotion', in E. Frankel, F. D. Miller and J. Paul (eds) *The Communitarian Challenge to Liberalism*, Cambridge: Cambridge University Press, pp. 27–58.

Obiora, L. Amede (1997) 'Feminism, Globalization, and Culture: After Beijing', *Indiana Journal of Global Legal Studies*, 4(2): 355–406.

Ogata, Sadako (2003) 'Foreword', in Antonia Chayes and Martha Minow (eds) *Imagine Coexistence. Restoring Humanity after Violent Ethnic Conflict*, San Francisco, CA: Jossey-Bass, pp. xi–xv.

Olsson, Louise (2000) 'Mainstreaming Gender in Multidimensional Peacekeeping: A Field Perspective', *International Peacekeeping*, 7(3): 1–16.

Olsson, Louise and Tryggestad, Torunn, L. (ed.) (2001) *Women and International Peacekeeping*, London: Frank Cass.

Omaar, Rakiya and Ibreck, Rachel (2004) *Women Taking a Lead. Progress Toward Empowerment and Gender Equity in Rwanda. Women for Women International Briefing Paper*, September. Kigali, Rwanda: Women for Women International – Rwanda.

O'Neill, Onora (1993) 'Justice, Gender, and International Boundaries', in Martha Nussbaum and Amartya Sen (eds) *The Quality of Life*, Oxford: Clarendon Press, 303–323.

Online Working Group on Women and Armed Conflict (1999) *Women and Armed Conflict. 'Good Practices, Lessons Learnt, Challenges and Emerging Issues' for Implementing the Beijing Platform for Action: Final Report*, 11 October–19 November, London: International Alert and Women Waging Peace. Online, available at: www.international-alert.org/women/idmakers/WomenwatchReport.pdf (accessed 1 February 2001).

Pankhurst, Donna (1999a) *Mainstreaming Gender in Peacebuilding: A Framework for Action. From the Village Council to the Negotiating Table*, London: International Alert and Women Waging Peace.

—— (1999b) 'Issues of Justice and Reconciliation in Complex Political Emergencies: Conceptualising Reconciliation, Justice and Peace', *Third World Quarterly*, 20(1): 239–256.

Paris, Roland (2004) *At War's End. Building Peace After Civil Conflict*, Cambridge: Cambridge University Press.

Peterson, V. Spike (2000) 'A "Gendered Global Hierarchy"?', in Grey Fry and Jacinta O'Hagan (eds) *Contending Images of World Politics*, London: Macmillan, pp. 199–213.

Pettman, Jan Jindy (1996) *Worlding Women. A Feminist International Politics*, London: Routledge.

Philipose, Liz (1996) 'The Laws of War and Women's Human Rights', *Hypatia*, 11(4): 46–62.

Phillips, Anne (2000) 'Multiculturalism, Universalism, and the Claims of Democracy', Geneva: UNRISD.

—— (1995) *The Politics of Presence*, Oxford: Clarendon Press.

Polgreen, Lydia and Rohter, Larry (2006) 'Where Political Clout Demands a Maternal Touch', *The New York Times*, 22 January: 4.

Porter, Elisabeth (2006a) 'Can Politics Practice Compassion?', *Hypatia*, 21(4): 97–123.

—— (2006b) 'No Just War: Political Reflections on Australian Churches' Condemnation of the Iraq War', *Australian Journal of Politics and History*, 52(3): 471–488.

—— (2005a) 'The Harm of Dualism', *Peace Review: A Journal of Social Justice*, 17(2–3): 321–237.

—— (2005b) 'Women and Security: You Cannot Dance if You Cannot Stand', *OpenDemocracy* 19 October. Online, available at: www.opendemocracy.net/democracy-resolution_1325/dance_2937.jsp.

—— (2003a) 'Women, Political Decision-Making, and Peace-Building', *Global Change, Peace and Security*, 15(3): 245–262.

—— (2003b) 'Security and Inclusiveness: Protecting Australia's Way of Life', *Peace, Conflict and Development: An Interdisciplinary Journal*, 3: 1–18. Online, available at: www.peacesutudiesjournal.org.uk.

—— (2000) 'Risks and Responsibilities. Creating Dialogical Spaces in Northern Ireland', *International Feminist Journal of Politics*, 2(2): 163–184.

—— (1999) *Feminist Perspectives on Ethics*, London: Longman.

—— (1998) 'Identity, Location, Plurality: Women, Nationalism and Northern Ireland', in Rick Wilford and Robert Miller (eds) *Women, Ethnicity and Nationalism. The Politics of transition*, London: Routledge, pp. 36–61.

—— (1997a) 'Diversity and Commonality; Women, Politics and Northern Ireland', *European Journal of Women's Studies*, 4(1): 83–100.

—— (1997b) 'Belonging and Citizenship: An Australian in Northern Ireland', in George Crowder, Hayden Manning, David Mathieson, Andrew Parkin and Leonard Seabrooke (eds) *Australasian Political Studies 1997: Proceedings of the 1997 APSA Conference vol. 3*, Adelaide: Flinders University, pp. 863–878.

—— (1991) *Women and Moral Identity*, Sydney: Allen and Unwin.

Porter, Norman (2003) *The Elusive Quest. Reconciliation in Northern Ireland*, Belfast: Blackstaff Press.

Powley, Elizabeth (2005) 'Rwanda: Women Hold Up Half the Parliament', in International IDEA (eds) *Women in Parliament: Beyond Numbers*, Stockholm: International Institute for Democracy and Electoral Assistance, pp. 142–151.

—— (2003) *Strengthening Governance: The Role of Women in Rwanda's Transition*, New York: Hunt Alternatives Fund.

Prager, Carol A. L. (2003) 'Introduction', in Carol A. L. Prager and Trudy Govier (eds) *Dilemmas of Reconciliation. Cases and Concepts*, Waterloo, Ontario: Wilfred Laurier University Press, pp. 1–26.

Prager, Carol A. L. and Govier, Trudy (eds) (2003) *Dilemmas of Reconciliation. Cases and Concepts*, Waterloo, Ontario: Wilfred Laurier University Press.

Prince-Gibson, Eetta (2005) 'Silent Screams', *Jerusalem Post*, 22 August. Online, available at: www.jpost.com/ (accessed 23 August 2005).

Reardon, Betty (1993) *Women and Peace: Feminist Visions of Global Security*, Albany, NY: State University of New York Press.

Rehn, Elisabeth and Johnson-Sirleaf, Ellen (2002) *Women, War and Peace: The Independent Experts' Assessment on the Impact of Armed Conflict on Women and Women's Role in Peace-Building*, New York: UNIFEM.

Reimann, Cordula and Ropers, Norbert (2005) 'Discourses on Peace Practices: Learning to Change by Learning from Change?' in Paul van Tongeren, Malin Brenk, Marte Hellema and Juliette Verhoeven (eds) *People Building Peace II. Successful Stories of Civil Society*, Boulder, CO: Lynnne Rienner Publishers, pp. 29–43.

Richmond, Oliver P. (2004), The Globalization of Responses to Conflict and the Peace-building Consensus, *Cooperation and Conflict* 39(2): 129–150.

Rigby, Andrew (2001) *Justice and Reconciliation. After the Violence*, Boulder, CO: Lynne Rienner Publishers.

Robinson, Fiona (2006) 'Care, Gender and Global Social Justice: Rethinking "Ethical Globalization"', *Journal of Global Ethics*, 2(1): 5–45.

—— (2001) 'Exploring Social Relations, Understanding Power, and Valuing Care: the Role of Critical Feminist Ethics in International Relations Theory', in Hakan Seckinelgin and Hideaki Shinoda (eds) *Ethics and International Relations*, Basingstoke: Palgrave, pp. 56–80.

—— (1999) *Globalizing Care. Ethics, Feminist Theory, and the International Relations*, Boulder, CO: Westview Press.

Rooney, Eilish (2000) 'Learning to Remember and Remembering to Forget: *Beloved* from Belfast', in Lynne Pearce (ed.) *Feminist Readings in Home and Belonging*, Aldershot: Ashgate, pp. 215–234.

Rose, Jacqueline (1993) *Why War?*, Oxford: Blackwell.

Ross, Fiona C. (2003) *Bearing Witness. Women and the Truth and Reconciliation Commission in South Africa*, London: Pluto Press.

Roynestad, Emily (2003) 'Are Women Included or Excluded in Post-Conflict Reconstruction? A Case Study from Timor Leste', *DAW Expert Group Meeting on Peace Agreements as a Means for Promoting Gender Equality and Ensuring Participation of Women*, 10–13 November, EGM/PEACE/2003/EP.8, New York: DAW.

Rubio-Marín (ed.) (2006) *Engendering Reparations: Recognizing and Compensating Women Victims of Human Rights Violations*, New York: International Centre for Transitional Justice.

Ruddick, Sara (1992) 'From Maternal Thinking to Peace Politics', in Eve Browning Cole and Susan Coultrap-McQuin (eds) *Explorations in Feminist Ethics. Theory and Practice*, Bloomington, in: Indiana University Press, pp. 141–155.

Sandel, Michael (1982) *Liberalism and the Limits of Justice*, New York: Cambridge University Press.

Sarkin, Jeremy and Daly, Erin (2004) 'Too Many Questions, Too Few Answers: Reconciliation in Transitional Societies', *Columbia Human Rights Law Review*, 35(3): 661–728.

Schirch, Lisa and Sewak, Manjrika (2005a) 'The Role of Women in Peacebuilding', European Centre for Conflict Prevention, Global Partnership for the Prevention of Armed Conflict. Online, available at: www.gppac.net (accessed 1 March 2005).

—— (2005b) 'Women: Using the Gender Lens', in Paul van Tongeren, Malin Brenk, Marte Hellema and Juliette Verhoeven (eds) *People Building Peace II. Successful Stories of Civil Society*, Boulder CO: Lynnne Rienner Publishers, pp. 97–107.

Schmeidl, Susanne and Piza-Lopez, Eugenia (2002) *Gender and Conflict Early Warning: A Framework for Action*, London and Bern: International Alert and Women Waging Peace/Swiss Peace Foundation.

Schott, Robin May (2004) 'The Atrocity Paradigm and the Concept of Forgiveness', *Hypatia*, 19(4): 204–211.

Schroeder, Emily, Farr, Vanessa and Schnabel, Albrecht (2005) *Gender Awareness in Research on Small Arms and Light Weapons. A Preliminary Report*, Bern: Swisspeace.

Scraton, P. (2002) 'The Politics of Morality', in Paul Scraton (ed.) *Beyond September 11. An Anthology of Dissent*, London: Pluto Press, pp. 40–47.

Sevenhuijsen, Selma (1998) *Citizenship and the Ethics of Care. Feminist Considerations on Justice, Morality and Politics*, trans. Liz Savage, London: Routledge.

Shoemaker, Jolynn (ed.) with Conaway, Camille Pampell (2005) *Inclusive Security: Women Waging Peace. Conflict Prevention and Transformation: Women's Vital Contributions*, Conference Report, 23 February, Washington, DC: Hunt Alternatives Fund.

Shriver, Donald W. (2003) 'Where and When in Political Life Is Justice Served by Forgiveness', in Nigel Biggar (ed.) *Burying the Past. Making Peace and Doing Justice after Civil Conflict*, Washington, DC: Georgetown University Bell, pp. 25–44.

—— (1995) *An Ethic for Enemies: Forgiveness in Politics*. Oxford: Oxford University Press.

Sluzki, Carlos E. (2003) 'The Process Toward Reconciliation', in Antonia Chayes and Martha Minow (eds) *Imagine Coexistence. Restoring Humanity after Violent Ethnic Conflict*, San Francisco, CA: Jossey-Bass, pp. 21–31.

Smith, David (2004) 'Why I Befriended My Dad's Killer', *The Observer*, 10 October 2004: 10.

Smyth, Marie (2003) 'Putting the Past in Its Place: Issues of Victimhood and Reconciliation in Northern Ireland's Peace Process', in Nigel Biggar (ed.) *Burying the Past.*

Making Peace and Doing Justice after Civil Conflict, Washington, DC: Georgetown University Bell, pp. 125–153.

Snyder, Anna (2006) 'Fostering Transnational Dialogue: Lessons Learned from Women Peace Activists', *Globalizations*, 3(1): 31–47.

Sommers, Marc and McClintock, Elizabeth (2003) 'On Hidden Ground. One Coexistence Strategy in Central Africa', in Antonia Chayes and Martha Minow (eds) *Imagine Coexistence. Restoring Humanity after Violent Ethnic Conflict*, San Francisco, CA: Jossey-Bass, pp. 35–58.

Sooka, Yasmin (2006) 'Dealing with the Past and Transitional Justice: Building Peace through Accountability', *International Review of the Red Cross*, 88(862): 311–325.

Soyinka, Wole (2000) 'Memory, Truth and Healing', in Ifi Amadiume and An-Na'im, Abdullahi (eds) *The Politics of Memory: Truth, Healing and Social Justice*, London: Zed Books, pp. 21–37.

Spees, Pam (2004) *Gender Justice and Accountability in Peace Support Operations. Closing the Gap.* London: International Alert and Women Waging Peace.

Spelman, Elizabeth (2003) 'Coexistence and Repair', in Antonia Chayes and Martha Minow (eds) *Imagine Coexistence. Restoring Humanity after Violent Ethnic Conflict*, San Francisco, CA: Jossey-Bass, pp. 235–251.

Squires, Judith (ed.) (1993) *Principled Positions. Postmodernism and the Rediscovery of Value*, London: Lawrence and Wishart.

Statement by Women Delegates to Darfur Peace Talks (2006) 'Statement by the Women Delegates to the Darfur Peace Talks, in Abuja, Nigeria, on the Occasion of the International Women's Day', 8 March, after *Sudan Tribune*, press release. Online, available at: www.sudanonline.com (accessed 10 March 2006).

Steans, Jill (1998) *Gender and International Relations. An Introduction*, Cambridge: Polity Press.

Stern, Maria (2005) *Naming Security – Constructing Identity. 'Mayan Women' in Guatemala on the Eve of 'Peace'*, Manchester and New York: Manchester University Press.

Sweetman, Caroline (ed.) (2005) *Gender, Peacebuilding and Reconstruction*, Oxford: Oxfam.

Sword Gusmao, Kirsty (2006) 'Women and Children First', *The Sydney Morning Herald*, 11–12 November: 29.

Sylvester, Christine (2002) *Feminist International Relations. An Unfinished Journey*, Cambridge: Cambridge University Press.

Taylor, Charles (1992) *Multiculturalism and 'The Politics of Recognition'*, Princeton, NJ: Princeton University Press.

Tickner, J. Ann (2001) *Gendering World Politics. Issues and Approaches in the Post-Cold War Era*, New York: Columbia University Press.

—— (1999) 'Why Women Can't Run the World: International Politics According to Francis Fukuyama', *International Studies Review*, 1(3): 3–11.

—— (1997) 'You Just Don't Understand: Troubled Engagements between Feminists and IR Theorists', *International Studies Quarterly*, 41(4): 611–632.

—— (1992) *Gender in International Relations. Feminist Perspectives on Achieving Global Security*, New York: Columbia University Press.

Toppinen, Pilvi (2005) 'Critical Reflections on Social Justice and Recognition', *Res Publica*, 11(4): 425–434.

Tripp, Aili Mari (2000a) 'Rethinking Difference: Comparative Perspectives from Africa', *Signs: Journal of Women in Culture and Society*, 25(3): 649–675.

—— (2000b) 'The Politics of Women's Rights and Cultural Diversity in Uganda', Geneva: UNRISD.

Tronto, Joan (1995) 'Care as the Basis for Radical Political Judgments', *Hypatia*, 10(2): 141–49.

—— (1993) *Moral Boundaries. A Political Argument for an Ethic of Care*, London: Routledge.

Turshen, Meredith (1998) 'Women's War Stories', in Meredith Turshen and Clotilde Twagiramariya (eds) *What Women Do in Wartime. Gender and Conflict in Africa*, London and New York: Zed Books, pp. 1–26.

Turshen, Meredith and Twagiramariya, Clotilde (eds) (1998) *What Women Do in Wartime: Gender and Conflict in Africa*, London and New York: Zed Books.

Tutu, Desmond (1999) *No Future Without Forgiveness*, London: Rider.

United Nations (UN) (2000) 'Windhoek Declaration: The Namibia Plan of Action on Mainstreaming a Gender Perspective in Multidimensional Peace Support Operations', 31 May, (S/2000/693), Windhoek, Namibia: United Nations.

UN Commission on the Status of Women (CSW) (2004) 'Women's Equal Participation in Conflict Prevention, Management and Conflict Resolution and in Post-Conflict Peace-Building. Agreed Conclusions', Forty-Eighth Session, 1–12 March. Online, available at: www.peacewomen.org/un/ecosoc/CSW/FinalACCSW48Womenpart.pdf (accessed 17 July 2004).

—— (CSW) (2000a) 'Agreed Conclusions on the Critical Areas of Concern of the Beijing Platform For Action, 1996–1999', New York: United Nations.

—— (2000b) 'Summary of the WomenWatch Online Working Groups on the 12 Critical Areas of Concern of the Beijing Platform for Action', E/CN.6/2000/PC/CRP.1, New York: United Nations.

UN Department of Political Affairs (DPA) (2002) 'Assisting Nations to Cultivate Peace after Conflict. The Work of the UN Peacebuilding Support Offices'. Online, available at: www.un.org/Depts/dpa/docs/conflict/text.html (accessed 9 February 2005).

UN Development Fund for Women (UNIFEM) and the NGO Working Group on Women, Peace and Security (NGOWG) (2005) 'The UN Peacebuilding Commission: A Blueprint for Amplifying Women's Voices and Participation. Discussion Paper', New York: UN Research Institute for Social Development. UN Research Institute for Social Development (UNRISD) (2005) *Gender Equality. Striving for Justice in an Unequal World*, Geneva: UNRISD.

UN Development Programme (UNDP) (2003) 'From Recovery to Transition: Women, the Untapped Resource', *Essentials*, 11 July: 1–12.

—— (1996) *An Inventory of Post-Conflict Peace-Building Activities*, New York: United Nations.

UN Development Fund for Women (UNIFEM) and the NGO Working Group on Women, Peace and Security (NGOWG) (2005) 'The UN Peacebuilding Commission: A Blueprint for Amplifying Women's Voices and Participation. Discussion Paper', New York: UN Research Institute for Social Development. UN Research Institute for Social Development (UNRISD) (2005) *Gender Equality. Striving for Justice in an Unequal World*, Geneva: UNRISD.

UN Division for the Advancement of Women (DAW) (2000) 'FWCW Platform for Action, Women and Armed Conflict' and 'FWCW Platform for Action, Women in Power and Decision-Making'. Online, available at: www.un.org/womenwatch/daw/beijing/platform/armed.htm and www.un.org/womenwatch/daw/beijing/platform/decision.htm (accessed 14 August 2000).

UN International Research and Training Institute for the Advancement of Women (INSTRAW) (2006) *Securing Equality, Engendering Peace: A Guide to Policy and Planning on Women, Peace and Security (UN SCR 1325)*, Santo Domingo: INSTRAW.

UN Office of the Special Advisor on Gender Issues and Advancement of Women (UN OSAGI) (2004a) *Women and Armed Conflict: New Challenges. Beijing at 10: Putting Policy into Practice*. New York: UN Department of Public Information.

—— (2004b), *Inventory of UN Resources on Women, Peace and Security*, New York: UN. Online, available at: www.un.org/womenwatch/osagi/resources/wps/Inventory-11Oct2004.pdf (accessed 21 February 2005).

UN Secretary-General (2005) *In Larger Freedom: Towards Development, Security and Human Rights for All*, Report of the Secretary-General, A/59/2005, New York: UN.

—— (2004a) 'Report of the Secretary-General on Women and Peace and Security', 13 October, S/2004/814.

—— (2004b) 'Report of the Secretary-General's High-level Panel on Threats, Challenges and Change', *A More Secure World: Our Shared Responsibility*, A/59/565, New York: United Nations.

—— (2004c) 'Learning the Lessons of Peace-Building', Tip O'Neill Lecture, Magee Campus, University of Ulster, 18 October.

—— (2002a) *Women, Peace and Security. Study Submitted by the Secretary-General Pursuant to Security Council Resolution 1325*, New York: United Nations.

—— (2002b) 'Report of the Secretary-General on Women, Peace and Security', 16 October, S/2002/1154, New York: United Nations.

—— (2000) 'Report of the Secretary-General on 'Review and Appraisal of the Implementation of the Beijing PFA', 19 January E/CN.6/2000/PC/2, New York: United Nations.

—— (1999) *Prevention of War and Disaster*, Report of the Secretary-General on the Work of the Organisation, 31 August, A/541, New York: United Nations.

—— (1992) *An Agenda for Peace. Preventive Diplomacy, Peacemaking and Peace-keeping*, Report of the Secretary-General, 17 June, A/47/277 – S/24111, New York: United Nations.

—— UN Secretary-General's High Level Panel (2006) 'Delivering as One', 9 November, New York: United Nations.

UN Security Council (2000a) 'Security Council Resolution 1325 on Women, Peace and Security', 31 October 2000 (S/RES/1325 2000), New York: United Nations.

—— (2000b) 'Namibia Background Paper. Women and Peace and Security'. Online. available at: www.unifem.undp.org/unseccouncil/namibiabg.htl (accessed 12 June 2001).

Valasek, Kristin (2006) *Securing Equality, Engendering Peace: A Guide to Policy and Planning on Women, Peace and Security (UN SCR 1325)*, Santo Domingo: INSTRAW.

van Tongeren, Paul, Verhoeven, Juliette and Wake, Jim (2005) 'People Building Peace: Key Messages and Essential Findings', in Paul van Tongeren, Malin Brenk, Marte Hellema and Juliette Verhoeven (eds) *People Building Peace II. Successful Stories of Civil Society*, Boulder, CO: Lynnne Rienner Publishers, pp. 83–93.

Verwoerd, Wilhelm (2003) 'Toward a Response to Criticisms of the South African Truth and Reconciliation Commission', in Carol A. L. Prager and Trudy Govier (eds) *Dilemmas of Reconciliation. Cases and Concepts*, Waterloo, Ontario: Wilfred Laurier University Press, pp. 245–278.

Vlachová, Marie and Biason, Lea (eds) (2005) *Women in an Insecure World. Violence Against Women. Facts, Figures and Analysis.* Geneva: Geneva Centre for the Democratic Control of Armed Forces.

Volf, Miroslav (1996) *Exclusion and Embrace. A Theological Exploration of Identity, Otherness, and Reconciliation*, Nashville, TN: Abingdon Press.

Wake, Jim (2004) 'Lessons Learned from Peacebuilding Practices in Asia Pacific', in Annelies Heijmans, Nicola Simmonds and Hans van de Veen (eds) *Searching for Peace in Asia Pacific. An Overview of Conflict Prevention and Peacebuilding Activities*, Boulder, CO: Lynne Rienner Publishers, pp. 105–134.

Walby, Sylvia (1996) 'Woman and Nation', in G. Balakrishnan (ed.) *Mapping the Nation*, London: Verso, pp. 235–254.

Walker, Margaret Urban (2006) 'The Cycle of Violence', *Journal of Human Rights*, 5(1): 81–105.

Walzer, Michael, (1997) *On Toleration*, New Haven, CT: Yale University Press.

—— (1977) *Just and Unjust Wars*, New York: Basic Books.

Warner, Marina (2002) 'Sorry'. *OpenDemocracy,* 7 November, 1–17. Online, available at: www.open democracy.net (accessed 12 June 2006).

Warren, Karen and Cady, Duane L. (1994) 'Feminism and Peace: Seeing Connections', *Hypatia* 9(2): 4–20.

Weiner, Eugene (2000) 'Coexistence Work: A New Profession', in Eugene Weiner (ed.) *The Handbook of Interethnic Coexistence*, New York: Continuum, pp. 13–24.

Welchman, Lynn and Hossain, Sara (eds) (2005) *'Honour' Crimes, Paradigms, and Violence Against Women*, London: Zed Books.

Whittington, Sherill (2003) 'Experience and Lessons Learned in UN Transitional Administration for East Timor', in *Economic and Social Commission for Asia Pacific: Putting Gender Mainstreaming into Practice* S7/ESCAP/2254, New York: United Nations.

Williams, Harriette E. (2006) 'Women and Post-Conflict Reconstruction in Africa', *Accord. Conflict Trends*, 1: 30–34. Online, available at: www.accord.org.za/ct/2006–1.htm (accessed 19 June 2006).

Wolff, Stefan (2006) *Ethnic Conflict. A Global Perspective*, Oxford: Oxford University Press.

Women's Commission for Refugee Women and Children (2000) *Rebuilding Rwanda: 'A Struggle Men Cannot do Alone'*, New York: Women's Commission for Refugee Women and Children.

Women for Women International (2004) *Women Taking a Lead. Progress Toward Empowerment and Gender Equity in Rwanda*, briefing paper, September, Kigali: Women for Women International. Online, available at: www.womenforwomen.org/Downloads/Rwpaper.pdf (accessed 17 October 2004).

Young, Iris Marion (2006) 'Responsibility and Global Justice: A Social Connection Model', *Social Philosophy and Policy Foundation*, 23(1): 102–130.

—— (2003) 'Feminist Reactions to the Contemporary Security Regime', *Hypatia*, 18(1): 223–231.

—— (1997) *Intersecting Voices. Dilemmas of Gender, Political Philosophy, and Policy*, Princeton, NJ: Princeton University Press.

—— (1993) 'Together in Difference: Transforming the Logic of Group Political Conflict', in Judith Squires (eds) *Principled Positions. Post-Modernism and the Rediscovery of Value*, London: Lawrence and Wishart, pp. 121–50.

—— (1990) *Justice and the Politics of Difference*, Princeton, NJ: Princeton University Press.

Youngs, Gillian (2004) 'Feminist International Relations: A Contradiction in Terms? Or: Why Women and Gender are Essential to Understanding the World '"We" Live In', *International Affairs*, 80(1): 75–87.

Yovel, Yirmiyahu (1998) 'Tolerance as Grace and as Rightful Recognition', *Social Research*, 65(4): 897–920.

Yuval-Davis, Nira (1994) 'Women, Ethnicity and Empowerment', in Kum-Kum Bhavnani and Ann Phoenix (eds) *Shifting Identities, Shifting Racisms. The Feminism and Psychology Reader,* London: Sage, pp. 179–197.

Zarkov, Dubravka and Cockburn, Cynthia (2002) 'Introduction', in Cynthia Cockburn and Dubravka Zarkov (eds) *The Post-War Moment. Militaries, Masculinities and International Peacekeeping. Bosnia and the Netherlands*, London: Lawrence and Wishart, pp. 9–21.

Zeitlin, June (ed.) (2005) *Beijing Betrayed. Women Worldwide Report that Governments Have Failed to Turn the Platform into Action*, New York: Women's Environment and Development Organization. Online, available at: www.wedo.org/files/gmr2005.html (accessed 1 April 2005).

Zorbas, Eugenia (2004) 'Reconciliation in Post-Genocide Rwanda', *African Journal of Legal Studies*, 1(1): 29–52.

Zuckerman, Elaine and Greenberg, Marcia (2005) 'The Gender Dimensions of Post-Conflict Reconstruction: An Analytical Framework for Policymakers', in Caroline Sweetman (ed.) *Gender, Peacebuilding, and Reconstruction*, Oxford: Oxfam, pp. 70–82.

Index